The Form and Function of Mark 1:1–15

The Form and Function of Mark 1:1–15

A Multi-Disciplinary Approach to the Markan Prologue

Bradley T. Johnson

FOREWORD BY
Ben Witherington III

◠PICKWICK *Publications* • Eugene, Oregon

THE FORM AND FUNCTION OF MARK 1:1–15
A Multi-Disciplinary Approach to the Markan Prologue

Copyright © 2017 Bradley T. Johnson. All rights reserved. Except for brief quotations in critical publications or reviews, no part of this book may be reproduced in any manner without prior written permission from the publisher. Write: Permissions, Wipf and Stock Publishers, 199 W. 8th Ave., Suite 3, Eugene, OR 97401.

Pickwick Publications
An Imprint of Wipf and Stock Publishers
199 W. 8th Ave., Suite 3
Eugene, OR 97401

www.wipfandstock.com

PAPERBACK ISBN: 978-1-5326-1721-8
HARDCOVER ISBN: 978-1-4982-4175-5
EBOOK ISBN: 978-1-4982-4174-8

Cataloguing-in-Publication data:

Names: Johnson, Bradley T. | Witherington, Ben, III (foreword)

Title: Form and function of Mark 1:1–15 : a mulit-disciplinary approach to the Markan prologue / by Bradley T. Johnson; foreword by Ben Witherington III.

Description: Eugene, OR: Pickwick Publications, 2017 | Includes bibliographical references.

Identifiers: ISBN 978-1-5326-1721-8 (paperback) | ISBN 978-1-4982-4175-5 (hardcover) | ISBN 978-1-4982-4174-8 (ebook)

Subjects: LCSH: Bible. Mark, I, 1–15—Criticism, interpretation, etc.

Classification: LCC BS2585.2 J68 2017 (PRINT) | LCC BS2585.2 (EBOOK)

Unless indicated otherwise, all Scriptural citations of the Greek NT are taken from Nestle and Aland, *Novum Testamentum Graece*, 27th ed. (Stuttgart: Deutsche Bibelstiftung, 1993); citations of the English NT are taken from Herbert Gordon May and Bruce Manning Metzger, eds., *The New Oxford Annotated Bible with the Apocrypha: Revised Standard Version, Containing the Second Edition of the New Testament and an Expanded Edition of the Apocrypha* (New York: Oxford University Press, 1977); and citations from the Septuagint are taken from Alfred Rahlfs, ed., *Septuaginta; Id Est, Vetus Testamentum Graece Iuxta LXX Interpretes* (Stuttgart: Privilegierte Wurttembergische Bibelanstalt, 1935).

Manufactured in the U.S.A.   10/27/17

This work is lovingly dedicated to my mother and late father, Linda and Bob Johnson, without whom none of this would have been possible.

Contents

List of Figures | viii
Foreword by Ben Witherington III | ix
Acknowledgments | xi
Abbreviations | xii
Introduction: Background and Rationale | xiii

1: A Survey of Recent Scholarship | 1
2: Formal Considerations | 30
3: Rhetorical Context | 66
4: Prologues in Antiquity | 95
5: The Function of Mark 1:1–15 | 117
6: Conclusions and Implications | 152

Appendix | 163
Bibliography | 165

List of Figures

Figure 1: Character Inversion | 63

Figure 2: Macro-Rhetorical Matrix | 77

Figure 3: The Nested Nature of Scenes in Mark's Prologue | 143

Foreword

Ancient Greek documents were not like our modern ones in so many ways. For one thing, they were written in *scriptio continua,* a continuous flow of Greek letters without separation of words, sentences, paragraphs, and there were no chapters and verses either. How was one to tell what a document was about under such circumstances? While some ancient documents had a *syllabus,* a small tag attached to the end of a scroll, which might indicate an abbreviated title and/or author of the document, this really did not help much with figuring out the contents of the document, especially not for a person who had never before gazed at the endless mass of Greek letters within the document itself.

Under these sorts of circumstances, the regular practice of those who were literate in the age we call the New Testament era, was to read out loud the first few lines of the document in order to figure out both the genre and the contents of the document itself. By reading the documents first few lines out loud, one was best able to figure out where words began and ended, where sentences began and ended, and in general where the reader ought to start to understand what was written. This put a premium on how a document began, for if one could not decipher the purpose and nature of a document from the outset, the puzzled reader was likely to roll up the scroll and give up the quest.

Mark's Gospel, generally recognized as the earliest written Christian telling of the story of Jesus of Nazareth in any sort of full form, begins abruptly, evaluating it from a modern point of view. It seems to have a heading, followed by a Scripture quotation, followed in turn by a brief summary of the ministry of John the Baptizer, followed by the description of a vision Jesus had while John was baptizing him, followed in turn by a telegraphic reference to the temptations of Jesus in the wilderness, followed finally by an equally succinct summary of the beginning of Jesus' ministry in regard to what was the content of his message—"the time is fulfilled, and the Dominion of God is at hand. Repent and believe in the Good News." What are we to make of this odd combination of items, none of which are explained at the outset?

Scholars have long pondered Mark. 1:1–15 and almost everything about these verses has been debated. What is the meaning of the word 'beginning' at the beginning of the document? Does it refer to just these first few sentences, or is John's baptizing ministry somehow the beginning of the Good News about Jesus, or is Mark suggesting that this whole Gospel is just the first installment of the telling of the Good News? Where exactly does the 'beginning' of Mark end? At v. 8, at v. 11, at v. 15? What are the reasons for thinking that is where the 'beginning' finally stops and why does it matter? And is this some kind of ancient biography? If so, what kind?

Brad Johnson has undertaken to write a clear and compelling presentation that addresses almost all the *start-up* questions the outset of Mark's Gospel has raised for interpreters of this document over many centuries. Taking into consideration both modern literary analysis and ancient rhetorical analysis, a pattern slowly and convincingly emerged into the light. Without giving away the argument, I think you will find this study both interesting, careful, and hopefully convincing in addressing the issues Mark's beginning raises.

At the end of the day, you may well find yourself saying "let the reader understand," as Mark himself was to say in Mark 13, by which is meant in this case—"finally I get it!" As it turns out, Mark 1:1–15 is the whole of the beginning, providing for us much of what we need to know to unpack not only the "beginning of the Good News about Jesus Christ" but also the beginning of this document and what follows it in Mark 1:16–16:8. As such, that is good news in itself. The puzzle of Mark's beginning may not be fully solved here, but at least we know the size of the puzzle, and what the major pieces of it are, and how they fit into the larger picture of the whole of our first Gospel.

Ben Witherington, III

Amos Professor of New Testament for Doctoral Studies
Asbury Theological Seminary

Acknowledgments

It is with heartfelt gratitude that I mention a short list of persons instrumental in the production of this work. I first thank David Thompson and Joe Dongell for serving on my Dissertation Qualifying Exam Committee. I also thank Craig Keener for serving on my Dissertation Defense Committee and David Bauer for serving as my able examiner on that occasion. I thank Patti Walker in the Office of Advanced Research Programs at Asbury Theological Seminary for her tireless energies, constant encouragement, and gentle patience with me as I plodded this course. Most of all, I wish to thank my Dissertation Supervisor, Ben Witherington III, who "talked me off the wall" more than once. Without his encouragement and direction, I would have excused myself from the program at the very start.

And I would be completely remiss if I failed to mention my personal cheerleader squad. My amazing wife (Christina) and our four equally-amazing sons (Sam, Luke, Matthew, and Caleb) in so many and various ways paid the price for this work, and did so with grace undeserved.

Abbreviations

AB	Anchor Bible
JBL	*Journal of Biblical Literature*
JETS	*Journal of the Evangelical Theological Society*
JSNT	*Journal for the Study of the New Testament*
JSNTSup	Journal for the Study of the New Testament Supplement Series
JSOT	*Journal for the Study of the Old Testament*
JTS	*Journal of Theological Studies*
NICNT	New International Commentary on the New Testament
NICOT	New International Commentary on the Old Testament
NIGTC	New International Greek Testament Commentary
NovT	*Novum Testamentum*
NTS	*New Testament Studies*
SBLDS	Society of Biblical Literature Dissertation Series
SNTSMS	Society for New Testament Studies Manuscript Series
WBC	Word Biblical Commentary

Introduction

Background and Rationale

ONE OF THE ONGOING interpretive tasks of NT exegesis is discovering and heeding the initial, heuristic literary devices at the beginning of documents. Whether those devices are called prescripts, superscripts, introductions, titles, *incipits*, prologues, forewords, *prolegomena*, or any of a number of other terms, the initial cues of written works serve not only to provide anticipatory cues as to what might be encountered, but also to prescribe a course along which the reader ought to travel. The Gospel of Mark is no exception to this rule, and most contemporary scholarship acknowledges that somewhere in the first chapter of Mark an introduction can be found. The problem lies in deciding what defines that introduction.

One might (perhaps rightly) ask why such concern should be given to Mark's opening unit. It is a dictum among navigators that the further one deviates from a prescribed heading, the wider the margin of error with regard to the intended mark.[1] Over great distances, even seemingly minor deviations in heading can compound over time to lead to unintended destinations. In a similar way, readers who fail to recognize authors' directional cues from the onset are subject to arrival at conclusions that those same authors may never have envisioned—or intended. In light of this reality, it is imperative that readers give careful consideration to the opening materials of any discourse, mining for and heeding their directional cues. However, one must recognize those cues in order to heed them. I surmise that some Markan problems may in fact be resolved, in whole or in part, if one is able to accurately discern Mark's initial clues and directives contained in his prologue.

Some of the issues related to Mark's Gospel have daunted interpreters for centuries. For instance, what explains the issue of the Markan citation

---

1. The reader will surely pardon the pun.

of Isaiah in 1:2, and does Mark represent the memoirs of Peter? Other issues have emerged with the advent of more recent developments in NT research. For example, what relationship does Mark share with the synoptic Gospels, and does Mark contain a secrecy motif? Although this project will not attempt to answer all of these questions, it is my hope that the results generated here may provide a way forward in regard to some of them. Of special interest to this present study are issues related to the function of Mark's opening verse, the Isaian citation in 1:2–3, and the extent of the "beginning" of the Gospel.

The impetus for this project actually dates back to about fifteen years prior to the present moment. As a student of Dr. Joel Green in a NT introduction class at Asbury Theological Seminary, I was tasked with my classmates to examine the first twenty verses of the Gospel of Mark and determine where, if at all, Mark's opening "scene" closed. The exercise was to demonstrate the role of literary boundary demarcation in NT interpretation, and in light of my work on that assignment, I initially determined that the opening unit closed with 1:15.

In the years since, I have taught extensively as a NT Greek instructor, regularly using the passage of Mark 1:1–15 as a proving ground for demonstrating various grammatical features. In that time, I have become increasingly convinced of the internal coherence of the passage. This present study is aimed at first determining the legitimacy of that conclusion with regard to the closing boundary of Mark's opening unit, and second, to determine for what purpose that unit functions.

I suggest that there is not only good cause to continue the quest for the ending to Mark's opening unit, but also grounds for confidence in such a quest. In chapter 1, I will conduct a survey of recent and relevant research pertaining to Markan studies in general and its opening materials in particular. There exists no shortage of work (both recent and ancient) regarding the conventions and roles of introductory materials in biblical discourse. Despite the wealth of scholarly work on Mark in recent years, contemporary research has failed to reach a consensus not only about the relationship of Mark's opening unit to the rest of his book, but also about the precise limits of the opening unit itself. What specifically seems missing from an initial survey of literature in this regard is the integration of: 1) a more comprehensive examination of Mark's opening materials, including the constellation of features serving to knit the unit into a cohesive whole; 2) the function of prologues, especially within the genre of ancient

INTRODUCTION

biography; and 3) the rhetoric in Mark. Although numerous studies have done admirable work in one or perhaps two regards, no single study to date has (to my knowledge) sought to explore the integration of form, prologue, and rhetoric into a holistic enterprise. This study proposes to fill that gap.

Prior to the last century or so, Mark was typically obscured by the shadow of Matthew and received comparatively little attention. Most interpreters, following Augustine's now (in)famous dictum that Mark was the "attendant and epitomizer" of Matthew,[2] seemed to suppose that Matthew was a better "value" insofar as most of Mark was found in Matthew. Matters changed significantly in the nineteenth century, however, when questions arose concerning the sources behind the Gospels as we now have them and the role of the author in giving shape to those sources. Specifically, it was observed that Mark appeared to be the basis of both Matthew and Luke, and as a result, Mark gained new significance not only as a source for those Gospels, but also as a theological work in its own right.

As the focus on Mark shifted from issues behind the text to issues within it, commentators began to ask questions about Mark's arrangement of his materials, his primary themes, and his intended audience. Recent years have thus seen a burgeoning interest in Mark, and the range of interpretive proposals and methods with regard to Mark's structure and aim has exploded.

There is little dispute about *the beginning* of Mark's Gospel—1:1 provides a fairly transparent opening bracket.[3] The extent of Mark's introduction, however, is highly disputed. It is not uncommon for exegetes to identify the closure of the opening material at v. 13, v. 15, or (in some cases) v. 8.[4] I thus wish to propose two things here: first, that Mark 1:1–15 is a definable literary unit; and second, that as a literary unit the passage performs a rhetorical function. The basis for the first assertion will derive from an inductive, *within the text* examination of the particular features of Mark 1:1–15. This will constitute chapter 2 where I will do a detailed analysis of the textual, syntactic, and literary features that contribute to the unit's integrity. At this stage, I will maintain a methodological commitment that privileges the text over against efforts to get behind or in front of it. In

2. Augustine, *Harmony of the Gospels* 1.2.4.

3. Suggestions that Mark's opening materials are redactional emendations by industrious scribes at a later date are almost entirely groundless. This issue will be addressed later in the study.

4. Guelich, *Mark 1—8:26*, 3–4, offers a concise survey of scholarship related to the delineation of Mark's opening material.

this second chapter I will address formal considerations, specifically noting how Mark 1:1–15 demonstrates a constellation of features that contribute to the overall coherence of the passage. I will rely largely on the principles of Inductive Bible Study as prescribed by David Bauer and Robert Traina.[5]

Chapter 3 will be a foray into the art of ancient rhetoric. Working on the assumption that form dictates function, I will survey the essential components of Greco-Roman rhetoric using deductive principles that grant access to the text of Mark from behind it. Recognizing the aural nature of Mark's first-century context, attention will be given both to rhetorical structures that shape the whole of a work (*macro*-rhetoric) and to the smaller units that comprise the particulars (*micro*-rhetoric). We will explore education in the Hellenized world of the first century, and Mark's location within that world. Before leaving this chapter, we will examine instances of Mark's use of rhetoric in the Gospel as a whole and in the prologue itself.

Once the essential form of Mark's opening and the rhetorical environment from which it likely originated have been established, chapter 4 will address the nature of prologues in antiquity. As my starting point, I will use the work of Richard Burridge and his identification of the Gospels as typical of ancient Greco-Roman biography.[6] Specifically, I will draw upon his selection and analysis of ten representative samplings of ancient bi,oi, inferring from those works the basic framework and guiding principles of prologues. This study will begin inductively by focusing on the primary sources themselves, but will then shift to a comparative analysis in which I assess Mark's prologue in light of those principles. I will give specific attention to the forms and functions of the *preface, prologue, incipit,* and *"virtual preface."* In conclusion, we will make some observations about the degree to which Mark does or does not comport with Greco-Roman practices.

Chapter 5 will then be a re-examination of 1:1–15 in light of rhetoric as it was practiced and taught in the NT world. Specifically, I will re-visit some unanswered questions arising from my earlier work on the form of Mark's prologue. The culmination of this chapter will be a re-reading of Mark in view of the relationship between Mark's form and function.[7]

---

5. Bauer and Traina, *Inductive Bible Study*.

6. Burridge, *What Are the Gospels?*

7. Because Mark's opening unit is coherently woven, and because his employment of form fully conveys his rhetorical function, it will be impossible for me to deal with individual issues as systematically as this outline suggests. I offer a word to my readers that, at numerous points along the way, they will encounter references and be redirected to other parts of this study. Such cannot be avoided, and to those for whom this is trying,

INTRODUCTION

In the chapter *Conclusions and Implications*, I will offer a brief summary of my conclusions and pose some possible directions for further research. Such directions include (but are far from limited to) Mark's role as the hermeneut of Peter, John's baptism in historical and theological context, and Mark's use of Isaiah. At the conclusion of this study, I will hope to have confirmed my thesis: first, that Mark 1:1–15 is a coherent unit; and second, that—as a prologue—it functions to legitimate Jesus as the Anointed Son of God through the rhetoric of inartificial proofs.

I offer my sincerest apologies.

1

A Survey of Recent Scholarship

With regard to the extent of Mark's opening remarks, scholars are divided.[1] The main contenders are that the section concludes at v. 13 or v. 15. Those who propose v. 13 as the terminus typically point to Mark's apparent change of setting in terms of geography (from the wilderness to Galilee) and time (from John the Baptizer to the period after his arrest). Such a conclusion is defensible. Since 2000, a number of articles,[2] monographs,[3] and full-length commentaries[4] have assumed or advanced this view. Alternatively, a number of studies since 2000 advocate that v. 15 is the terminus for the Markan prologue. These studies often cite the parallelism between John in 1:2–8 and Jesus in 1:9–15, and vv. 14–15 are often viewed as transitional with respect to the narrative continuing with v. 16. This position is likewise well-grounded and (not surprisingly) also appears in a number of publications, including articles and essays,[5] monographs,[6] commentaries,[7] and at least one dissertation.[8] In addition, recent decades have witnessed a number of studies dedicated to the proposition that Mark

---

1. For a comprehensive listing of various attempts to outline Mark's Gospel, see the excellent (though now dated) survey by Cook, *The Structure and Persuasive Power of Mark*, 11–86.

2. Nightingale, *Don't Be Late*, 107–18; Nouis, *Proposition de plan de Marc*, 32–60.

3. Cook, *The Structure and Persuasive Power of Mark*; Davidsen, *The Narrative Jesus*; Humphrey, *Narrative Structure and Message in Mark*; Moloney, *Mark; Beginning the Good News*.

4. Beavis, *Mark*; Culpepper, *Mark*; Donahue and Harrington, *The Gospel of Mark*; France, *The Gospel of Mark*; Healy, *The Gospel of Mark*; Stein, *Mark*.

5. Guijarro, *Why Does the Gospel of Mark*, 28–38; Shepherd, *The Narrative Role*, 151–68.

6. Danove, *The Rhetoric of the Characterization*; Dechow, *Gottessohn und Herrschaft Gottes*; Incigneri, *The Gospel to the Romans*.

7. Boring, *Mark*; Edwards, *The Gospel according to Mark*.

8. Black, *John, Elijah, or One of the Prophets*.

1:1–15 is a definable unit.⁹ Taken together, works arguing that Mark's opening concludes either at v. 13 or v. 15 predominate.

Such is not to suggest that other views are unattested. In fact, the view that 1:1–8 is the extent of Mark's opening was presumed for generations, largely reflected in the fact that the Westcott-Hort text featured a conspicuous typesetting break between vv. 8 and 9, clearly reflecting the idea that 1:1–8 was Mark's opening. In a 1949 lecture, R. H. Lightfoot was the first to seriously challenge this position, yet a few proponents of this view remain.¹⁰ Others suggest that the ending concludes with v. 11.¹¹

Some would extend Mark's closure beyond v. 15. Whitney Shiner, for instance, places the conclusion to Mark's prologue (which is to be taken functionally as an *exordium*) at v. 16.¹² Nor is it uncommon for scholars to include the double call narrative of 1:16–20 with Mark's opening.¹³ What is less common is the proposal that Mark's opening ends as far as v. 28.¹⁴

What follows is a survey of scholarship related in small measure to recent Markan studies in general and in larger measure to Mark's opening materials in particular. It is not in any way meant to be exhaustive. Such surveys on Mark as a whole are plentiful, and I do not intend here to retread ground that has already been thoroughly worked. One need only consult such comprehensive studies as Sean Kealy's two-volume history of

---

9. Boring, *Mark 1:1–15*, 43–81; Dautzenberg, *Die Zeit des Evangeliums*, 219–34; Dormeyer, *Mk 1,1–15 als Prolog*, 181–211; Drury, *Mark 1:1–15*, 25–36; Gibbs, *Mk 1,1–15*, 154–88; Guelich, *The Beginning of the Gospel*, 5–15; Lambrecht, *John and Jesus in Mark 1.1–15*, 357–84; Sankey, "Promise and Fulfilment," 3–18.

10. Bryan, *A Preface to Mark*; Mack, *A Myth of Innocence*; Sapaugh, *An Appraisal*; Schmithals, *Das Evangelium nach Markus*; Scott, *Chiastic Structure*, 17–26; Wallis, *Mark's Goal-Oriented Plot Structure*, 30–46; Zimmermann, *Jesus Christus*; Zmijewski, *Markinischer Prolog und Täufertradition*, 41–62.

11. Barber, *Mark as Narrative*; Feneberg, *Der Markusprolog*; although it should be noted here that Feneberg's selection of v. 11 as the terminal point of his study is somewhat arbitrary by his own admission, his presentation comes down more firmly on this suggestion than any other.

12. Shiner, *Proclaiming the Gospel*, 183; however, this is a change of position with respect to his earlier work where he defines Mark's opening unit as 1:13 without comment. See *Follow Me*, 171.

13. Abbott, *What Happened to Mark's Infancy Story*, 202–16; Myers, *Binding the Strong Man*; Palmer, *The Markan Matrix*; Winn, *Mark and the Elijah-Elisha Narrative*.

14. Radaelli, *I Racconti*.

the interpretation of Mark,[15] or William Telford's compilation of various works on Mark.[16] Concise summaries are also available in abundance.[17]

I will primarily recount the treatment of Mark over the past forty years or so, with a particular emphasis on works dealing with Mark's opening materials. Choosing a point forty years prior to the present moment is helpful because a number of salient studies emerged within a relatively narrow timeframe. These studies laid the basis for the proliferation of those studies that followed in subsequent decades and are reflective of a growing number and diversity of methods and interpretive conclusions. Of course, it is simply not possible to list every source. However, I hope that what I provide here will serve the reader in terms of providing works that are both representative and normative of various approaches and methodological commitments. Because methods are not always clearly distinguishable, and further, because scholars sometimes employ multiple methods in their work, my schematization will not be without fault. What I offer will (I trust) sketch in broad strokes the canvas of scholarly research into Mark as a whole, with particular attention on those works that in some way address Mark's opening materials.

My aim in establishing this survey is to demonstrate two things: first, that the number of interpretive methods in approaching Mark has burgeoned in recent decades; and second, the proliferation of these methods has only widened the range of suggestions about where Mark's opening unit concludes and with what effect. Thus, the movement toward consensus with regard to Mark's opening unit has stalled. This chapter will therefore serve to provide a warrant for my study.

The Present Shape of Mark's Gospel

Before addressing higher critical questions, a preliminary task is to address the present shape of Mark. Because my focus lies with Mark's beginning, I will avoid the complex web of issues related to the uncertainty of Mark's ending, where such issues are legion.[18] This is not to suggest, though, that

---

15. Kealy, *A History of Mark*.
16. Telford, *Writing on the Gospel of Mark*.
17. See Anderson and Moore, *Mark & Method*, 1–22; Moloney, *Beginning the Good News*, 19–42; Yarbro Collins, *Mark*, 103–19; van Iersel, *Een Evangelist Kijkt Terug*, 228–43; and Young, *Whoever Has Ears to Hear*, 385–496.
18. For a current discussion related to the Markan ending, see the recent dissertation

the stability of the Markan beginning is unchallenged. Clayton Croy[19] and J. K. Elliott,[20] for example, have argued that the opening of Mark is defective. While it must certainly be noted that Mark 1:1–15 is not without its textual difficulties, views of a lost or damaged beginning of Mark have not been widely embraced largely because of their highly conjectured assumptions.[21] In light of more convincing text-critical evidence, we will assume that Mark's opening unit is generally as we find it in 1:1–3.[22]

Mark's Editorial Activity

Well into the twentieth century, the dominant questions in biblical studies related to matters of source materials. The advent of form criticism created a temporary detour from the logical progression of questions of source to questions of arrangement. The redaction-critical era corrected that course deviation, yet any discussion of Mark's handling of sources raises a series of questions. How has Mark arranged his sources? Where has he emended those sources? At what points can "Markan seams" be

---

done under the supervision of Dan Wallace by Sapaugh, "An Appraisal." The thesis of this dissertation is that the three longer endings of the Gospel of Mark have not been adequately investigated from the standpoint of intrinsic probability. The dissertation evaluates the internal evidence of each of the three longer endings of Mark—the Freer Logion, Intermediate Ending, and Long Ending. This includes both linguistic and literary patterns. The same evaluation was performed on seven anomalous pericopae in the main body of Mark (1:1—16:8).

19. Croy, *Where the Gospel Text Begins*, 105–27.

20. Elliott, *Mark 1.1–3*, 584–88; in a previous study, however, Elliott notes with respect to Mark 1:2 that the NT never uses καθώς at the beginning of a clause to introduce an OT citation, therefore 1:2 must be understood to relate to 1:1. See *Mark and the Teaching of Jesus*, 37–45; Dan Wallace points this out in his review of Elliott's most recent compilation, *New Testament Textual Criticism*. I will say more about this later in our discussion.

21. The minority status of this view is perhaps nowhere more evident than in a private conversation reported by Eugene Boring with C. F. D. Moule, in which Moule claimed in 1988 that, "My secret heresy is that *both* the beginning and the ending of Mark have been lost, and just as it has been given a secondary ending, it has been given a secondary beginning (emphasis original)." Boring, *Mark 1:1–15*, 72.

22. Closely related to issues of the stability of Mark's opening material is the matter of the text of the entire Gospel itself. Larry Hurtado has demonstrated compellingly that our present form of Mark is more reliable than many have earlier been believed. Hurtado, *P45 and the Textual History of Mark*, 132–48; most recently, Didier LaFluer has produced a monograph on the textual basis of Mark and it relationship to the minuscule family, f13. Lafleur, *La Famille 13 dans Marc*.

detected? Is Mark a conservative redactor in handling his traditions or is he more of a creative theologian?

Responding primarily to the tendencies and excesses of form criticism, Willi Marxsen challenged the early twentieth-century preoccupation with form critical studies by undertaking instead an earnest investigation of the theological aims and compositional strategies of the evangelist himself.[23] In so doing, Marxsen broke the hegemony of the form critics (who largely minimized the role of the author in Gospel construction) by shifting attention from the isolated units of tradition contained in the Gospels to the redactional activity of the author. Said differently, Marxsen moved from the particulars to the whole, especially with regard to Mark's contribution to the shaping and "consolidating" of the material. Although Marxsen's work may not pay immediate dividends for my study, it does provide the basis for redactional and (consequently) narrative studies that move from issues behind the text to issues within the text.

Leander Keck followed Marxsen's lead, likewise affirming the creative role of Mark as redactor.[24] Keck's more specific task was to challenge the dominant view that Mark's opening unit ends at v. 13. He acknowledged not only that no consensus had as of that time been reached regarding the purpose of Mark's opening, but even worse that "almost never does the introduction figure in discussions of Mark's purpose."[25] He attributes this inattention largely to form criticism's singular concern to isolate the various pre-Markan traditions in the Second Gospel and the attempts of various Jesus Questers to extract data from Mark for purposes of historical reconstruction.[26] Keck's study is foundational to my thesis insofar as he sets about asking the precise questions I am posing, namely with respect to "the *extent* of the introduction and the *intent* of the author (emphasis his)."[27] I am less apt, however, to accept Keck's appraisal of *discipleship* as the organizing theme to Mark. This conclusion seems to be forced onto the text rather than inferred from it.

If Keck (and Marxsen to an even larger extent) represents a perspective on the Second Gospel that views the author as exercising creative control

---

23. Marxsen, *Der Evangelist Markus*.
24. Keck, *The Introduction to Mark's Gospel*, 352–70.
25. Ibid., 352.
26. Ibid., 356.
27. Ibid., 352; see also Malbon, *Ending at the Beginning*, 175, who raises the same two questions.

over the redactional process, Rudolf Pesch[28] might be said to represent the opposite extreme, although it must be noted that the distinction here is one of degree and not of category. For Pesch, any claims purporting Mark to have been creative in his redaction are largely overstated.[29]

Methodologically, he is chiefly concerned to separate Mark's redactional effort from the traditions available to him. Noting his location as only one of a number of recent redactional critics taking Mark under consideration,[30] Pesch follows Keck in suggesting "at least the possibility" that the terminus of Mark's prologue might be v. 15.[31] Mark, according to Pesch, is very selective in his emendation of the traditions, the only evidence being his original contribution of the superscription of 1:1 (which serves a programmatic interest for the Gospel)[32] and his slight expansion of v. 15.[33] Aside from minor "interferences" at vv. 2–3 (which bear the stamp of redactional activity through expansion and emendation to bring the tradition of the Baptizer into alignment with the early Christian tradition),[34] the addition of τῆς Γαλιλαίας in v. 9,[35] and the possible insertion of εὐθὺς for editorial purposes in v. 10,[36] Mark is content to leave the traditional materials alone. Thus, we see the contribution of original material "only at the edges."[37] The value of Pesch's findings for my own inquiry lies in his careful demonstration of the plausibility of Mark 1:1–15 as a coherent unit of tradition.

Ernest Best likewise pursues a conservative tack with regard to Mark's editorial activity. Mark is "neither author, nor editor" but rather "an artist putting together a collage, creating a new unity out of existing material."[38] From his hand come only linking verses and minor editorial changes—he has written no pericope. Evidence of his redactional work can be found in his connecting seams, his insertion of explanatory clauses,

---

28. Pesch, *Anfang des Evangeliums Jesu Christi*, 108–44.
29. Ibid., 311; see also *Das Markusevangelium*, 15.
30. Pesch, *Anfang des Evangeliums Jesu Christi*, 343.
31. Ibid., 313.
32. Ibid., 336.
33. Ibid., 337.
34. Ibid., 318–20, 323–24.
35. Ibid., 335.
36. Ibid., 317, 335.
37. Ibid., 315.
38. Best, *Mark*, 121.

and his ordering of events.³⁹ But this poses a dilemma for Best: if Matthew and Luke had Mark available as a source, then the issue of their redaction of Mark is relevant. However, if we do not know for certain what Mark's sources were, is it appropriate to speak of Mark as a "redactor"? Best prefers, for this reason, to think of Mark's work as perhaps "compositional" rather than "redactional." ⁴⁰ This is a subtle but important point and lends itself to my inquiry insofar as I am interested in the "compositional" unity of Mark's opening unit.

It becomes readily apparent that a tension exists within redactional approaches between the *creative theologian* views of Marxsen and Keck, and those of the *conservative editor* views of Pesch and Best. Robert Stein has attempted to establish guidelines for discerning the differences between Mark's editorial activity and his source material. Some of his criteria include seams, insertions, summaries, creation of pericopes, modification of material, comparison with Matthew and Luke, investigation of "misformed" pericopes, investigation of inconsistency between Mark's account and what actually happened, Markan selection, omission, and/or arrangement of material (including arrangement of individual pericopes, placing of one pericope within another, and geographical scheme), the Markan introduction and conclusion, vocabulary, and Christological titles. His methodology leads him to conclude that the Markan prologue is defined by Mark 1:1-15 and serves two emphases: 1) to convey Jesus as the fulfillment of OT prophecy; and 2) to highlight the advent of Jesus as ushering in a new era of salvation history. ⁴¹ Others have followed suit in various ways.⁴² Although some commentators strive for a centrist position by maintaining a more balanced view,⁴³ the trend has been decidedly in the direction of viewing Mark as an author in his own right, as the following instances will illustrate.

By combining exegesis with redactional analysis, Ramon Trevijano Etcheverría feels confident that the historical context of Mark's composition (in terms of source materials and textual tradition) and his theological

---

39. Ibid., 11.

40. Ibid., 14.

41. Stein, *Proper Methodology*, 48-49.

42. See, for example, Schreiber, *Die Christologie des Markusevangeliums*, 154-55; *Theologie des Vertrauens*, 1-21; Neirynck, *Duality in Mark*, 13; or Best, *Mark*, 11.

43. For example, Ernst, *Das Evangelium nach Markus*, who, although exercising caution in attempting to separate tradition from Markan redaction, moves away from a purely historical approach toward one that is more engaged with theological concerns and usefulness for the church.

thrust (in response to doctrinal questions in the early Christian era) can be inferred, each of which is readily apparent throughout Mark's Gospel and with special emphasis in 1:1–15.[44] He sees Mark's redactional activity largely aimed at highlighting the salvific dimension of the gospel as initiated by the activity of the Baptizer. Whereas Matthew and Luke tend to emphasize the eschatological dimensions with regard to the coming judgment, Mark offers the ministry of the Baptizer as a means of reconciling Israel to God in an effort to avoid the coming wrath. Thus, baptism is primarily understood as a reconciling, salvific act.[45]

The point of departure between Trevijano Etcheverría and Pesch lies in each commentator's views of the manner in which Markan redaction has occurred.[46] Arguing from a very conservative stance, Pesch sees the tradition largely intact with only minor interference by the redactor—primarily at the "edges." Trevijano Etcheverría, on the other hand, sees evidence of a more creative theologian in Mark. An example of the evangelist's willingness to "re-touch" inherited, written sources is evident in Mark's use of the haggadic *pesher* underlying the conflation of Ex 23:20, Isa 40:3, and Mal 3:1 in Mark 1:2–3:

> La conciencia profética del cristianismo primitivo reforzaba el derecho a la adaptación targúmica. La reproducción exacta de las frases se subordinaba a su significado esencial y aplicación inmediata. Esta alteración de los textos, para apoyar la perspectiva teológica del escritor, se encuentra. en todo el N. T., sobre todo en Jn. En Mc. las resonancias del A. T. colorean la narración evangélica; pero también asume el lenguaje del A. T. a partir de los hechos evangélicos.[47]

While agreeing with Pesch at multiple points with regard to theology and methodology (especially with regard to the overall trajectory of the prologue as defined and its terminus in the climactic sentence in vv.

---

44. Trevijano Etcheverría, *Comienzo del Evangelo*, xxii–xxiii. "La preparación de un comentario breve al evangelio entero de Marcos nos ha permitido constatar que los versículos que delimitamos como prólogo constituyen la sección de más honda riqueza temática y ofrecen de entrada las perspectivas más amplias. El estudio que ofrecemos queda centrado en el análisis exegético de Mc. 1, 1–15, para discernir sus implicaciones históricas y su alcance teológico."

45. Ibid., 68.

46. Even in the arrangement of well-preserved source materials the creativity of a redactor can in some way be sensed.

47. Trevijano Etcheverría, *Comienzo del Evangelo*, 240.

14–15⁴⁸), Trevijano Etcheverría does break with him in terms of the degree to which Mark has exercised creative control over his sources. "*Disentimos de la interpretación de R. Pesch* [. . .] *en cuanto que en 1, 2–8 vemos más en obra al evangelista Marcos. Es cierto que sigue su tradición, pero con omisiones y retoques de gran alcance.*"⁴⁹ Once again, the differences here are of a degree rather than a category.

Hugh Anderson likewise ascribes to Mark more credit for his authorial contribution. Arguably the first English commentary written from a decidedly redaction-critical perspective, Anderson's volume on Mark highlights the value of form criticism's healthy skepticism and pursuit of scientific study by means of the various criteria of authenticity. However, it likewise lodges some significant critiques of form criticism.⁵⁰ Ralph Martin follows Anderson in seeing Mark's contribution as more kerygmatic than historical, but is unwilling to completely jettison the latter. His principal aim is to "detach Mark from the apron-strings of Peter and set him on his own two feet,"⁵¹ since Mark is "an independent theologian and creative Christian writer and not simply [. . .] a stenographic reporter or scissor-and-paste compiler of Petrine traditions."⁵² As will be argued later, evidence of Mark's role as Peter's hermeneut should not be too quickly dismissed.

Theodore Weeden also presents Mark as "a much more deliberate theologian than had earlier been assumed."⁵³ He suggests that Mark was writing to correct a presumed push toward a θεὸς ἀνήρ Christology by interlopers into the Christian community.⁵⁴ Jack Kingsbury provides a decisive critique of Weeden's defense of a corrective Christology.⁵⁵ Proceeding from a literary analysis, Kingsbury demonstrates how titles of majesty in Mark are in no way defective and in no need of reinterpretation (as a corrective theological approach would suggest). Rather, such titles as *Son of God* and *Messiah* should be read within their literary context (i.e., within the plot of the story).⁵⁶ And since the issue with regard to

---

48. Ibid., 244.
49. Ibid., 242.
50. Anderson, *The Gospel of Mark*, 15.
51. Martin, *Mark, Evangelist and Theologian*, 15.
52. Ibid., 14.
53. Weeden, *Mark*, 3.
54. Ibid., 164.
55. Kingsbury, *The Christology of Mark's Gospel*.
56. Ibid., xii.

the variant reading of υἱοῦ θεοῦ in 1:1 cannot be decided on the basis of external textual evidence, Kingsbury's study will perhaps be helpful to us as we seek to establish the text at this point.

From Redaction to Oral Performance and Written Composition

The advent of redactional analysis launched a new era in synoptic studies. Attention began to shift from the historical processes operating *behind* the text to evidence of the author's activity *within* the text. As more attention was directed toward the role of the author, scholars began to infer structuring principles controlling the shape of the text itself. These inferences generally arise from observations at both the macro- and micro-textual levels. On one hand, macro-textual structures can be observed with regard to the overall shape of Mark as a whole. These structures provide an overall pattern, trajectory, or outline to the Gospel. On the other hand, micro-textual structures and devices can be observed operating within individual units of text—even within the very grammar itself.

One such example is the work of Frans Neirynck, who observes a tendency to communicate by means of *duality*. Dualities for Mark create "a sort of homogeneity in Mark, from the wording of sentences to the composition of the gospel. After the study of these data one has a strong impression of the unity of the gospel of Mark [. . .] no pericope in Mark can be treated in isolation."[57] Further, Mark's two-step progression is a distinctive characteristic of Mark. A view of the whole of the gospel reflects Mark's own manner of writing.[58]

Joanna Dewey notes even more sophisticated structures in Mark. She proceeds in light of the following presuppositions: 1) that Mark is a compiler; 2) that, contrary to Bultmann, Mark "is in fact master of his material"; and 3) that the Second Gospel, despite its relative austerity, is nevertheless a literary work.[59] She points to a number of literary devices evident in Mark,[60] highlighting (among others) Mark's arrangement of 1:1–8 on the basis of a concentric structure.[61] Dewey champions James Muilenburg's call

---

57. Neirynck, *Duality in Mark*, 37.
58. Ibid., 72.
59. Dewey, *Markan Public Debate*, 18–19.
60. Ibid., 31–34.
61. Ibid., 144–47; see also her emphasis on the centrality of these concentric structuring devices, 1. However, her tendency to see concentric structures where they may or

for rhetorical analysis (to be discussed below) and argues that the structured literary units (the *forms*) comprise the basis of rhetorical force. At a number of points she exercises caution with regard to the precise prehistory of these literary devices. For example, are they grounded in oral or written literature? Are the techniques Greek or Semitic? Are they conscious or subconscious products?[62] Such questions become grist for the mill of scholarly inquiry. One line of inquiry seeks to recover the socio-historical basis for the written forms as they exist and necessarily raises questions related to genre. Another line of inquiry aims to investigate the oral and aural contexts of Mark's Gospel. We will treat each in turn, acknowledging the blurred lines that enter the discussion at this point.

Oral and Performance Criticism

Some of the recent efforts to highlight the oral dimension of the text of Mark demonstrate, in various ways, the effect of Mark when read aloud in a single sitting. Christopher Bryan poses two primary questions. First, what is the literary genre of Mark? Second, was it meant to be read aloud?[63] For him, the answer to the second question is a resounding "Yes." Bryan grounds his argument for the aural nature of Mark on the work of Walter Ong in support of his identification of various oral features of Mark and Mark's aural context.[64] Elizabeth Struthers Malbon also argues for the aural texture of Mark and the fact that it could and should be read aloud in one sitting.[65] Likewise, P. Mourlon Beernaert argues for a single sitting.[66] He laments that Mark is read piecemeal through a typical lectionary cycle—a move that compromises the dramatic integrity of the Gospel. He proposes instead that Mark should be intonated with a strong voice by speaking slowly and reading Mark in its entirety. In this way, the listening audience will discern the scene demarcations, which he argues consist of a prologue (1:1–13), six scenes depicting various attributes of the kingdom (e.g., its approach, mystery, and expansion), and an epilogue (16:1–8). Alec Mc-

---

may not exist is perhaps nowhere more apparent than her failure to recognize the strong literary parallelism between the narratives of John in 1:2–8 and Jesus in 1:9–15.

62. Ibid., 29–30.
63. Bryan, *A Preface to Mark*, 3.
64. Ong, *Orality and Literacy*.
65. Malbon, *Hearing Mark*, 5.
66. Mourlon Beernaert, *Saint Marc*.

Cowan has brought just such a reading to the stage through his dramatic presentation of Mark.[67]

Whitney Shiner further develops the case for the orality of Mark. He concludes that: 1) the oral performance of an ancient work in the NT world was of primary importance; 2) the performance of that narrative would have been semi-dramatic in style; 3) the recitation would have routinely emphasized emotional impact; 4) the accepted and expected style of delivery would have been more bombastic than today; and 5) the audiences themselves would have been equally bombastic in their responses and actually would have played a role in the performance.[68]

Others have undertaken to compare the dramatic dimensions of Mark to Greek drama. Gilbert Bilezikian seeks to enlarge upon Stein's criteria for identifying redactional elements by suggesting that Mark's orchestration of various features reflects a strong affinity for Greek tragedy. "Once recognized, the dramatic structure of the Gospel provides that integrating, comprehensive perspective that makes possible the delineation of both the distinctive redactional features of each part and the interdependence of the components."[69] The genre of Greek tragedy naturally lends itself to the intrinsic tragedy of Mark's story as that story recounts the painful tearing away of Gentile Christianity from its Jewish roots.[70] In a similar way but for a different purpose, Friedrich Lang identifies Mark's Gospel with Greek drama.[71] He observes a five-part structure prefaced by a prologue of 1:1–13. The aim of the drama is to answer two primary questions: who is Jesus, and why was he crucified?

Stephen Smith compares Mark specifically to Sophocles' *Oedipus Rex*. He notes both a general arrangement consisting of a seven-part scheme bracketed by a prologue and epilogue, and the binding of the parts by transitional passages that stand in for *choral odes*.[72] Several elements serve to connect Mark with Sophocles, the most notable of which is foreshadowing (clearly evident, he claims, in the Markan prologue). For example, Smith observes that the ἄγγελος of 1:2 appears at the close in 16:5–7; ὁδός in 1:2–3 appears central to 8:27—10:52; John *qua* Elijah in 1:6–8 appears again in

67. McCowen, *Personal Mark*.
68. Shiner, *Proclaiming the Gospel*, 4–5.
69. Bilezikian, *The Liberated Gospel*, 139.
70. Ibid., 141, 145.
71. Lang, *Kompositionsanalyse des Markusevangeliums*, 1–24.
72. Smith, *A Divine Tragedy*, 246–47.

9:11–13; the divine voice of 1:11 appears again in 9:7; and the temptation narrative of 1:12–13 appears in multiple accounts between Jesus and the adversary/demons, especially in Peter's rebuke of 8:31–33.[73] He defends the terminus for the prologue as 1:13 on the ground that the protagonist (Jesus) is introduced in the following verse.[74]

On the heels of redaction criticism and its interest in the role of the editor in giving shape to his materials (and in light of the emergence of investigations of orality in Mark), several studies have emerged seeking to identify a macro-structure to Mark. One of the more dominant "findings" for such studies is Mark's purported use of literary chiasm. A. Nouis, for instance, notes a number of *inclusions* (beginning and ending elements that are parallel) that define individual sections of the Gospel.[75] The central feature of a chiasm in this sense is the structuring of nested inclusions—often with a feature at the center. Whatever is at the center, argues Nouis, is the most important matter: "le centre du chiasme correspond à l'idée principale au coeur du passage."[76] One of the key functional elements is its ability to help readers memorize passages as oral units. Mark stitches together his individual materials as an aural means of improving retention and recall.

Benoît Standaert typifies this commitment to concentric structuring.[77] He believes that the oral *Sitz im Leben* of Mark was most likely a Christian Easter vigil based on a Passover *Haggadah* in which initiates prepared for early morning baptism followed by Eucharist.[78] He specifically highlights the numerous references to *night* evident throughout the Gospel.[79] Mark's structure follows widely-used conventions in the Greco-Roman world and consists of three parts: a prologue (1:1–13), a *narratio* (1:14—6:13, itself comprised of two major sections sandwiched between three diptych summaries), an *argumentatio* (6:14—10:52), a *dénouement* (11:1—15:47), and an epilogue (16:1–8).

Bas van Iersel, Standaert's adviser, pressed his student's method into service and refined it. It seems intuitive to van Iersel that longer works

---

73. Ibid., 241–42.
74. Ibid., 240.
75. Nouis, *Proposition de Plan de Marc*, 33.
76. Ibid., 34.
77. Standaert, *Évangile selon Marc*.
78. Hengel also suspects that Mark was used for liturgical purposes (*Studies in the Gospel of Mark*, 52).
79. Standaert, *Évangile selon Marc*, 41.

(such as Mark's Gospel) would take longer to read aloud and would have a greater need for structuring elements.[80] He sees these structuring elements at work both at the macro- and the micro-levels of the Gospel. Appealing to concentric structuring principles, he observes an ABCBA structure with *hinges* between A and B elements at 1:14–15 and 15:40–41.[81] The transition from blindness to sight frames the internal C element. The overarching chiasm is clearly evident to him, especially in view of the parallelism of the two major sections organized topographically with respect to the locales of Galilee and Jerusalem.[82] Augustine Stock shares Standaert's conclusions at multiple points.[83] First, he sees Mark heavily informed by the Passover event. Second, he sees a baptismal context as the most likely *Sitz* for Mark, especially in view of the preponderance of baptism language in the Gospel. The prologue and the epilogue frame the catechetical material within.[84] The center of that material is Jesus' threefold mention of baptism in 10:38–39.[85] Third, Stock gives chiasm a prominent location in his analysis by claiming that the device was the functional equivalent of paragraph breaks, punctuation, and capitalization (among others),[86] and that the central element served a climactic function in view of the structuring principles of balance and inversion.[87] "A literary work should begin and end in the same way [. . .] with the most important material in the middle."[88] (Of course, one might rightly ask how likely an aural reader would be to identify a central element in a work as large as Mark's.)

Robert Humphrey's analysis challenges the conclusions of both Standaert and Stock. He argues that Mark is *not* primarily following

---

80. Van Iersel, *Reading Mark*, 18.

81. The challenge confronting such observations is to demonstrate how an aural reader would keep pace with these unfolding structures, especially over such large stretches of text. Admittedly, a "reader" might successfully navigate these on the basis of access to and careful study of a physical manuscript, but the burden on that reader to effectively communicate such nuance to an aural audience would be extraordinary.

82. Van Iersel, *Reading Mark*, 20–26.

83. Stock, *The Method and Message of Mark*.

84. Ibid., 16–17.

85. Ibid., 18–19. Scott, *Chiastic Structure*, 18–19, goes one step further by pointing out that Mark 9:7 is the exact center of the Gospel ("This is my son; listen to him"), with 5,375 words on one side and 5,376 words on the other.

86. Stock, *The Method and Message of Mark*, 20.

87. Ibid., 19.

88. Ibid., 23.

Greco-Roman conventions.[89] He does hold that Mark is carefully structured around chiasms, even more so than Standaert and Stock presume. Humphrey has attempted to isolate three major sections in Mark, each organized by an ABCXCBA principle, each of approximately equal length, and each framed by three episodes at the beginning and three parallel episodes at the end (with a central element that interprets the whole section). The outline consists of a superscription (1:1), first major section (1:2—6:29), second major section (6:30—11:19), and third major section (11:20—16:8).[90]

In a self-published work, David Palmer applies what he calls a literary-structural analysis to Mark.[91] Drawing on his background as an architect, Palmer is comfortable working with structures. The ordering principle for his analysis is a series of twenty-eight *days* arranged in four series of seven days each. Each *day* is understood as the period from dawn of one day to the dawn of the next.[92] This structuring excludes the prologue, which he defines as 1:1–20 (a period minimally consisting of fifty days).[93]

Vernon Robbins observes a three-step progression intrinsic to Mark's organization.[94] At a micro-level, the first step of the progression involves Jesus in motion with his disciples (usually employing either ἐξέρχομαι or ἐκπορεύομαι) from one venue to another. The second step recounts the interaction between Jesus and his disciples. The third step culminates in a narrational *summons* (προσκαλέομαι), *call* (καλέω, φωνέω), or *sending* (ἀποστέλλω).[95] The first instance of a three-step progression is 1:14–20 (thus ascribing to 1:1–13 introductory status). Subsequent progressions include 3:7–19; 6:1–13; 8:27—9:1; 10:46—11:11; 13:1–37.[96]

---

89. Humphrey, *Narrative Structure and Message in Mark*, 10.
90. Ibid., 13.
91. Palmer, "The Markan Matrix."
92. Ibid., 36.
93. Ibid., 75.
94. Robbins, *Summons and Outline in Mark*, 97–114; in his development of this three-step model, Robbins is building on the two-step progression pioneered by Neirynck, *Duality in Mark*. Mark 8:27—10:45 contains a unified structure that gives the section a central position in the theology of Mark. Recent analysis has shown a more subtle three-part progression in this section of Mark. Each one of the passion predictions itself stands within a unit characterized by three parts (8:27-30, 31-33, 8:34—9:1; 9:30-32, 33-34, 35-50; 10:32-34, 35-41, 42-45
95. Robbins, *New Boundaries in Old Territory*, 133.
96. Robbins, *Jesus the Teacher*, 25.

In his commentary on Mark, Robbins further explains that the three-step progression describes the natural life-cycle of a story insofar as stories have *beginnings*, *middles*, and *ends*. This pattern can also be applied to the natural life-cycle of a teacher-student relationship. At a macro-level, we see in the *beginning* of Mark the willingness of both the teacher (Jesus) and his potential students (the disciples) to assume their respective roles (1:14—3:6). The *middle* of Mark features a "rhetorical give-and-take" between the teacher and his students (3:7—12:44). Finally, at the *end*, the teacher encourages his students to trek forth on their own (13:1—16:8). In this way, "the Markan story concerns the natural, socio-biological life cycle of a male human being."[97] The abrupt ending of Mark achieves the desired result of inviting the reader into the role of discipleship.[98] It can be easily noted, he maintains, how the three-step progressions at the micro-level combine to create the larger matrix for a three-step progression at the macro-level. At this macro-level, Jesus' identity changes incrementally in correspondence to the three-step units.

Perhaps the most elaborate assessment of Mark's ordering principles is that of Ethel Wallis.[99] Viewing 1:1–8 as a prologue, she observes four discrete units in the plot of Mark's narrative. On the *base* side of her configuration lie the core and amplification. Mirroring the base is the *goal* side featuring complication and resolution. The conflict episodes constitute the central backbone of Mark's unified plot structure.[100] The balance and symmetry of the plot structure suggest Greek poetic influence, the purpose of which is to highlight the deity of Jesus.[101]

Though compositional critics have shed light on the need for heeding Mark's structuring principles, it seems to me that appeals to concentric circles, *inclusions*, and step-progressions are largely overplayed. The sheer breadth and diversity of recent formulations about the "key" to Mark's structure are indicative of the tendentious nature of these formulations. Further, it is not at all clear how, in an aural context, the readership would recognize the central element of the chiasm as a text was delivered orally. In my mind, the closing bracket is far more likely to serve a climactic or paramount function once the repeating element is brought back to mind. Nevertheless, compositional

---

97. Ibid., xx–xxi.
98. Ibid., 192–93.
99. Wallis, *Mark's Goal-Oriented Plot Structure*.
100. Ibid., 32.
101. Ibid., 43–44.

critics have raised important and legitimate questions about the shape of Mark's Gospel, and two structuring devices in particular will be central to my own analysis: the literary prologue and the summary statement.

Prologues

In a seminal issue of *Semeia*, contributors share thoughts about the opening materials of the Gospels. Dennis Smith offers an overview of the types and functions of narrative beginnings in antiquity as a way of contextualizing the discussion.[102] One common type of beginning is the *preface* (προοίμιον or φροίμιον; *exordium*).[103] Another type is the *dramatic prologue*.[104] Through these means, authors could address hearers in the first person, defend themselves against attacks of critics, and appeal to audiences for favor. By contrast, a third type (known as an *incipit*) is a less formal, brief phrase that simply introduces a document or selection from a document (e.g., the *Gospel of Thomas* begins with, "These are the secret sayings which the living Jesus spoke and which Didymus Judas Thomas wrote down."). An *incipit* could even function as a title or scroll tag (σίλλυβος; *titulos*).[105] Smith also notes, almost as an afterthought, the existence of a *virtual preface*.[106] Citing Xenophon as an example, Smith highlights the fact that Xenophon can undertake his narrative account *in media res* because there was no apparent need to elaborate upon the specific background or context.

J. Kudasiewicz argues that each of the Synoptics begins with a prologue (Matt 1:1; Mark 1:1; Luke 1:1-14), identifying that work's respective function and genre (for Matthew, a βίβλος γενέσεως; for Mark, a εὐαγγέλιον; for Luke, a διήγησις).[107] In Mark's case, εὐαγγέλιον fulfills a literary function by integrating the entire work, specifically by establishing 1:1 in its relationship to 1:14-15; 8:35; 10:29; and 14:9. In this way, claims Kudasiewicz, Mark has effectively created a new literary genre.

---

102. Smith, *Narrative Beginnings*, 1-9.

103. Ibid., 1-3.

104. Ibid., 3-4.

105. Ibid. For a discussion of Mark's "title," see Hengel, *Studies in the Gospel of Mark*, 64-84.

106. Smith, *Narrative Beginnings*, 6-7.

107. Kudasiewicz, *Poczatek Ewangelii*, 89-109.

J. Gibbs provides an inventive way of understanding the Gospel prologues.[108] Although he maintains an eye on redaction-critical concerns (and positions his efforts as such), the main thrust of his analysis is literary. His thesis is that each canonical Gospel begins with a prologue that: 1) offers a guide to the structure of the whole; 2) creates a context for the whole; and 3) functions as a table of contents with regard to the themes and motifs of the whole.[109] He presumes that the extent of each prologue can be determined in this way: "We only need to look at the end of each gospel and then to see how far we have to go from the beginning of that gospel in order to reach something which corresponds to its end."[110] In his estimation, each of the Gospels contains in its conclusion references to a mission to all persons, the locales of Galilee (Matthew, Mark, and John) or Rome (Luke), and the presence of Jesus. Because Mark 1:14–15 features all three elements, the prologue of Mark must end at this point.[111]

In a more contemporary treatment, Danelle Nightingale[112] posits an interesting scenario for an evangelical lay audience: Mr. and Mrs. Long attend a dramatic performance of the Gospel of Mark. Mr. Long is delayed parking the car and subsequently misses the opening of the performance. The question is this: Would Mr. and Mrs. Long ultimately experience the scope of the performance in the same way given the variability of their access to the prologue?[113] She presumes that they would not. For Mark, the prologue stitches together both the volatility of the "road of uncertain faith" and the "solid assurance" of the divine hand behind the curtain; thus, "the dual reality of a life of discipleship" is intimated as early as the prologue. Mark is therefore to be understood as serving a pastoral function by presenting "a picture of discipleship, in which the affirmations of the prologue balance the turbulence of the remainder of the gospel."[114] Although Nightingale offers a helpful and contemporary analogy for understanding the importance of a prologue, she fails to recognize the centrality of other

---

108. Gibbs, *Mk 1,1–15*.

109. Ibid., 154.

110. Ibid., 156–57.

111. Ibid., 157–59.

112. Nightingale, *Don't Be Late*.

113. Ibid., 115; Nightingale sets the boundaries of the prologue at 1:1–13, but acknowledges the possibility of a 1:1–15 delineation.

114. Ibid., 117–18.

moments of "divine assurance" that stand apart from the prologue—namely, the divine affirmation at the transfiguration in Mark 9.

Summary Statements

Just as a prologue serves a particular function within a work, so also does a *Sammelbericht*, or "summary statement." Because the focus of this present study relates to the definition and role of Mark's opening material, the issues of prologue (as an opening unit) and summaries (as a possible means of marking the transition or separation between units) will be central to the discussion. Karl Schmidt has arguably set the initial agenda for any exploration of summary statements in the Gospels.[115] He argues that summarizing reports in the Gospel apparently coincide with geographical references and thus yield clues with regard to natural divisions within the structure of the work. As such, they function essentially as narrative "pegs" within the Gospel structure. C. H. Dodd[116] and Norman Perrin[117] subsequently followed suit. Charles Hedrick[118] has issued a slight challenge to this trend, however, with his suggestion that the summary reports stand alone as individual units independent of their surrounding pericopae. Their function is to introduce new information in a generalizing manner.

One of the possible Markan *Sammelberichte* is 1:14–15. Whereas Pesch has been noted to see 1:14–15 as original to Mark's source material with only minimal interference by Mark, others suggest that the summaries (such as 1:14–15) are editorial emendations sitting in the seams between larger units. G. van Oyen maintains that the Markan summaries perform a transitional function between various sections of the narrative.[119] For him, all of Mark's summaries are redactional and that list consists of 1:14–15, 21–22, 32–34, 39, 45; 2:1–2, 13; 3:7, 12; 4:1–2; 6:6b, 30–34, 53–56; and 10:1. Whereas Pesch argues that the summaries already existed in the tradition, Joachim Gnilka[120] joins van Oyen in viewing them as the products of Markan creativity. Wil-

---

115. Schmidt, *Der Rahmen der Geschichte Jesu*.
116. Dodd, *The Framework of the Gospel Narrative*, 396–400.
117. Perrin et al., *The New Testament*.
118. Hedrick, *The Role of Summary Statements in Mark*, 289–311.
119. Van Oyen, *De Summaria in Marcus*. Access to van Oyen's work was made possible by the following English review: Gillman, "De Summaria in Marcus En de Compositie van Mc 1:14-8:26," 760–62.
120. Gnilka, *Das Evangelium nach Markus*,.

helm Egger finds a middle position.¹²¹ Of such summaries, three (1:22; 2:13; 6:30) tend to be the least disputed with regard to editorial activity. As will be argued in this work, vv.14–15 do represent a *Sammelbericht*, the specific outcome of which is a climactic moment at the end of Mark's opening.

Narrative Criticism

The discussions above concerning the nature and function of literary devices such as prologues and summary statements provide a natural segue into literary analysis specifically as found among practitioners of narrative criticism. Mary Ann Tolbert applies her narrative approach to Mark, noting a general beginning, middle, and end ordering of Mark's overall work in ways that comport with typical Hellenistic practices. However, Boring's critique of her tendency to force 1:1–13 into a chiastic structure based on word repetition is probably well-founded.¹²² Further, her tendency to subsume nearly any written work under the category of "fiction" renders the term essentially meaningless.¹²³

A related attempt to employ narrative-critical methods with less-than-satisfying results is that of Robert Funk. For Funk, one aspect of narrative analysis involves the identification of *participants* in the narrative, and Funk asserts that Jesus is not depicted as "the 'subject' (viz., the agent)" until v. 14, thus serving to justify his identification of 1:13 as the closing scene to Mark's opening unit. This argument fails on multiple counts, only two of which will be highlighted here. First, Funk claims that "Jesus does not appear in 1:4–8, and in 1:9–11 he is the patient (something happens to him)."¹²⁴ Setting aside for the moment the fact that Jesus is identified directly and indirectly in 1:1–8, Funk fails to note that Jesus is introduced in v. 9 as an agent (i.e., a non-patient) in its purest form with the statement ἐγένετο ἐν ἐκείναις ταῖς ἡμέραις ἦλθεν Ἰησοῦς ἀπὸ Ναζαρὲτ τῆς Γαλιλαίας. Here, it can clearly be seen that Mark introduces Jesus in 1:9 as a principal agent.

Second, Funk suggests that Jesus remains in the shadows of John's ministry throughout v. 13 as evidenced by the passive voice of ἐβαπτίσθη in v. 9. However, that Jesus is listed here as the *grammatical subject* despite

---

121. Egger, *Frohbotschaft und Lehre*.
122. Boring, *Mark 1:1–15*, 59.
123. Tolbert, *Sowing the Gospel*, 30.
124. Funk, *The Poetics of Biblical Narrative*, 223.

the fact that "something happens to him"[125] clearly indicates that Mark's interest lies in the placement of Jesus on center stage. Thus, Funk's attempt to make John the unifying participant focus of 1:1-13 fails.

On the other hand, Frank Matera deploys his narrative-critical method to discern the way Mark utilizes his prologue to present the reader with information and background knowledge that is both essential for the reader and yet unknown to the actors in the narrative. As such, Matera constructively posits Mark's prologue (defined as 1:1-13) as the hermeneutical key to Mark's Gospel.[126] Detlev Dormeyer likewise considers the function of a narrative prologue, specifically comparing Mark's opening to that of the Hellenistic ideal biography.[127] P. Sankey views Mark's prologue (albeit from a more reader-oriented perspective) as demonstrating a series of fulfilled promises, thus giving literary coherence to 1:1-15: "There is always a gap between promise and fulfillment. Not only is fulfillment always partial, but its nature is never quite what was expected [. . .]. The effect of this misfit is to increase the reader's creative role in finding coherence."[128] (Sankey's argument will be given more attention in my final chapter.)

Other narrative treatments offer further promise. Tom Shepherd employs standard narrative categories in demonstrating the literary coherence of 1:1-15. These include settings, characters, actions and plot, time relationships, and narrator/implied reader.[129] In his monograph on the nature and role of 1:1-15, Hans-Josef Klauck broadens his employment of narrative-critical methods to interface with other disciplines, especially that of historical criticism. For him, "*ahistorisch, wie oft befürchtet, muß Erzählforschung also nicht sein.*"[130] Like Shepherd, Klauck's analysis leads him to confirm the unity of 1:1-15, where the appearance of John and the appearance of Jesus fund a parallelism conveyed via a diptych of 1:4-8 and 9-15, with 1:1-3 functioning as a "*Prolog im Prolog.*"[131] At the other end of the unit, 1:14-15 serves

---

125. Ibid.

126. Matera, *The Prologue as the Interpretative Key to Mark*, 15.

127. Dormeyer, *Mk 1,1-15 als Prolog*.

128. Sankey, "Promise and Fulfillment," 16, but its nature is never quite what was expected. The effect of this misfit is to increase the reader's creative role in finding coherence.

129. Shepherd, *The Narrative Role*, 152.

130. Klauck, *Vorspiel im Himmel*, 67.

131. Ibid., 33; this follows the conclusions of Feneberg, *Der Markusprolog*, 195; Klauck argues that this mimics the pattern of the introit to John's Gospel.

as the *propositio*.[132] After addressing the literary unity of Mark's prologue, Klauck goes on to argue that the Markan prologue serves a distinct purpose in introducing the reader to Mark's Gospel. That purpose is to provide a *leser-psychologischen Effekt* that initiates the reader.[133] The value of Klauck's work for my own study is great insofar as he not only asks the same questions I am asking (What is Mark's opening unit, and to what effect?), but also because he provides a multi-disciplinary approach that resists the temptation of allowing one approach to silence others.[134]

Perhaps no other narrative analysis is as comprehensive and judicious as that of Ohajuobodo Oko.[135] Oko sets out to examine the various passages in Mark that address the identity of Jesus. This, for Oko, is the central concern of Mark. For each passage, he conducts an analysis at the three levels of *story*, *discourse*, and *historical/theological mediation*. His analysis leads him to conclude that 1:1–15 does indeed represent a unit and, as a prologue, serves to introduce the whole of the Gospel.[136] With Klauck, Oko seeks to preserve the historical context of the narrative. For him, John the Baptizer functions as an historical nexus to Elijah's expected return in Mal 3:1. That return, contra Q, is not apocalyptic, but preparatory for the way of Jesus.[137] Oko follows the narrative categories of Funk with regard to such matters as participants and temporal/geographical indicators as markers of segments,[138] but does so with a consistency that renders his outcomes more defensible.[139]

---

132. Klauck, *Vorspiel im Himmel*, 34–35.

133. Ibid., 112–15.

134. Where my own study diverges from Klauck's is threefold. First, I intend to demonstrate that Mark 1:1 is an incipit standing over the prologue, and that 1:2–3 should be read as substantiation of John's appearance in 1:4. Klauck, on the other hand, argues that 1:1–3 is a "prologue within a prologue." Second, I will emphasize the rhetorical devices at play within the prologue, specifically as they provide legitimation of Jesus' identity as the Anointed Son of God. Third, I will emphasize the narrative trajectory of the prologue within a *Heilsgeschichte* framework.

135. Oko, *Who Then Is This?*

136. Ibid., 60.

137. Ibid., 75–76.

138. Funk, *The Poetics of Biblical Narrative*, 63–67.

139. Oko, *Who Then Is This?*, 60.

Genre Criticism

As the literary and compositional features of Mark come into view, questions emerge about the type of writing Mark best represents. Richard Burridge's landmark study shifted the balance of the debate decidedly in favor of reading Mark within the literary genre of Greco-Roman biography.[140] While some early trends in Gospel studies sought to recover the historical Jesus (and by extension represented biographical works in some measure),[141] others sought to read the Gospels in light of their parallels with popular Greco-Roman biography.[142] The advent of form and redaction criticisms derailed this initial trajectory toward biographical analysis. Charles Talbert's pioneering work, however, called into question the mythical claims of form criticism by classifying ancient Greco-Roman biography into five types. He assigns the Gospels to the category of biography on this basis insofar as they satisfy such criteria,[143] namely by attempting to "dispel a false image of the teacher and to provide a true model to follow."[144]

Burridge advanced and modified Talbert's position by comparing the canonical Gospels to ten examples of approximately contemporaneous Hellenistic *lives*.[145] He analyzes these ten works on the basis of their opening features (including titles and prologues), subjects (noting the allocation of space to subjects and their frequency as controlling subjects of verbs), various external features (including mode of representation, size, structure, scale, literary units, use of sources, and methods of characterization), and various internal features (setting, topics, style, atmosphere, quality of characterization, social setting and occasion, authorial intention, and purpose). After noting close affinities between the Synoptics and Greco-Roman βίοι, he concludes that "the next question, therefore, concerns how many shared features are necessary to make a genre."[146] His conclusion is that the Gospels meet that standard. "If genre is the key to a work's interpretation, and the genre of the gospels is βίος, then the key to their interpretation must be the person of their subject, Jesus of Nazareth."[147] Burridge's work will be

---

140. Burridge, *What Are the Gospels*.
141. For example, Renan, *The Life of Jesus*.
142. Votaw, *The Gospels and Contemporary Biographies*.
143. Talbert, *What Is a Gospel?*, 92–98.
144. Ibid., 94.
145. Burridge, *What Are the Gospels?*, 150–56.
146. Ibid., 211.
147. Ibid., 248.

THE FORM AND FUNCTION OF MARK 1:1–15

central to my study as I set out in part to compare Mark's opening with the various openings of the works Burridge used in his own study.

Bryan follows Burridge by suggesting that the genre of Mark can be inferred not from explicit markers, but rather from the dominance of a cluster of elements.[148] This is an important observation. One of Bryan's arguments for the biographical nature of Mark is Mark's use of a prologue among his opening features. Bryan defines this prologue as 1:1–8.[149] Santiago Guijarro likewise builds on Burridge's findings, using Mark's biographical prologue to indicate Mark's means of ascribing honor to Jesus.[150] Although he concedes that Mark does not completely follow traditional patterns of Hellenistic *lives* (notably due to the absence of Jesus' ancestry and upbringing in the opening of the Gospel), its beginning (Mark 1:1–15) functions as the normal introduction to a βίος by ascribing honor to the subject's character. According to Guijarro, Mark had a dilemma: how to present Jesus with honor despite his humble origins and dishonorable death.[151] "He did not praise Jesus' descent and education, but pointed to his virtues [. . .]. To understand adequately how Mark accomplished this and the connotations of his presentation of Jesus at the beginning of the Gospel, we must read these verses in light of the social values shared by him and his readers."[152] These values are drawn from Bruce Malina's anthropological assessment of the honor and shame culture of the first-century Greco-Roman world.[153] Guijarro suggests that the specific type of honor associated with Jesus is *ascribed* honor, revealed specifically at the climax of the second diptych of the prologue; the three episodes of 1:9–11, 12–13, 14–15, thus constitute a "status transformation ritual."[154] Ben Witherington follows suit in terms of viewing Mark as a Hellenistic *life*,[155] but also notices a strong Christological undercurrent funded by a series of identity questions concerning Jesus, such as those found at 1:27; 2:7, 16, 24; 4:41; 6:2; and 7:5.[156]

---

148. Bryan, *A Preface to Mark*, 13.

149. Ibid., 33–35.

150. Guijarro, *Why Does the Gospel of Mark*.

151. Ibid., 31.

152. Ibid., 32.

153. Malina, *The New Testament World*; see also deSilva, *Honor, Patronage, Kinship & Purity*.

154. Guijarro, *Why Does the Gospel of Mark*, 34.

155. Witherington III, *The Gospel of Mark*, 1–9.

156. Ibid., 37.

Some of the work related to the Christological aspects of Mark has already been discussed, specifically that of Weeden and Kingsbury's critique of Weeden. Eugene Boring further accentuates Mark's Christology by challenging the notion that Mark is an example of Hellenistic biography.[157] Although Mark demonstrates multiple points of contact with ancient βίοι, it is nevertheless a "quantum leap" from that genre, falling just short of *sui generis*. He highlights several principle departures from ancient biography. "These features," he asserts, "are all Christological. The Gospel of Mark is narrative Christology."[158] He further claims that "the orientation of a biography is toward the principal subject, to magnify his or her greatness. The orientation of Christology is away from the subject to the hidden actor, away from the Christ-figure as a character in the story to God the author of the story."[159] This aspect is especially evident in the way Boring highlights the passive sense and implied divine agency of χριστός.[160]

For Boring, the Christological narrative is structured in two major units: 1:16—8:21 and 11:1—16:8.[161] The prologue, as the introduction to the bi-partite structure, functions in four "literary-theological" ways by: 1) introducing the main characters; 2) introducing the five main themes of power, story, weakness, secrecy, and disciples; 3) focalizing[162] the narrative that follows the prologue; and 4) relating the time of the Gospel to the time of its readers.[163] Although I largely concur with Boring's conclusions, I question some of the avenues by which he arrives at those conclusions. For example, are the five main themes really "main themes" of Mark, and if so, are they indicated within the prologue in ways that would be transparent to his readers? I am not convinced that they are. Another question raised by his work pertains to the historical underpinnings of the narrative itself. By refracting Mark through a narrative-Christological lens, it seems to me that the historicity of the essential narrative is compromised.

---

157. Boring, *Mark*, 6–9.

158. Ibid., 8; see also *The Christology of Mark*, 125–53, and Tannehill, *The Gospel of Mark as Narrative Christology*, 57–96.

159. Boring, "Mark 1:1–15," 70.

160. Boring, *Mark*, 249–50.

161. Boring, "Mark 1:1–15," 46.

162. Here Boring relies on the work of Funk, *The Poetics of Biblical Narrative*.

163. Boring, "Mark 1:1–15," 61–69.

U. Mell also sees a trans-temporal dimension to Mark.[164] He bases his observations on the assumption that Mark 1:9–15 represents the earliest baptism tradition of Jesus. In the tradition, two primary features support the notion that Mark is primarily apocalyptic fulfillment-Christology: 1) Jesus is the suffering Son of God; and 2) Jesus is the re-created Adam—the ideal of God's creation.[165] Robert Guelich's defense of Mark 1:1–15 is likewise firmly grounded in a trans-temporal reading of Mark that finds in the prologue the satisfaction of Isaian expectations for salvation.[166]

Rhetorical Criticism

Thus far in this survey, I have explored questions related to the form of Mark's opening unit primarily through methods aimed at treating the text itself. As our view of Mark's opening material shifts from the particulars to the whole, we begin to get a sense of the basic framework of his introduction and can likewise begin to get a sense of what his purposes might be. This speaks to questions related to the function of Mark 1:1–15.

Assuming that Mark wrote with purpose in mind, what specific aim(s) can be inferred from his opening unit? Said differently, how does his prologue attempt to establish his reader upon the proper course for engaging the material that follows? I intend to demonstrate how rhetorical criticism in particular will be useful in providing an answer to this question.

In his 1968 Presidential Address to the annual meeting of the Society of Biblical Literature, James Muilenburg issued a call to move beyond form criticism's primary occupation with the observable and repeatable patterns of texts.[167] Without jettisoning the enterprise of form criticism, Muilenburg sought to establish a new trajectory in biblical studies that would give attention to the unique features and particularities of a text.

> What I am interested in, above all, is in understanding the nature of Hebrew literary composition, in exhibiting the structural patterns that are employed for the fashioning of a literary unit, whether in poetry or in prose, and in discerning the many and various devices by which the predications are formulated and

---

164. Mell, *Jesu Taufe durch Johannes*, 161–78.
165. Ibid., 177.
166. Guelich, *The Beginning of the Gospel*.
167. Muilenburg, *Form Criticism and Beyond*, 1–18.

ordered into a unified whole. Such an enterprise I should describe as rhetoric and the methodology as rhetorical criticism.[168]

In this summons, Muilenburg opened the conversation to matters of purpose and effect. He specifically outlined his method as principally involving two stages. The first stage consists of determining the scope of the literary unit—where the unit begins and ends. Indicators of demarcation can appear as "climactic or ballast lines."[169] Indicators can also appear via repetition, especially where a word, phrase, or concept appears at the beginning and is repeated at the end with emphasis. This creates what is known as a ring composition, or *inclusio* (discussed above).[170] The second stage consists of recognizing the various structures of composition, such as parallelism, refrains, strophes, turning points or breaks or shifts, particles, vocatives, rhetorical questions, and repetition (among others). The task of the exegete at this stage,

> is to recognize the structure of a composition and to discern the configuration of its component parts, to delineate the warp and woof out of which the literary fabric is woven, and to note the various rhetorical devices that are employed for marking, on the one hand, the sequence and movement of the pericope, and on the other, the shifts or breaks in the development of the writer's thought.[171]

Responding to Muilenburg's call for a rhetorical approach to the study of the Bible, George Kennedy proposed a reading that would follow that of an early Christian situated in a Greek-speaking world where rhetorical instruction was at the heart of education.[172] For him, all religious systems are rhetorical insofar as they attempt to communicate religious truth.[173] Rhetoric for Kennedy is "that quality in discourse by which a speaker or writer seeks to accomplish his purposes." This involves not merely delivery techniques, but *invention*— "the treatment of the subject matter, the use of evidence, the argumentation, and the control of emotion" especially as

---

168. Ibid., 8.
169. Ibid., 9.
170. Ibid.
171. Ibid., 10.
172. Kennedy, *New Testament Interpretation through Rhetorical Criticism*, 5.
173. Ibid., 158.

understood by Greeks and Romans.[174] The NT is thus positioned at the nexus of Greek and Jewish cultural currents. As such, the reader must accept that rhetoric is a universal, trans-cultural phenomenon—Aristotle's formulations are applicable in large measure anywhere and anytime.[175]

Central to such formulations is the idea that rhetoric is built on *enthymemes*, or statements with supporting reasons. What distinguishes Mark and much of the NT is its Jewish character that tends to rely upon non-enthymatic rhetoric. For Kennedy, this is "radical Christian rhetoric," and it appears not only in a variety of individual NT pericopae, but also largely characterizes Mark as a whole.[176] Because speech is linear in its deployment, it is cumulative. What follows can therefore only be understood in light of what precedes it.[177] Precisely because Mark sits at the junction of Greek and Jewish influences, we should expect to find that his rhetorical characteristics, like those of the other Gospel writers, are established in the opening chapters.[178]

Despite Kennedy's minimization of the role of genre in his methodological approach,[179] his commitment to reading within a first-century Hellenistic context will be fruitful for my own purposes. Likewise, the work of Ben Witherington seeks to recover the basic mindset of a first-century readership. Following Kennedy, Witherington notes the Greco-Roman aspects of the NT writings (and the corresponding commitment to rhetoric intrinsic to that world), as well as the importance of the "opening signals" in a work.[180] Mark, he suggests, is largely shaped by the aims of deliberative rhetoric in narrative form. Although the rhetoric at play is elementary, it is apparent that Mark is competent with basic rhetorical practices. His narrative has the distinctive form and feel of the ancient βίος genre and provides hortatory overtones suggesting the emulation of Jesus as an exemplar. The persuasive force can be seen largely in the way the smaller units (often consisting of *chreiai*, enthymemes, and short parabolic discourses) are stitched together seamlessly to give the narrative a sense of forward motion.

---

174. Ibid., 3.
175. Ibid., 10.
176. Ibid., 7, 104.
177. Ibid., 5.
178. Ibid., 101.
179. Ibid., 37, 97.
180. Witherington III, *The Gospel of Mark*, 3–4.

Mark's use of *chreiai* is distinctive, and shows clear evidence of condensation (distilling the ample amount of material available to Mark) rather than amplification (conflating from an insufficient amount of material). Elaborations (*ergasiae*) do occur, but this is a result of Mark's linking of *chreiai* together (often by means of εὐθύς, which should simply be understood as a marker of sequence, like *next*, rather than the overdrawn use of *immediately*).[181] If we are to take seriously the fact that Mark's beginning has a particular shape that was written for a particular effect, then the work of rhetorical critics like Kennedy and Witherington will be indispensable for this present study.

Summary

It should be evident by now that there is clearly no consensus as to what constitutes the extent of Mark's opening unit. As a result, there can be no clear consensus as to what Mark's purpose—if any—may have been in drafting his opening material. Moving forward, I intend to not only demonstrate that 1:1–15 is the scope of Mark's prologue, but also that, as such, it serves to legitimate Jesus as the Anointed Son of God.

---

181. Ibid., 24–28.

2

Formal Considerations

As already indicated in the preceding material, my aim in this study is twofold. The second aim is to address what purpose Mark's opening unit might possibly serve. The first is to establish the formal integrity of 1:1–15 as that opening unit, and the thrust of this chapter is to demonstrate that integrity. Such a demonstration will take place in three steps.[1] First, I will briefly address textual issues related to the passage. Second, I will conduct a syntactic analysis that identifies the main clause structures in use, as well as those subordinating clause structures that animate the main clauses. Third, I will survey the constellation of features that give the passage its literary unity.

Textual Analysis

"Son of God" (1:1)

My first task is to establish 1:1–15 on textual grounds. Broadly speaking, the passage reflects a fairly stable text. Of potential concern, though, is the υἱοῦ θεοῦ variant in 1:1, which cannot be resolved on the basis of external evidence. The debate largely centers on whether or not the phrase was likely to have been added by creative scribes—or omitted by careless ones. Those who suggest that υἱοῦ θεοῦ is a scribal emendation include Adela Yarbro Collins,[2] Bart Ehrman[3] and Peter Head.[4] Tommy Wasserman (among

---

1. Although it is customary for the writer of a work such as this to provide his or her own translation of the text in question early in that study, I will instead provide mine as part of my conclusion in hopes of demonstrating how the passage would read in view of the forgoing work.
2. Yarbro Collins, *Mark*, 130; *Establishing the Text*, 111–27.
3. Ehrman, *The Text of Mark*, 143–56.
4. Head, *A Text-Critical Study of Mark 1:1*, 621–29.

others) has launched a more compelling case that argues for the originality of the phrase, and I am inclined to follow him.[5] My approach will be to illustrate how the matter can be resolved by looking at the prologue as a whole. My inclination is that the phrase is original, although I concur with Craig Evans, who maintains that Mark's Christology is in no way compromised if the words are omitted.[6] Much more will be said about this matter toward the conclusion of this study.

"In the Prophets" (1:2)

A second textual matter relates to the ascription of the citation in 1:2–3 to Isaiah. In the KJV we note, instead of *written in Isaiah the prophet*, it is simply *written in the prophets*. This version reflects an alternate reading consistent with the Western text type—a reading presumably created to eliminate the embarrassing matter. So high is their confidence in the received text (which reads, *in the prophets*) that Rendel Harris and Vacher Burch suggest it is actually "right, and the earliest codices of the New Testament [with the reading *in Isaiah the prophet*] are wrong."[7]

While some MSS (A L W)[8] read τοῖς προφήταις in place of τῷ Ἠσαΐᾳ τῷ προφήτῃ, support for the move is slim. The variant is most likely accounted for by the seeming difficulty of associating 1:2 directly with Isaiah. This makes τῷ Ἠσαΐᾳ τῷ προφήτῃ the more difficult reading, and the one to be preferred.

John "the Baptizer" (1:4)

Two other matters present themselves. One is the variance of the definite article before βαπτίζων in 1:4. Whereas the inclusion of the article is consistent with a titular reference to John, that decision likely reflects a later, more developed sense of John's role and purpose within the tradition of the early

---

5. Wasserman, *The Son of God*, 20–50; see also Boring, *Mark*, 30; Guelich, *Mark 1—8:26*, 6; Pesch, *Das Markusevangelium*, 1:77; Anderson, *The Gospel of Mark*, 67.

6. Evans, *Mark's Incipit*, 68.

7. Harris and Burch, *Testimonies*, 22. They further declare that "[e]very student knows that the second verse of the Gospel has been replaced by modern editors in the form, 'As it is written in the prophet Isaiah,' in place of the conventional, 'As it is written in the prophets,'" 21.

8. Guelich, *Mark 1—8:26*, 6.

church. The decision to include it also tends to accompany an additional emendation, namely the removal of καὶ immediately before κηρύσσων in the same verse.[9] In order to make grammatical sense of the passage, the καὶ must be removed to create a smooth sense if the variant article is accepted.[10] As with the υἱοῦ θεοῦ phrase, the variant ὁ can only be resolved by an appeal to internal evidence, and that will also be addressed in light of my view of the prologue as a whole.

The "Kingdom" of God (1:14)

The other issue relates to the insertion of τῆς βασιλείας between τὸ εὐαγγέλιον and τοῦ θεοῦ in 1:14. France is likely correct in maintaining that the insertion is an "improvement" meant to smooth out the presumed oddity of "the gospel of God." The fact that "the kingdom of God" appears in the immediately following verse confirms, for France, the likelihood of scribal emendation.[11]

In sum, the textual issues that present themselves in Mark's opening unit will most likely be resolved only by careful consideration of the internal evidence, and one of the possible outcomes of this present study is a better sense of how the whole of the Markan prologue might address such matters. Regardless of one's commitments, none of the variants is likely to directly impact the results of this study related to the overall form of Mark's opening unit.

Syntactic Analysis

The second task in exploring the formal features of 1:1–15 is to survey the passage, specifically making note of the high-level assertions and attendant modifiers that populate the unit. Drawing on the work of Constantine Campbell,[12] I will provide an outline of the essential contours of the pas-

---

9. Although France, *The Gospel of Mark*, 60–61, explains the circumstance in constructive ways, his conclusions are, in my estimation, problematic for internal reasons, as I will show later in this study.

10. Compare "John appeared baptizing in the wilderness and proclaiming a baptism" to "John [add *the*] Baptizer appeared in the wilderness [delete *and*] proclaiming a baptism."

11. France, *The Gospel of Mark*, 89.

12. Campbell, *Basics of Verbal Aspect in Biblical Greek*.

sage by noting the aorist indicative verbs at work. The aim of this move is to isolate the primary subject-verb relationships that provide the backbone of the narrative so as to establish its main foci.

It must be said with all clarity that Mark's original audience would have most likely encountered Mark's Gospel aurally rather than visually.[13] That said, we must pay careful attention to the linear nature of the text, specifically considering the way the narrative unfolds. As readers in a twenty-first-century context, we have the disadvantage of being removed from Mark's writing chronologically, linguistically, and culturally. It is simply not possible for us to recreate the environment in which Mark would have likely been heard. Such is not to say that we ought not try, though. In that spirit, my tactic at this point is to proceed verse-by-verse (or better said, clause-by-clause) through 1:1–15, noting areas of ambiguity or concern along the way.

The Relationship between 1:1 and 1:2–3

We no sooner embark upon our journey than we encounter a huge exegetical issue for modern interpreters of Mark. Should the text identified as 1:1 be read with the material that follows or considered as a title set apart from what follows? Grammatically, the subordinating conjunction καθὼς will be the deciding factor. Everything depends on whether the term looks backward (to a verbless clause) or forward (to a verbal clause) in this case. My suspicion is the latter, and I will offer two primary reasons for believing so: 1) the subordinating conjunction καθὼς is far more likely to relate grammatically to the verb ἐγένετο in 1:4 than it is to the verbless text string in 1:1; and 2) 1:1 is likely to stand as a heading or title.

"Just As" . . . "John Appeared"

Even though we cannot read through first-century lenses, one of the advantages of being a modern reader is having easy access to written texts. However, we must constantly remind ourselves that the writings of the ancient world (especially those of the NT) were aural texts written to be *heard* more than *seen*. Written texts give us the opportunity to examine and re-examine written materials from any angle and any number of times. That skews our

---

13. Bryan, *A Preface to Mark*.

hearing a bit. Aural texts unfold, and it is imperative that we as readers keep that in mind, specifically noting how words and concepts accumulate meaning in a linear direction.

Such is not to say, however, that aural reading takes place mechanically and unvaryingly from one word to the next. An illustration of how such reading is dynamic and responsive is that of today's voice recognition software. In my limited engagement with it, I have noted a seeming irony: the slower and more carefully I speak into a voice recognition device, the more the device struggles to recognize my speech. However, when I speak more fluidly and naturally, the device renders my speech surprisingly well. If I observe the display screen of my device as I speak into it, I note that the device is constantly adjusting and correcting based on the steady stream of inputs it is receiving. The device is in fact engaged in aural reading. For example, if I dictate, *I will see you when there* . . . , the device will likely pause, waiting to hear if for the last word spoken I mean *their*, *there*, or *they're*. It may initially register *their*, but if the following words are *is more time*, the device uses this additional information and quickly backs up to update its understanding of *their*, changing it to *there*, so that the device's understanding is, *I will see you when there is more time*.

This is generally how aural reading works. With that in mind, I suspect that when Mark's listeners heard the phrase καθὼς γέγραπται, they would have initially indexed it to 1:1 since that would be their only reference point thus far. That indexing would likely be uncomfortable. However, the phrase would have likely created a simultaneous expectation for an appeal to Scripture. The citation of Isaiah in 1:2–3 would have immediately satisfied that expectation, but what would have remained unresolved is the relevance of the citation: does it provide the *basis* for the opening text string of 1:1? Mark's listeners might have initially assumed so, but as the utterance would have unfolded, I suspect that they would have quickly updated their understanding of the citation as the basis for the advent of John the Baptizer in 1:4. Said differently, the mention of John and his wilderness ministry of baptism would most likely have caused the listeners to quickly back up and reformulate their understanding of *just as it has been written*.

Not all commentators agree, however. Guelich, for instance, suggests that "1:2 clearly requires a close syntactical relationship with 1:1."[14] He bases this assumption on two points: "First, καθὼς never introduces a sentence in either Mark or the rest of the NT documents except in the unrelated

---

14. Guelich, *Mark 1—8:26*, 7.

καθώς/οὕτως combination [. . .]. Second, when καθώς occurs in a formula with γέγραπται, it always refers to the preceding rather than to the succeeding material [. . .].[15] This initial argument (that καθώς never introduces a sentence) can be challenged on at least three grounds.

First, the conjunction καθώς nowhere else subordinates a clause to a verbless phrase in Mark. This is not to suggest that it could not be happening in 1:1–2, but rather that it is unlikely. In fact, such a move would be a bit incoherent, especially as the opening of a document. Here is a list of all of the occurrences of καθώς in Mark (not including 1:2). In each case, the conjunction clearly subordinates a clause to a verbal clause (the subordinate verb is italicized in each case):

Mark	Main Clause	καθώς	Subordinate Clause
4:33	Jesus was speaking parables	as	they *were able* to hear
9:13	They did to him	as	it *has been written*
11:6	They spoke to them	as	Jesus *spoke*
14:16	They found	as	he *told* them
14:21	The Son of Man goes	as	it *has been written*
15:8	The crowd began to ask	as	he *was accustomed to do*[16] for them
16:7	You will see him	as	I *told* you

Guelich's first argument requires a direct relationship to exist between καθώς and the preceding verbless phrase, which is an unattested phenomenon elsewhere in Mark.

Perhaps we should widen our net a bit to see if there is evidence in Mark of the use of a synonym for καθώς that might function to substantiate a verbless clause elsewhere in Mark. The range of conjunctions that Mark uses to introduce the formulaic expression γέγραπται (specifically where an OT text is cited or directly alluded to) includes ὡς (7:6), πῶς (9:12, positing a question then answered with a καθώς clause in 9:13), οὐ (11:17, establishing a question that assumes a positive response relative to the citation), and ὅτι (14:27, understood in a causal sense). It will be observed that in every case, the conjunction/γέγραπται formula connects to a clause based on a finite verb. Here is a listing of those occurrences:

---

15. Ibid.

16. Here, a customary or habitual use of the imperfect tense is most likely at play. See Wallace, *Greek Grammar beyond the Basics*, 548.

Mark	Main Clause	Conj.	Subordinate Clause
7:6	Isaiah prophesied correctly	ὡς	γέγραπται
9:12	Elijah comes and restores ...	πῶς	γέγραπται
11:17	You have made it a den of robbers ...	οὐ	γέγραπται
14:27	All of you will fall away ...	ὅτι	γέγραπται

As with καθώς, none of these other subordinating conjunctions that introduce a scriptural citation ever point to a verbless clause in Mark.

Perhaps, then, we ought to broaden our nets even further to include the Synoptics. A quick survey of Matthew and Luke reveals the following passages in which the formulaic γέγραπται is governed by a subordinating conjunction:

Passage	Main Clause	Conjunction	Subordinate Clause
Matt 2:4–5	Messiah is to be born in Bethlehem	οὕτως γὰρ	γέγραπται
Matt 4:6	Cast yourself down	γὰρ	γέγραπται
Matt 4:10	Go away from me, Satan	γὰρ	γέγραπται
Matt 26:24	The Son of Man will go	καθὼς	γέγραπται
Matt 26:31	All of you will fall away	γὰρ	γέγραπται
Luke 2:22–23	They took him to Jerusalem	καθὼς	γέγραπται
Luke 3:3–4	He went proclaiming	ὡς	γέγραπται
Luke 4:9–10	Cast yourself down	γὰρ	γέγραπται
Luke 24:26	For the Christ to suffer and be raised	οὕτως	γέγραπται

These are the uses of subordinating conjunctions with γέγραπται in Matthew and Luke. In no case does such a formulation point to a verbless clause. It should also be noted that no such instances can be found in John's Gospel, either. The net could be widened so far as the entire corpus of the NT, but I believe the analysis above adequately demonstrates the improbability of Mark 1:1 being syntactically connected to 1:2. To suggest that 1:1 is connected to 1:2 creates the kinds of problems of which Mark has unjustifiably been accused. The plain sense of the passage reads comfortably if one acknowledges a full stop after 1:1, then reads 1:2–3 as the subordinated basis for 1:4—John appeared in the wilderness baptizing *just as it has been written.*

Second, Guelich specifically makes an exception of the καθώς/οὕτως combination on the ground that it is unrelated. The sense of the καθώς/οὕτως combination is comparative, as Wallace notes.[17] This comparative sense can be seen explicitly in a number of Gospel passages, but three in particular stand out. In each case, καθώς begins the sentence (or is immediately preceded by καί), a direct reference to an OT person is made, and οὕτως then introduces a contemporary circumstance or future event that is brought to bear alongside the OT reference. Here is how Mark 1:2-4 reads when brought alongside these other three passages (here translated and abridged):

	(καὶ) καθώς Clause	οὕτως Clause
Luke 11:30	*Just as* Jonah became a sign	*so* also will the Son of Man be
Luke 17:26	And *just as* occurred in the days of Noah	*so* also will be in the days of the Son of Man
John 3:14	And *just as* Moses lifted the serpent	*so* must the Son of Man be lifted
Mark 1:2-4	*Just as* has been written in Isaiah	(implied *so*) John appeared

As the reader will note, Mark's citation of Isaiah maintains continuity with citations of Jonah, Noah, and Moses in the καθώς clauses. The only significant differences are: a) whereas the passages from Luke and John are explicitly Christological with respect to Son of Man language, the Markan passage is less so (although only by a matter of degree); b) Mark's reference is to the past whereas the others are to the future; and b) Mark's passage omits an explicit οὕτως. This really does not create an obstacle for seeing the similarity with the other three passages if one is willing to grant Mark the literary license to imply the term. It may be the case that he was not familiar with the combination or simply preferred not to use it (since nowhere in Mark does the exact combination appear in this comparative sense).[18] It can be seen, however, that Mark's use of καθώς here is consistent *in principle* with the common καθώς/οὕτως combination. The Greek NT[19] captures this sense—rightly, I think—when it assigns an upper case letter to Καθώς in 1:2 and a comma after the last word of 1:3, thus subordinating the conjunction to the first finite verb outside of the citation—ἐγένετο.[20] The sense, then, is this: *just as it has been written, John*

---

17. Ibid., 662–63, 674–75, 762.

18. Incidentally, the exact combination appears in this comparative sense nowhere in Matthew, and only twice in Luke (11:30; 17:26) and four times in John (3:14; 12:50; 14:31; 15:4).

19. Nestle and Aland, *Novum Testamentum Graece*.

20. See also Haenchen, *Der Weg Jesu*, 38; Lane, *The Gospel of Mark*, 41.

appeared. To assume instead that Mark is using the term in 1:2 as a means of substantiating 1:1 is quite problematic.[21]

Acknowledging that language is at times more of an art than a science, it would actually seem to be the case that Mark and the other Gospel writers take some liberties in the ways they create their comparisons. Introducing a parallel account into the previous table and tweaking the arrangement of the table only slightly, we see how this is the case:

	Initial Comparative Clause	Subsequent Comparative Clause
Luke 17:26	And just as (καθώς) occurred in the days of Noah	so (οὕτως) also will be in the days of the Son of Man
Matt 24:37 (parallel)	As (ὥσπερ) the days of Noah	so (οὕτως) will be the coming of the Son of Man
Matt 24:38–39 (extended parallel)	As (ὥς) was in those days	so (οὕτως) will be the coming of the Son of Man
Luke 17:28–30	As (καθώς) happened in the days of Lot	so (κατὰ τὰ αὐτά) will be the day
John 3:14	And just as (καθώς) Moses lifted the serpent	so (οὕτως) must the Son of Man be lifted
Mark 1:2–4	Just as (καθώς) has been written in Isaiah	so John appeared

These data suggest the following possible combinations where the initial component of the comparative structure begins or appears at the beginning of a sentence: καώς/οὕτως, ὥσπερ/οὕτως, καθώς/κατὰ τὰ αὐτα, ὥς/οὕτως. Mark's choice to imply the subsequent conjunction appears to be within tolerances.

This brings us to the third way Guelich's first argument can be challenged. Given the diversity of patterns above, it does not seem a stretch to believe that Mark's preferred combination might be καθώς in tandem with an implied conjunction that connects the comparative clauses. What is even more suggestive is the form of Luke 17:28, which matches the pattern of 1:2–4. That pattern consists of: 1) a sentence or definable utterance that begins with καθώς and is immediately followed by 2) a lengthy reference to an OT circumstance and 3) culminating in a comparison initiated by something *other than* οὕτως. Here are the two passages alongside one another:

---

21. Among those who agree that the conjunction begins a new thought and is thus distinct from 1:1 are Taylor, *The Gospel According to St. Mark*, 153; and Anderson, *The Gospel of Mark*, 67–68.

FORMAL CONSIDERATIONS

	Initial Conjunction	Initial Clause	OT Restatement	Subsequent Conjunction	Subsequent Clause
Luke 17:28-30	ὁμοίως καθὼς	ἐγένετο ἐν ταῖς ἡμέραις Λώτ	ἤσθιον, ἔπινον, ἠγόραζον, ἐπώλουν, ἐφύτευον, ᾠκοδόμουν· ᾗ δὲ ἡμέρᾳ ἐξῆλθεν Λὼτ ἀπὸ Σοδόμων, ἔβρεξεν πῦρ καὶ θεῖον ἀπ' οὐρανοῦ καὶ ἀπώλεσεν πάντας	κατὰ τὰ αὐτὰ	ἔσται ᾗ ἡμέρᾳ ὁ υἱὸς τοῦ ἀνθρώπου ἀποκαλύπτεται
Mark 1:2-4	καθὼς	γέγραπται ἐν τῷ Ἠσαΐᾳ τῷ προφήτῃ	ἰδοὺ ἀποστέλλω τὸν ἄγγελόν μου πρὸ προσώπου σου, ὃς κατασκευάσει τὴν ὁδόν σου· φωνὴ βοῶντος ἐν τῇ ἐρήμῳ· ἑτοιμάσατε τὴν ὁδὸν κυρίου, εὐθείας ποιεῖτε τὰς τρίβους αὐτοῦ	(implied)	ἐγένετο Ἰωάννης βαπτίζων ἐν τῇ ἐρήμῳ καὶ κηρύσσων βάπτισμα μετανοίας εἰς ἄφεσιν ἁμαρτιῶν

I have offered three responses to Guelich's first objection to taking 1:1 as grammatically independent of 1:2. He suggests that Mark 1:1 must be read in continuity with 1:2, since καθώς (which introduces 1:2) nowhere introduces a sentence in the NT except for in καθώς/οὕτως combinations. As I have just shown, the καθώς in 1:2 *is* part of a καθώς/οὕτως combination in principle, and is fully comfortable in an initial position. The range of variations under very similar circumstances confirms that.

His second objection relates to the formulaic expression καθὼς γέγραπται, which he claims never substantiates material that follows the citation. This objection can be likewise dismissed—as with the previous point—on the grounds that writers exercise latitude in the ways they structure their utterances. By enlarging our view of formulae used to introduce OT citations, we can acknowledge that the field of options is a bit larger than Guelich suggests.

The phrase καθὼς γέγραπται is not the only formula that can be used to point to a direct citation of OT Scripture. In fact, not all scriptural citation formulae in the NT are built on καθὼς γέγραπται (see below), and not all occurrences of καθὼς γέγραπται are direct scriptural citation formulae (e.g., Mark 9:13; 14:21). Therefore, the question is not whether καθὼς γέγραπται as a citation formula ever points to succeeding material, but whether any citation formula can point to its fulfillment or resolution in a subsequent rather than a preceding passage.

We have already seen uses of καθὼς γέγραπται where it points to a scriptural citation, but we need to also recognize that other formulae are available and attested in the Gospels, such as οὕτως γέγραπται (Matt 2:5; Luke 24:46), ὡς γέγραπται (Mark 7:6; Luke 3:4), and simply γέγραπται (most notably in the temptation accounts; see Matt 4:4, 7; Luke 4:4, 8). The author of the Fourth Gospel opts for a slightly different construction involving γεγραμμένον in a periphrastic phrase. It is to this use that we now turn.

John tends to allude to OT citations a bit differently than the Synoptic authors do. Rather than employ the perfect indicative, John seems to prefer a periphrastic participle: ἐστιν γεγραμμένον. In five instances, this construction points to an explicit OT citation.[22] What is of most interest for our present discussion, though, is what appears in 6:45. Here, the concept of *teaching* is the bond between the citation (καὶ ἔσονται πάντες διδακτοὶ θεοῦ) and the contemporary circumstance (πᾶς ὁ ἀκούσας παρὰ τοῦ πατρὸς καὶ μαθὼν ἔρχεται πρὸς ἐμε,). It will be noted that the contemporary circumstance, as in Mark 1:4, appears *after* the citation rather than before it. In this way, John 6:45 provides a basis for the coherence of Mark 1:2–4. The following table will illustrate:

	Citation Formula	OT Citation	Subsequent Clause
John 6:45	ἔστιν γεγραμμένον ἐν τοῖς προφήταις	καὶ ἔσονται πάντες διδακτοὶ θεοῦ	πᾶς ὁ ἀκούσας παρὰ τοῦ πατρὸς καὶ μαθὼν ἔρχεται πρὸς ἐμέ
Mark 1:2–4	καθὼς γέγραπται ἐν τῷ Ἠσαΐᾳ τῷ προφήτῃ	ἰδοὺ ἀποστέλλω τὸν ἄγγελόν μου πρὸ προσώπου σου, ὃς κατασκευάσει τὴν ὁδόν σου· φωνὴ βοῶντος ἐν τῇ ἐρήμῳ· ἑτοιμάσατε τὴν ὁδὸν κυρίου, εὐθείας ποιεῖτε τὰς τρίβους αὐτοῦ	ἐγένετο Ἰωάννης βαπτίζων ἐν τῇ ἐρήμῳ καὶ κηρύσσων βάπτισμα μετανοίας εἰς ἄφεσιν ἁμαρτιῶν

One further observation is worth sharing in this regard. My case in point is the first volume of *Plutarch's Lives* in the Loeb Classical Series.[23]

---

22. John 2:17; 6:31, 45; 10:34; 12:14.
23. Perrin, *Plutarch's Lives*.

That volume contains the *Theseus*. We find here—in the very first words of Plutarch's very first *Life*— the following opening:

> Just as geographers, O Socius Senecio, crowd on to the outer edges of their maps the parts of the earth which elude their knowledge, with explanatory notes that "What lies beyond is sandy desert without water and full of wild beasts," or "blind marsh," or "Scythian cold," or "frozen sea," so in the writing of my Parallel Lives, now that I have traversed those periods of time which are accessible to probable reasoning and which afford basis for a history dealing with facts, I might well say of the earlier periods: "What lies beyond is full of marvels and unreality, a land of poets and fabulists, of doubt and obscurity." (Plutarch, *Theseus* 1.1; Perrin)

The relevance and significance of the passage for the question at hand may not be immediately apparent. However, a comparison of the text alongside Mark's opening material and in the original Greek will quickly reveal both the relevance and the significance.

	Subordinating Conjunction	Reference to Writings	Excerpt from Writings	Comparative Conjunction	Main Clause
Theseus 1.1	Ὥσπερ	ἐν ταῖς γεωγραφίαις	Τὰ δὶ ἐπέκεινα θῖνες ἄνυδροι καὶ θηριώδεις...	οὕτως	ἐμοὶ... καλῶς εἶχεν εἰπεῖν....
Mark 1.2–4	Καθὼς	γέγραπται ἐν τῷ Ἠσαΐᾳ τῷ προφήτῃ	ἰδοὺ ἀποστέλλω τὸν ἄγγελόν μου...		ἐγένετο Ἰωάννης βαπτίζων....

Perrin, in his rather free translation above, fails to convey the parallels. Here is a more wooden translation of the two passages:

	Subordinating Conjunction	Reference to Writings	Excerpt from Writings	Comparative Conjunction	Main Clause
Theseus 1.1	(Just) as	in the earth-writings	"Now the further reaches are dry sand-heaps and beast-infested ...	so	it is right for me to say ....
Mark 1.2–4	(Just) as	it is written in Isaiah the prophet	"Behold, I am sending my messenger ... "		John appeared baptizing ....

Plutarch opens his βίος of Theseus with a subordinating conjunction of comparison, just as Mark does. He then references a text for the basis of the comparison, as does Mark. He then cites from that text, as does Mark. He then provides an explicit counterpart for the comparison by means of the conjunction οὕτως. He then provides the comparison, as does Mark. The only difference of any potential significance is that Mark implies his comparative conjunction in the main clause, which creates no syntactic difficulties and fits within the range of options available to writers. Thus, with the opening statement of the *Theseus*, we have concrete demonstration by an unquestioned authority of the same construction as we see in Mark 1:2–4. In a word, reading 1:1 independently of 1:2 is both attested and coherent.

In sum, Guelich's objections can be dismissed on a number of grounds. First, that Mark does not elsewhere use a citation to support a following— as opposed to a preceding—claim does not rule out the possibility of such use here. Singularity is no basis for exclusion. Second, Guelich's sampling size is far too small to be statistically significant. By restricting his sample exclusively to καθὼς γέγραπται formulae (and specifically excluding καθὼς/ οὕτως combinations), he fails to consider a number of circumstances in which the sense is shared—despite minor formal differences. Third, his determination of the "syntactical impossibility" of placing a period at the end of 1:1 is rather a moot point.[24] The placement of the period is obviously editorial and is simply meant to set off 1:1 from 1:2; it is not necessarily meant to suggest that 1:1 is a syntactic sentence requiring final punctuation. Fourth, the parallel of Plutarch's introduction to his biography of Theseus demonstrates the syntactic viability of Mark's construction. This reference to Plutarch is perhaps the highest court of appeal when it comes to matters of grammar and syntax. Fifth, the suggestion that each of the other citation formulae in Mark points to the preceding rather than the following material fails to acknowledge the fact that the citations outside of the prologue all originate from Markan characters. In Mark 1, we have an entirely different circumstance—we have a formula coming straight from Mark's pen. The objection is therefore an apples-to-oranges comparison. Finally, Mark's placement of the citation ahead of its reference enables him to accomplish a critical task in his prologue, namely this: to create an historical trajectory that begins with the prophet Isaiah, transitions through John, and culminates with Jesus.

24. Guelich, *Mark 1—8:26*, 7.

I therefore maintain that the reading as given in the NA27 is the most plain sense and likely solution. Further support for this plain sense view comes from the parallel accounts in the other Gospels. These provide explicit warrant for understanding the early church's common conviction that relates the Isaiah prophecy to the advent of John the Baptizer: Matt 3:1; 11:10; Luke 3:3–4; 7:27; and John 1:19.

1:1 as Title of the Prologue

Having attempted to demonstrate the syntactic independence of 1:1 from 1:2, I now want to demonstrate how 1:1 is coherent as a title of the prologue.

We know for certain that Mark is at least acquainted with the OT. In fact, he makes that clear immediately in 1:2. Verses 2–3 represent the only citation of the OT that Mark himself employs; all others come on the lips of Markan characters. This suggests that Mark may be holding the OT as his primary framework for his narrative. Therefore, if we want to understand how Mark might have structured his beginning, we might look no further than the OT corpus.

Much has been made of Mark's use of ἀρχή in 1:1, specifically as it relates to or conjures images of Gen 1:1 (ἐν ἀρχῇ).[25] Genesis 1:1 generalizes and summarizes details that are then particularized in 1:2—2:3/4,[26] culminating in the parallel bracket of 2:3/4 where we hear direct echoes of 1:1, including *God, created, heavens,* and *earth*. It seems initially apparent, then, that Gen 1:1 plausibly represents a title that stands minimally over 1:2—2:3/4, if not a larger swath of literary real estate.[27] In a similar way, we see that Mark 1:1 generalizes and summarizes the details that are particularized in 1:2–15, culminating in the parallel bracket (or *inclusio*; see below) of 1:14–15 where we hear echoes of 1:1, including *gospel, Jesus,* and *God* (if one allows for the textual variant).

Scholars have also noted resonance between Mark 1:1 and other introductory formulae in the OT. Evans highlights the various points of contact between Mark's *incipit* and those of the Priene Calendar Inscription.

---

25. For example, Lohmeyer, *Das Evangelium des Markus*, 10; Edwards, *The Gospel according to Mark*, 23; Cole, *Mark*, 103; Witherington III, *The Gospel of Mark*, 69.

26. Because of the transitional nature of Gen 2:4, it is difficult to discern whether it should represent the conclusion of the opening unit, or the entry to the next.

27. For a helpful and highly accessible survey of the interpretative range of options regarding Gen 1:1, see Arnold, *Encountering the Book of Genesis*, 24–26.

He specifically notes the parallel use in the inscription of εὐαγγέλια (used twice, both instances in the plural), ἄρχειν (used in infinitival form), and reference to a divine agent.[28] E. Lohmeyer has observed similarities in form between 1:1 and various OT introductory citations in wisdom literature, including Prov 1:1; Song 1:1; Ecc 1:1.[29] Pesch notes specifically the high degree of comportment between Mark 1:1 and Hosea 1:2a, calling the latter *die beste Parallele* with Mark 1:1.[30] Here are the passages in comparison:

Prov 1:1	Σαλωμῶντος υἱοῦ Δαυιδ ὃς ἐβασίλευσεν ἐν Ισραηλ
Song 1:1	ᾆσμα ᾀσμάτων ὅ ἐστιν τῷ Σαλωμων
Ecc 1:1	παροιμίαι Σαλωμῶντος υἱοῦ Δαυιδ ὃς ἐβασίλευσεν ἐν Ισραηλ
Hos 1:2a	ἀρχὴ λόγου κυρίου πρὸς Ωσηε
Mark 1:1	Ἀρχὴ τοῦ εὐαγγελίου Ἰησοῦ Χριστοῦ [υἱοῦ θεοῦ]

Less noted are the titular headings in the prophetic material, which for our study may be especially significant given Mark's appeal to Isaiah in Mark 1:2. Isaiah 1:1a reads, ὅρασις ἣν εἶδεν Ησαιας υἱὸς Αμως. John Oswalt identifies this as a superscript:

> (It) is typical of the prophetic books in general, in that it identifies the prophet at the outset. Furthermore, it follows the pattern of all but Ezekiel, Jonah, Haggai, and Zechariah in the structure of the rubric, i.e., "The word of the Lord/oracle/vision which came to the prophet/the prophet saw at such and such a time."[31]

Generally, these superscriptions invoke some sort of utterance that originates from God. In Mark 1:1, the utterance is the announcement of good news via τὸ εὐαγγέλιον, which has as its initial origin (ἀρχή) the offstage divine discourse between the Father and the Son in 1:2-3. Like Isa 1:1, Mark 1:1 seems to serve to identify the work, or—in this case—the opening of the work. It also locates John within the stream of OT prophetic tradition.

We see similar evidence in the NT, whether it is an epistolary prescript, a prescript such as Luke provides in Luke 1:1-4, or the introduction of Revelation 1:1. In fact, it seems to be typical for a NT writer to identify his work by means of some sort of introductory superscription or

---

28. Evans, *Mark's Incipit*, 69.
29. Lohmeyer, *Das Evangelium des Markus*, 1:10.
30. Pesch, *Anfang des Evangeliums Jesu Christi*, 336.
31. Oswalt, *The Book of Isaiah, Chapters 1-39*, 81.

title. Matthew's Gospel is especially noteworthy in this regard insofar as it specifically features a superscription (βίβλος γενέσεως) in 1:1 that is then paralleled in 1:17 (αἱ γενεαί), forming a clear *inclusio* where the first line establishes and the last line completes the trajectory.

Arguing from different grounds, Eugene LaVerdiere maintains that 1:1 should be understood as a *title* as opposed to a *name* for the Gospel, but is nevertheless syntactically independent from 1:2. "Mark's Gospel has a name," he maintains, "[it is] the 'Gospel According to Mark.'"[32] Following suit, L. de Santis,[33] E. Krentz,[34] J. Kudasiewicz,[35] and S. Samuel[36] have all contributed articles defending or assuming 1:1 as syntactically independent from 1:2, as have several monographs and full-scale commentaries.[37]

Thus, evidence is ample that 1:1 is an independent thought, both in terms of syntax and in terms of biblical and extra-biblical parallels. A question that will remain unanswered at the moment relates to the extent of the title: Does it relate to the prologue exclusively, or should it be understood to serve as a title for the entire Gospel? I will address that matter in my final chapter.

Clause-Level Analysis

At this point, my reader may lament the amount of ink spilled pursuing what may seem to be a pedantic issue. This issue of the relationship between 1:1 and the text following, however, is essential for establishing a clause-level analysis. In essence, the most irreducible unit of a sentence is the subject-verb relationship, where the subject can be understood as the main topic or focus of the sentence and the verb as the assertion or predication about that subject. Whereas I prefer to think of a grammatical phrase as a group of related words that function as a single part of speech, for me a clause is the next order of magnitude insofar as the clause

---

32. LaVerdiere, *The Beginning of the Gospel*, 19.
33. De Santis, *Mc 1,1*, 175–92.
34. Krentz, *The Starting Point of the Gospel*, 412.
35. Kudasiewicz, *Poczatek Ewangelii*.
36. Samuel, *The Beginning of Mark*, 405.
37. Pesch, *Das Markusevangelium*, 1:74–77; Lane, *The Gospel of Mark*, 42–45; Donahue and Harrington, *The Gospel of Mark*, 59–60; Boring, *Mark*, 29–32; LaVerdiere, *The Beginning of the Gospel*, 19; Yarbro Collins, *Mark*, 130; Cook, *The Structure and Persuasive Power of Mark*, 138–40, 173; Schmithals, *Das Evangelium nach Markus*, 73–76.

enlarges a phrase to include a subject-verb relationship. These subject-verb relationships function organically to give structure to a discourse. As the organizing elements, subject-verb relationships are like individual bones in a skeleton. By extension, I might suggest that the remainder (and bulk) of the text outside of and beyond the subject-verb relationship—as with human bodies—comprises the *flesh* of the narrative. To carry the analogy one step further, we can observe that conjunctions (I specifically have in mind here subordinating conjunctions) join dependent (or subordinate) clauses to independent (or main) clauses like ligaments join tissue to bone. Mark's Gospel is no exception.

Stemming from nearly ten years of teaching first-year Greek courses at the graduate-level, I have developed an approach to the text that has served me well as an instructor. That approach involves the demarcation of *sentences* in the Greek New Testament. Because final punctuation in the text is either scribal or editorial, such indications can be subjective at times— and open to debate. Therefore, my next step in treating the text is to break the sentences (which I use as my starting point) down into clauses. Here, again, marks such as commas and semi-colons are non-native to the text. However, the syntax of the Greek NT (with Mark certainly being no exception) lends itself to clause-level analysis. So, to begin my analysis of the text of Mark 1:1–15, I will identify the skeletal structure (i.e., the subject-verb relationships) of main clauses first,[38] and then animate that structure with subordinate clauses. This should give us a well-grounded sense of the essential assertions of Mark's opening narrative.

Here is a summary of the subject-verb relationships in the main clauses of Mark 1:1–15. In essence, these short, pithy statements form the core structure of Mark's opening unit and thus provide the major pegs on which his narrative hangs.

	Subject(s)	Finite Verb(s)	Inflectional Attributes
1:4	Ἰωάννης	ἐγένετο	Aorist
1:5	χώρα καὶ Ἱεροσολυμῖται	ἐξεπορεύετο καὶ ἐβαπτίζοντο	Imperfect
1:6	Ἰωάννης	ἦν ἐνδεδυμένος καὶ ἐσθίων	Imperfect (Periphrastic)
1:7	Ἰωάννης (implied)	ἐκήρυσσεν	Imperfect
1:9	Ἰησοῦς	ἦλθεν	Aorist
1:9	Ἰησοῦς (implied)	ἐβαπτίσθη	Aorist

---

38. Here, I must clarify that by "main clause" I mean a clause that is grammatically independent and is established upon one or more finite verbs.

FORMAL CONSIDERATIONS

	Subject(s)	Finite Verb(s)	Inflectional Attributes
1:10	Ἰησοῦς (implied)	εἶδεν	Aorist
1:11	φωνή	ἐγένετο	Aorist
1:12	πνεῦμα	ἐκβάλλει	Present
1:13	Ἰησοῦς (implied)	ἦν πειραζόμενος	Imperfect (Periphrastic)
1:13	Ἰησοῦς (implied)	ἦν	Imperfect
1:13	ἄγγελοι	διηκόνουν	Imperfect
1:14	Ἰησοῦς	ἦλθεν	Aorist

The careful reader of the Greek of Mark's Gospel will note a number of things about this analysis. First, 1:1 contains no verb, and is thus not a clause; and because it is not a clause it is unlikely to be governed by a subordinating conjunction. Second, 1:2–3 represents a dependent clause beginning with a subordinating conjunction (καθώς), which I associate with the initial aorist indicative of the narrative (ἐγένετο) in 1:4. Third, and because direct discourse typically stands in a subordinate relationship to the main verb giving it expression, I have not included direct discourse in the mainline of the narrative.

What can also be observed is the interchange of aorist and imperfect tense forms. At key points of character introduction (e.g., John in 1:4; Jesus in 1:9[39]; the voice in 1:10) or plot movement (Jesus is baptized in 1:9; Jesus sees the heavens separated in 1:10; Jesus goes into Galilee in 1:14), the aorist tense punctuates the shift in the narrative.

> Because the aorist indicative provides a bird's-eye view of an action (or a helicopter view) and portrays actions in summary, it is often used to outline the skeletal structure of a narrative. The basic outline of events in the story is presented by the aorist in quick succession: Jesus went . . . this happened . . . Jesus said . . . and so on. This basic outline, or skeletal structure, is called the mainline of a narrative.[40]

The imperfect tenses then tend to animate the narrative with vivid detail, typically serving as a dramatic backdrop. Said differently, if the aorist

---

39. Καὶ ἐγένετο ἐν ἐκείναις ταῖς ἡμέραις in 1:9 does not fit neatly into this matrix. Most likely it is a formulaic expression and should be understood as a temporal marker rather than a marker of action. Therefore, I will (for the moment) exclude it from the ranks of the highest-level assertions since its assertion is temporally subordinate to the movement of Jesus from Nazareth to the region of the Jordan River.

40. Campbell, *Basics of Verbal Aspect in Biblical Greek*, 38.

tense draws the lines, the imperfect tense colors them in. In a similar way, subordinate clauses (including infinitival and participial phrases) accentuate the image by creating nuance. The following outline illustrates how John is initially at the center of the narration that begins with his dramatic entrance in 1:4, but is overshadowed by the advent of Jesus. (References to John, whether by implied verbal subject or substantive, are <u>underlined</u>; references to Jesus are in **bold**.)

1. ἐγένετο <u>Ἰωάννης</u>
    i. Καθὼς γέγραπται
    ii. <u>βαπτίζων</u>
    iii. <u>κηρύσσων</u>
    A. ἐξεπορεύετο πρὸς <u>αὐτὸν</u> χώρα καὶ Ἱεροσολυμῖται
    B. ἐβαπτίζοντο ὑπ' <u>αὐτοῦ</u>
        i. ἐξομολογούμενοι
    C. ἦν <u>Ἰωάννης</u>
        i. ἐνδεδυμένος
        ii. ἐσθίων
    D. <u>ἐκήρυσσεν</u>
2. ἦλθεν **Ἰησοῦς**
3. **ἐβαπτίσθη** ὑπὸ <u>Ἰωάννου</u>
4. **εἶδεν**
    A. **ἀναβαίνων**
5. φωνὴ ἐγένετο
    A. πνεῦμα **αὐτὸν** ἐκβάλλει
    B. **ἦν**
        i. πειραζόμενος
    C. **ἦν**
        i. (μετὰ τῶν θηρίων)
    D. ἄγγελοι διηκόνουν **αὐτῷ**
6. ἦλθεν **Ἰησοῦς**
    i. Μετὰ δὲ τὸ παραδοθῆναι <u>τὸν Ἰωάννην</u>

ii. κηρύσσων

iii. λέγων

This scheme serves to illustrate a number of points. First, the grammatical role of John is significantly greater in 1:2–8 than it is in 1:9–15. Second, the grammatical role of Jesus is significantly greater in 1:9–15 than it is in 1:2–8. Third, aorist tense verbs punctuate the action at decisive points, whereas imperfect tense verbs (and the present tense verb ἐκβάλλει in 1:12, which will be considered alongside the imperfects on the basis of its internal aspectual orientation) provide texture for the aorists. This is especially true in two places. In 1:4, John steps into the spotlight and the ensuing imperfects fall under the aegis of his character and activity (1:5–7). In 1:9, Jesus steps into the spotlight, but the ensuing imperfects are not assigned descriptively to him (although he is subjected to these imperfects), but rather to *the voice* in 1:10. Interestingly, the voice appears on the scene and seems to govern the litany of imperfect tense agents, including the Spirit, the adversary, the wild beasts, and the messengers. Only in 1:14 does Jesus step out in his own right and in his own voice. The impression is that God is behind the scenes orchestrating matters for his son—the star of the show.

The payoff for conducting these analyses is not immediately forthcoming; however, the results generated here will serve to fund the subsequent literary analysis, as well as matters related to the function of Mark's prologue (later in this study).

Literary Analysis

Having established the text of 1:1–15 and assessed its clause structure, I now proceed under the assumption that Mark begins his Gospel account with an intentional, well-defined prologue, the purpose of which will be explored later in this study. The task immediately at hand, though, is to establish the veracity of 1:1–15 as a definable unit. In order to make such a case, I will further observe that Mark's narration is largely episodic. Mark's Gospel is a product of judicious appropriation of certain events which—for Mark—are seminal. Each appropriation conveys its own glimpse into the character, work, or teaching of Jesus, or the various responses to him. We might very well think of these as scenes in a dramatic presentation, each of which in some way advances the larger agenda of the writer.

These episodes, or scenes, vary widely in their size and shape. Consider, for example, the lengthy apocalyptic discourse of Mark 13, especially in contrast to the concise double call narrative of 1:16–20. In each case, we have readily discernible units, but each has its own particular set of features contributing to the episodic nature of the passage. I suggest that well-defined scenes are comprised not only of a number of attributes, but also that such attributes work together to create a cohesive web of meaning, so much so that it can be difficult to isolate attributes. The integrity of such units increases proportionally with the number and inter-relatedness of its attributes. This is precisely what we find with Mark 1:1–15. In this opening unit, the number and inter-relatedness of those attributes is quite large.

Many commentators have advanced the notion that Mark's opening unit ends at v. 13.[41] In suggesting this, those commentators commonly note two variables: 1) a change of location from the wilderness to Galilee; and 2) a change of time from before John's arrest to after it. Without doubt, these two attributes do serve in some way to set apart 1:14–15 from the preceding material; but do these attributes provide enough differentiation between v. 13 and the following to warrant the conclusion that Mark's opening unit terminates with 1:13? I think not.

As I examine 1:1–15, I notice a much larger constellation of features that give a particular shape to the passage. Further, and as mentioned just a moment ago, these features reinforce one another so strongly that it is difficult to isolate one feature for discussion without necessarily implicating another. What follows will be my attempt to discuss an initial set of features that I observe in 1:1–15. These include: 1) the *inclusio* of εὐαγγέλιον at 1:1 and 1:14–15; 2) the recurrence of key words and motifs; 3) the parallelism of John and Jesus, specifically as depicted in 1:8; 4) temporal markers that establish a trajectory toward climax with the initial words of Jesus in 1:14–15; and 5) a readily discernible break with v. 16.[42] The cumulative effect of these features conveys a sixth attribute: namely, an inversion of character focus that presents itself by means of a literary chiasm. Before discussing each of these in turn, it may be helpful to offer a preliminary summary of the more general structural features of the unit.

41. Such views have already been mentioned in the preceding chapter.

42. As will be demonstrated in chapter 3 (Rhetorical Context), a *chreia* would typically conclude with a climactic statement by the subject of the work. Mark 1:14–15 certainly represents such a tactic. It would likewise be rather odd for the opening of a work whose main figure is Jesus to end on a note where Jesus is a passive character being cared for by *the angels* who are positioned as the grammatical subject of the final clause of 1:13.

FORMAL CONSIDERATIONS

I intend to demonstrate that Mark 1:1–15 consists of an opening heading (1:1) for the prologue, followed by a *synkrisis* of John (1:2–8) and Jesus (1:9–15). As Jesus comes to the forefront of the narrative, John retreats to the background. John's ministry begins with a prophetic announcement offered *ipsissima vox* of Isaiah (1:2–3) and culminates in a generalizing statement *ipsissima vox* of John (1:7–8). On the other hand, Jesus' ministry begins with his movement from Galilee to the wilderness (1:9) and ends with his return to Galilee (1:14). The climactic utterance of Jesus in 1:15 is likewise given *ipsissima vox* and serves to summarize the essential nature of Jesus' ministry by providing a proper closure to the prologue with direct points of contact with the material that precedes it.

"Good News" (Inclusio)

The first feature contributing to the unity of 1:1–15 is the term εὐαγγέλιον, which provides the basis for a literary *inclusio* of 1:1 and 1:14–15.[43] This is among the more salient literary features that demarcate the extent of Mark's opening. The unit literally begins and ends with the *good news*.[44] The function of the *inclusio*, consistent with its typical usage, is to establish "the main thought of the book (or passage), pointing to the essential concern of the book (or passage)."[45] The effect of the *inclusio* is even more pronounced when two additional factors are considered: 1) εὐαγγέλιον occurs twice in the closing bracket of 1:14–15, thus equating to three appearances within the space of fifteen verses; and 2) the term occurs only five additional times in Mark,[46] with the next appearance (as indicated earlier) not occurring until Mark 8. Keck notes the theological relationship between 1:1 and 1:14–15 on the basis of the term, but does not explain the relationship in literary terms.[47] Guelich employs the term "inclusion" to describe that

---

43. Painter, *Mark's Gospel*, 35; Witherington III, *The Gospel of Mark*, 68; Guelich, *Mark 1—8:26*, 4; see also Guelich, *The Beginning of the Gospel*, which provides an especially helpful survey of issues related to the structuring of the unit.

44. In chapter 5, I will defend the notion that 1:1 functions as an *incipit* of the prologue itself.

45. Bauer and Traina, *Inductive Bible Study*, 117–18; see also Aune, *Inclusio*, 229; and Boismard, *Procédé Rédactionnel dans le Quatrième Évangile*, 235–41.

46. 8:35; 10:29; 13:10; 14:9; 16:15.

47. Keck, *The Introduction to Mark's Gospel*, 359–60.

literary relationship, but does not provide an explicit case in regard to how the relationship works.[48]

The nature of a literary *inclusio* is well understood by commentators in terms of its form: a word, phrase, or grammatical structure is repeated later in the text, creating a set of brackets that unify the internal contents and differentiate those contents from the external materials. What is less discussed is the *how* of this process.

The function and utility of an *inclusio* are especially apparent in an aural text such as Mark. The initial utterance of εὐαγγέλιον in 1:1 creates an expectation on the part of the reader. The reader is now in tune with the frequency generated by the term, and anticipates some sort of explanation in terms of definition (What is the *good news*?) or relevance (How is this news *good* for me?). Since the term appears twice in 1:14–15 in regard to the initial proclamation of Jesus (who stands as either the object or subject of the term in 1:1) and does not appear again until 8:35, the form of the *inclusio* is evident.

Key Words and Motifs (Recurrence)

The second noteworthy feature is the concentration of key words and motifs. This is perhaps the most rudimentary way of demarcating and differentiating a textual unit. At this point, an important matter must be clarified. It has just been shown that εὐαγγέλιον is a feature that functions as an *inclusio* in demarcating the opening and closing brackets of the prologue. It is not necessary (or even expected) that all features of the prologue will appear in those brackets. Rather, it *is* necessary that the features of the prologue contribute to the unique shape of the prologue to the degree that such features help to distinguish the unit from what follows. Just as a particular sub-pattern or theme appears within the larger pattern of a tapestry, so do sub-themes appear in Mark's prologue. The important point is this: the prologue must contain a sufficient number of internal elements to distinguish it from the material beyond it. It is the *sum total* of such elements that characterizes the unit as a whole, not the *individual* capacity of each element to define that whole.

As seen in the previous section, one of the primary terms used with a heightened frequency in the passage is εὐαγγέλιον, not appearing again until Mark 8. In fact, three of Mark's eight uses of the term occur within

48. Guelich, *Mark 1—8:26*, 4.

the first fifteen verses of his Gospel (1:1, 14, 15). What we can also note is the concentration of *wilderness* language, specifically the employments of ἐρημος at 1:3, 4, 12 , 13 (representing four of nine total occurrences in Mark and not occurring again until 1:35).[49] We also observe Mark's indication of John's diet of insects and *wild* honey (1:6), the presence of *wild* animals during Jesus' temptation period (1:13), and the Jordan River as a remote setting (1:5, 9). Also of interest is Mark's deployment of the cognates μετανοία (1:4) and μετανοέω (1:15). The only other occurrence of either word in Mark comes at 6:12; thus, two of the three instances of these words occur within the span of 1:1–15.

In addition, the concept of baptizing has special prominence in Mark's opening. We observe that John appears not only for the purpose of baptizing in the wilderness (1:4), but he specifically proclaims a baptism of *repentance* leading to the forgiveness of sins (also 1:4). In the very next verse, all the Judean countryside and all of the Jerusalemites turn out to be baptized by John. In 1:8, John contrasts his former baptism of water to the forthcoming baptism of Holy Spirit by Jesus. We then read that Jesus was baptized by John in 1:9. If one excludes for a moment the hyper-concentration of uses of the term in 10:38–39 (containing six total occurrences), these employments of baptismal language in 1:4–9 constitute six of fifteen total occurrences in Mark.[50]

Finally, the centrality of κηρύσσω cannot be overlooked. This term underscores the proclaiming function of John and Jesus, occurring three times in the unit (1:4, 7, 14). This raises an important point: whereas terms related to baptism are limited to 1:4–9, and whereas wilderness language

---

49. Although one might contend that this serves to support claims that Mark's opening unit concludes with 1:13, I will argue below that the narrative locus remains "in the wilderness" through 1:14–15. I further maintain that the wilderness motif is but a single sub-theme that contributes to the overall character of the opening unit. That wilderness language does not specifically appear in 1:14–15 in no way minimizes the function of 1:14–15 as the closing boundary. Just as language related to baptizing is concentrated in the prologue (but does not appear in 1:14–15), so too is language related to a wilderness setting. Such sub-themes—taken as a whole—give the prologue a distinctive character in contrast to what follows. To use an example, it is not necessary for one to discern a morsel of carrot in a spoonful of vegetable soup to recognize the spoonful *as* vegetable soup. The presence of carrot in the soup *as a whole* helps to distinguish the soup from the grilled cheese sandwich sitting next to it.

50. What is of interest to me is that, of those other nine uses of words built on the βαπτ- root, one of them is in the disputed passage of Mark 16:16, four of those terms are titular in denoting John (6:14, 24–25; 8:28), and two of them involve a sense of the word that involves the *dipping* of objects instead of persons (7:4b; 14:20).

seems to conclude at 1:13, it might be argued that this provides a warrant for more narrowly defined boundaries (perhaps 1:4-13). I maintain that the influence of these words and concepts extends more widely—to the margins of the unit. I will offer two points of evidence.

In the first instance, one might rightly suggest that the extent of baptism as a topical focus is limited to 1:4-9, since the cognates are confined to these verses. However, and as we know, verse demarcations do not necessarily correspond to sentence limitations. As I have argued already in this chapter, the opening citation in 1:2-3 should be read as part of the sentence containing 1:4. As a result, the baptismal motif in 1:4 is very much at play in 1:2-3 insofar as baptism serves as the means for preparation prescribed in 1:2-3. In the same way, and although the last mention of baptism in the opening unit comes in 1:9, the baptismal scene continues to unfold through 1:11-12. Thus, we see the scope of influence of *baptism* extending from 1:2 to at least 1:12.

In the second instance, we can see that the wilderness as the geographical locus for the scene actually extends past 1:13 and includes 1:14-15, despite the seeming transition to a Galilean setting in 1:14. A point to be made here relates to the translation of ἦλθεν in 1:14. A quick survey of about a dozen modern English versions reveals a fairly even split between *came* and *went* as the translation for ἦλθεν.[51] This highlights the fairly dynamic nature of the word.[52] I suspect that translators probably did not invest a great deal of energy deliberating whether or not they should choose *came* or *went*, as such a matter seems rather pedantic for translational purposes (and perhaps rightly so). However, for my purposes, it makes a significant difference which word one chooses.

A primary reason to construe ἦλθεν as *went* in 1:14 is because it creates a reversal of Mark's employment of the same term in 1:9, where ἦλθεν is attended by ἀπὸ Ναζαρὲτ τῆς Γαλιλαίας; in 1:14, the verb is attended by εἰς τὴν Γαλιλαίαν. The pivotal terms in this instance are the prepositions ἀπό (with a focus on origin) and εἰς (with a focus on destination),[53] which—when attending ἦλθεν—create framing elements for the wilderness scene featuring Jesus. It might thus be argued that Mark's narrative strategy in 1:9-15 is to

---

51. Those works translating the term as *came* include the CEB, ESV, NAB, RSV, NRSV, and NKJV. Those translating the term as *went* include the NET, NIV, TNIV, NJB, and NLT.

52. See Decker, *Mark 1-8*, 17.

53. For the senses of ἔρχομαι with ἀπό and εἰς, see Danker, et al., *BDAG*, 3143.1.a.b.

suggest that *Jesus came from and went (back) to Galilee*. My suspicion is that this is precisely the case, especially when taking into consideration the other contextual evidence that ties 1:14-15 to the material prior. One can observe the key words comprising 1:14-15: Ἰωάννης in 1:14 is mentioned explicitly by name in 1:4, 6, 9, and is the implied subject of verbs in 1:5, 7; Ἰησοῦς of 1:14 is mentioned explicitly by name in 1:1, 9, and remains the dominant subject in 1:10-13; Γαλιλαία of 1:14 is mentioned explicitly in 1:9; κηρύσσω in 1:14 is used in 1:4, 7; εὐαγγέλιον in 1:14-15 (*bis*) appears in 1:1; (τοῦ) θεοῦ of 1:14-15 (*bis*) appears in 1:1 (if one allows for the textual variant); and μετανοεῖτε in 1:15 appears with its cognate (μετανοία) in 1:4.

Taken in sum, then, we can see that these words not only appear with unprecedented frequency within 1:1-15, but also that their presence and influence permeate the entire passage. Further, 1:14-15 represents a clear commitment to the trajectory of thought and vocabulary established in 1:1-13. Thus, the passage of 1:1-15 exhibits a unity on the basis of the recurrence of key words and concepts.

John and Jesus (Parallelism)

The third feature appears in 1:8. What is conspicuous about the text is the high degree of parallelism between the two clauses. Schematically, they can be represented in this way:

Verse	Subject	Verb	Direct Object	Preposition	Instrumental Dative
Mark 1:8a	ἐγώ	ἐβάπτισα	ὑμᾶς		ὕδατι
Mark 1:8b	αὐτός	βαπτίσει	ὑμᾶς	ἐν	πνεύματι ἁγίῳ

Whereas the overall pattern of parallelism marks the similarity between the works of John and Jesus, the conjunction δέ (here taken adversatively) serves to highlight the contrast between those works. This contrast is necessary if the parallelism is to hold true, for just as the two rails of a modern rail line run parallel, they are not one and the same—there is differentiation.

This verse occurs at the midpoint of the literary unit and brings into resolution the implicit comparison between these two characters. Just as John appears in the wilderness (1:4), Jesus spends forty days in the wilderness (1:13). Just as John finds sustenance (by eating insects and wild honey, 1:6), so does Jesus find sustenance (at the hands of the ministering messengers, 1:13). Just as John is a proclaimer (1:4, 7), so also is Jesus a proclaimer (1:14). Just as John is legitimated by Isaiah's prophecy (1:2–3), so is Jesus legitimated by the voice from the heavens (1:11). Just as John demands repentance (1:4), so does Jesus (1:15). Just as John baptizes (with water, 1:8), so will Jesus baptize (with Holy Spirit, 1:8).

The comparison built on the parallel clause structure anticipates the "passing of the baton" that is about to happen in the following verse, initiating the closure to the ministry of John and ushering in the new era of Jesus' ministry.[54]

Temporal Markers (Climax)

The fourth literary feature is climax, specifically as it is formed by five temporal markers. These are ἀρχή in 1:1; ἐν ἐκείναις ταῖς ἡμέραις in 1:9; μετὰ δέ in 1:14; πεπλήρωται and ἤγγικεν in 1:15; and μετανοεῖτε and πιστεύετε in 1:15.

"The Beginning"

Ἀρχή is the first word aural readers of Mark would hear. It is typically translated as *beginning* (either with or without an article), and as such, carries a temporal sense.[55] This is somewhat consistent with Mark's narrative insofar as it has a basic chronological arrangement; however, *beginning* is not the only translational option. The word can also carry a causal sense, often used for one who begins a work (thus, a *beginner*)[56] or initiates an activity on the basis of one's authority.[57] This latter sense is also attested in relationship to angelic and transcendent powers, which is intriguing in light of the transcendent conversation that takes place in 1:2–3, especially referencing an ἄγγελος.

In any case, the word has an initiating sense to it, whether logical or temporal, and thus stands at and marks the starting point.

---

54. For perspectives on the parallelism between John and Jesus, see Ernst, *Das Evangelium nach Markus*, 31; Gnilka, *Das Evangelium nach Markus*, 1:39; and Pesch, *Das Markusevangelium*, 1:71–72, who sees 1:9–15 as a parallel to 1:2–8.

55. Danker, BDAG, 1153.1.a.

56. Ibid., 1153.2.

57. Ibid., 1153.6.

FORMAL CONSIDERATIONS

"In Those Days"

This phrase marks a subtle shift in the narrative. That shift is not linear, however, pointing to one thing that happens after another; rather, the shift is concentric. The introduction of Jesus into the storyline takes place *within* the scope of John's ministry. Thus, ἐν ἐκείναις ταῖς ἡμέραις frames the baptism and temptation of Jesus within the larger temporal sphere of John's activity. The focus narrows with the insertion of this phrase, and the spotlight that was broadly on John is now more narrowly focused on Jesus.[58]

"Now After"

Those commentators who argue that Mark's opening concludes with 1:13 typically note μετὰ δέ in 1:14 as marking a temporal deviation from Mark's paratactic use of καί.[59] A quasi-temporal shift does indeed occur with the arrest of John. (I dub this shift "quasi-temporal" inasmuch as the shift is more synchronic than diachronic.) One notes up to this point the paratactic tendency of Mark to conjoin clauses and scenes by means of καί, where the conjunction can be seen introducing vv. 5, 6, 7, 9, 10, 11, 12, and 13. The conjunction continues to function as a marker of scenes in its introductions of these units: the double-call narrative (1:16–20), the Capernaum demoniac (1:21–28), the healing of Peter's mother-in-law (1:29–34), Jesus' attempt to seek solitude (1:35–39), and the healing of the leper (1:40–45). In every case, Mark introduces a scene with καί. This is Mark's tendency.

What is disruptive about the pattern of scene introductions in Mark's first chapter, though, is the occurrence of μετὰ δέ at the beginning of 1:14. Although some have argued that this temporal marker serves to establish a new pericope,[60] the phrase is actually marking *con*junction rather than *dis*junction. Mark has amply demonstrated that his primary choice for

---

58. For more on this, see chapter 5.

59. Stein, *Mark*, 69; Donahue and Harrington, *Mark*, 70; Gundry, *Mark*, 62; and noteworthy is Kuthirakkattel, *The Beginning of Jesus' Ministry*, 21, who suggests not only that 1:14 is set off from 1:13 by δέ but also that δέ could in fact "mark a contrast or a turning point within the same story or trend of thought (5,11; 13,14.28.32; 15,6.16)." Nevertheless, he claims that the primary *connecting words* that unite 1:1–13 (βαπτίζειν, πνεῦμα, and ἔρημος) are missing from 1:14 and therefore constitute a break. What is puzzling is his choice of these *connecting words* (e.g., πνεῦμα does not appear until 1:8) and his failure to recognize the wealth of correspondence between the language of 1:14–15 and 1:1–13 (see my earlier comments under *Key Words and Motifs*).

60. See, for example, Gundry, *Mark*, 1:62.

marking the beginning of a new scene is καί. The shift to μετὰ δέ must then indicate (if one assumes that it is marking transition) a shift of either greater or lesser magnitude in comparison to καί.

If one employs a flat reading of the passage in which the individual sub-scenes are simply observed as beads on a string, one will fail to appreciate the trajectory intrinsic to Mark's opening materials. The transition generated by μετὰ δέ certainly conveys a temporal shift, but not in a linear sense. I suggest that the shift occurs parenthetically, as the postpositive conjunction δέ so often does. John's arrest has been inserted into the narrative to provide a collateral comment; it is not a part of the flow of the narrative, for we are given no details about John's exit (at least not until Mark's sixth chapter). Thus, the arrest of John is not to be understood simply as a scene-changing device for Mark, but as something more significant.

Rather than conduct a study of each word (hoping that the sum of the parts does in fact equal the whole), I would prefer to examine the phrase as a formulaic expression; it is extensively attested elsewhere in the Septuagint and NT. Though it may be fairly innovative to suggest this about the combination of a temporal preposition and postpositive conjunction, the evidence is readily apparent that this construct can not only mark climactic events in a series, but does so in some perhaps surprising ways. I will use three illustrations.

Daniel 7:7

Daniel 7 is a clearly defined unit. It begins at 7:1 with a time demarcation (the first year of Belshazzar's reign) when Daniel is reported to have had his dream. It ends at 7:28 with a statement concluding the narrative, and then 8:1 introduces a new narrative, also demarcated by time (the third year of Belshazzar's reign). The space between relates exclusively to the dream and its interpretation. The dream proper goes at least as far as 7:8, thus constituting a smaller scene within the larger scene. That dream takes place in four movements, each depicting the appearance of a terrible beast. The first beast is described in 7:4. The second is described in 7:5. The third is described in 7:6. The fourth beast, however, requires the space of six verses beginning with 7:7, and is described as "terrible and dreadful and exceedingly strong [. . .] different from all the beasts that were before it" (Dan 7:7). This fourth unit is introduced by μετὰ δὲ.

FORMAL CONSIDERATIONS

Matthew 1:12

Like Daniel 7, the genealogy of Jesus in Matt 1:1–17 is a well-defined unit. It arguably features an *inclusio* of 1:1 and 1:17 (listing the progression from Jesus to Abraham chiastically) that brackets three stanzas of fourteen generations each. The culmination is the birth of Jesus, who is identified as the final generation of the third stanza. Matthew's periodization of the genealogy into literary stanzas is made explicit in Matt 1:17, and it is the final stanza that bears particular importance insofar as it brings the reader to the intended destination: the birth of Jesus. This third stanza is introduced by μετὰ δὲ.

Luke 1:24

After his prescript, Luke begins his narrative with the account of Zechariah and Elizabeth in 1:5. The moment is identified as the time of King Herod, and the narrative continues through 1:25 featuring Zechariah primarily and Elizabeth secondarily. A change of scene occurs at 1:26 when time is identified as the sixth month, and the character focus shifts to Mary. Elizabeth is, as mentioned, a secondary character in the unit, but in Lukan fashion serves as the unexpected exemplar for faithfulness.[61] This stands in sharp contrast with Zechariah who, as a priest, should have demonstrated trust in the Lord more than anyone—especially his barren wife of reproach. Luke's opening scene concludes with a moment that, on one level, is anti-climactic (Elizabeth *privately* rejoices in the Lord's favor in a space of *only two verses*). Read in view of Luke's theology of reversal, however, Elizabeth's response is the crowning moment of the passage. Her response is introduced by μετὰ δὲ.

Three features shared by these passages serve to underscore the role of μετὰ δὲ as a marker of climax. First, the units are clearly defined.[62] It would be a bit precarious to suggest otherwise. Second, there is a movement from the lesser to the greater in each case. Third, the final moment in each scene culminates the scene and is set off by μετὰ δέ. In sum, these passages demonstrate how the phrase functions as a means of marking climax, about which Bauer and Traina note that the movement is consistently from

---

61. On Luke's theology of reversal, see York, *The Last Shall Be First*.
62. With regard to Daniel, I have in mind here the dream scene specifically, 7:1–8.

the lesser to the greater.[63] As it pertains to Mark 1:1–15, we likewise see a clearly defined unit (certainly with regard to the beginning of the passage), a movement from the lesser role of John to the greater role of Jesus (see 1:7, which makes this explicit), a scene that arguably ends on a climactic note (Jesus' words are given their first expression), and an introduction of that scene with μετὰ δὲ.

"Has Been Fulfilled" and "Has Approached"

Another temporal marker is the employment of fulfillment language at 1:15. The scene finds its culmination in πεπλήρωται and ἤγγικεν, each of which marks achievement both lexically and grammatically. From a grammatical perspective, the perfect tenses convey accomplishment of a past event with imminent results; the net effect is that the landscape of reality is altered in the wake of that event. From a lexical perspective, the two words likewise have a sense of imminence: πληρόω with respect to time, and ἐγγίζω with respect to place. The language thus posits a moment of actualization, contributing to the climactic nature of the utterance.

"Repent" and "Believe"

Immediately on the heels of the two-part fulfillment declaration, we hear two imperatives of command: μετανοεῖτε and πιστεύετε . Here again, the verbal inflections are significant. In light of the preceding proclamation, people are admonished to *repent and believe in the good news*. Both verbs are inflected for the imperative mood. Although technically timeless (as a non-indicative verb), the imperative tense looks forward to a future temporal moment for satisfaction of the command. Because the imperative is intrinsically unrealized at the moment of utterance, it is laden with expectancy.

In sum, then, we observe the following trajectory established by Mark's temporal markers: 1) Mark initiates his narrative with a starting point (ἀρχή); 2) the narration narrows to focus on Jesus (ἐν ἐκείναις ταῖς ἡμέραις); 3) the climax of the unit is anticipated with the quasi-temporal break initiated by μετὰ δέ; 4) the first words of Jesus bring to fullness both God's appointed time and his approaching kingdom (πεπλήρωται and

---

63. Bauer and Traina, *Inductive Bible Study*, 99.

ἤγγικεν); and 5) the yet-untold drama is alluded to through the utterance of tandem imperatives awaiting actualization (μετανοεῖτε and πιστεύετε).

Break with 1:16–20 (Contrast)

Ched Myers is one of the few Markan commentators willing to press the boundaries of the opening unit beyond 1:15.[64] For him, Mark's prologue concludes with 1:20. His primary evidence is the parallel of the call of the first disciples in 1:16-20 with that of 8:27—9:13. Myers observes a bipartite structure in Mark, and to support that commitment 1:16-20 must be included with 1:1-15. As with so many ideological readings, however, Myers first creates an interpretive extrusion tube that approximates his political views, and then forces the text of Mark through that tube. Not surprisingly, his output neatly fits the shape of his tube. What gets lost in the process, though, is anything that defies that shape; those materials are left on the floor of the extrusion room.

We can see a fairly distinct break between 1:1-15 and 1:16-20 on a number of grounds. Only two common denominators connect the two passages: Jesus as a character and Galilee as a locale.[65] A host of other factors separates them from one another. One factor is the addition of four new characters into the story: Simon, Andrew, James and John. Another factor relates to the first instance of Mark identifying a dative indirect object as the target of a speech utterance. For the first time, we hear Jesus speak concretely *to persons*. Third, the concept of discipleship (understood here as following Jesus) is the dominant theme of 1:16-20, yet that theme appears nowhere in 1:1-15.[66] Fourth, none of the major themes (or even minor themes) of 1:1-15 (like gospel, baptism, repentance, or proclamation) appear in 1:16-20. In sum, there is a fairly incisive break between 1:1-15 and 1:16-20 that creates a dramatic contrast between the generalities of 1:1-15 and the concrete particularities of 1:16-20.

---

64. Myers, *Binding the Strong Man*, 109-36.

65. And even here the relationship is tenuous, for whereas the general direction of Jesus' movement in 1:14 from the wilderness is toward Galilee, the setting in 1:16-20 is specifically beside the Sea of Galilee.

66. Cf. Keck, *The Introduction to Mark's Gospel*, 364; and Boring, *Mark 1:1—15*, 65-67.

Inversion of Character Focus (Chiasm)

The orchestration of the preceding literary features into a whole brings us to the final meta-feature of the text. That meta-feature is the inversion of character focus from John to Jesus. Specifically, Mark begins his account with a title (1:1), and then undertakes his narrative in earnest with 1:2–3, which serves as preparatory material realized in the person and work of John. In 1:4–6, we learn of John, his nature, and his work, but there is a conspicuous absence of references to Jesus. In 1:7–8, John proclaims a message of a coming, *stronger* one, alluding to the advent of Jesus. In 1:9–13, Jesus arrives from Nazareth and is baptized by John. John is still on stage, but has been removed from the spotlight. What is distinctive about this text is the employment of the passive voice form, ἐβαπτίσθη. Mark does not tell us that *John baptized Jesus*; rather, he tells us that *Jesus was baptized by John*. The difference may again seem pedantic, but it is important here because it represents an intentional change of grammar on Mark's part, resulting in an explicit shift of focus from John to Jesus—Jesus is now the subject of the controlling verb and remains in focus as the subject throughout Mark. Richard Burridge has calculated that roughly one-fourth of the verbs in Mark's Gospel feature Jesus as the subject, and 1:9 provides the onset of that character focus.[67]

The switch in subject-focus from John to Jesus is pivotal. Thus, and because of the *pivot* of the passive voice employment, Jesus is now in the spotlight as the central actor on the Markan stage. The passive verb is the exact moment of transfer. John's work is almost finished. The Fourth Gospel captures the essence of the pivot in the clearest of terms when the Baptizer says, "He must increase, but I must decrease" (John 3:30).

The baptism and temptation scenes close and 1:14–15 provides the first words of Jesus in the narrative, where he proclaims a message of the arrival of God's kingdom (although, as already suggested and will be argued later, the utterance is given *ipsissima vox* of Jesus rather than *ipsissima verba*). At this point, Mark also provides an exit cue for John at 1:14 ("Now after the arrest of John"). The material following on the heels of 1:15 marks an exclusive and totalizing focus on Jesus and his ministry with no further involvement from John, save for the retrospection on his demise in Mark 6. The chart below provides a visualization of this character inversion:

---

67. Burridge, *What Are the Gospels?*, 190; he further notes that an additional one-fifth of Markan verbs are conveyed through Jesus' teaching and parables.

Character Inversion

1:2-6	1:7-8	1:9-13	1:14-15	1:16ff.
John's ministry	··············	··············	·············▶	Jesus' ministry
	John's proclamation ········	··············	▶ Jesus' proclamation	
		John baptizes Jesus (Jesus is baptized by John)		
	Jesus' coming ministry ········	··············	▶ John's passing ministry	
[no Jesus*] ············	··············	··············	··············	▶ [no John*]

The asterisks in the lower corners suggest that, although Jesus and John are not explicitly referenced in 1:2 and 1:16 respectively, they are alluded to. Taking 1:1 as a title, we note that Jesus is given explicit mention prior to 1:2 in a prospective way. Likewise, John is given explicit mention subsequent to 1:15, but in a retrospective way (see Mark 6).

What we will note about this character inversion is that it in fact provides the basis for the macro-structure of 1:1–15—a structure girded by the support mechanisms of the recurrence of key words and motifs, the *inclusio* of εὐαγγέλιον, the parallelism between John and Jesus, temporal markers leading to climax, and a significant break with 1:16 and the remainder of the Gospel. Taken together, these features form a literary chiasm.

I must issue at this point a caution with regard to chiasm, for this structure is often seen where it likely does not exist. I concur with Bauer and Traina when they suggest that chiasm "is not nearly as ubiquitous as most scholars have claimed; many scholars see chiasm almost everywhere [. . .]."[68] David deSilva also laments excesses in the application of chiasm, especially when those excesses ignore the ancient conventions as they are discussed within the milieu that generates them. He specifically observes how frequently *hysteron proteron* ("the technique of taking up the last

---

68. Bauer and Traina, *Inductive Bible Study*, 119–20; also see Ben Witherington III's critique of Ken Bailey's use of chiasm in *Paul through Mediterranean Eyes*.

point or question first and the first point or question last"⁶⁹) is confused with *commutatio* ("a contrast built upon the crosswise repetition of two word-stems with change of word order and, for example, case"⁷⁰). It is the latter that is the far more widely attested type of chiastic device in ancient Greek and Latin literature, argues deSilva. Although related to chiasm, *hysteron proteron* is to be distinguished from *commutatio*. He notes Aristarchus' commentary on Homer's explicit use of the structuring device.⁷¹ Of special note is the manner in which Homer balances parts of his narrative with one another: "[E]verything in the second half of this 'chiastic' passage relates to its counterpart in the first half as answer relates to specific question. If scholars limited their conversations to chiasms whose components were this closely and unmistakably linked, there would be no debate over their validity."⁷²

Because the purpose of this chapter is largely to make observations, I will hold off with further comments about chiasm and its relationship to Mark 1:1–15. That argument will be resumed nearer the end of this study. For the moment, I will leave this discussion with the observation that the constellation of features that give Mark 1:1–15 its formal integrity converge into a holistic shape that presents itself as shown in the figure above. The shape of that structure suggests chiasm, or at least something in that vein.

Summary

In sum, I have attempted to demonstrate how Mark 1:1–15 has a formal consistency that is sustained by syntactic and literary features. The opening verse functions as an identifying marker or heading of the prologue and is distinct from 1:2 and the material that follows. Further, I have noted that the citation in 1:2–3 is to be understood as providing the basis for John's appearance in 1:4. The clause structure of the passage indicates a consistent use of aorist tense verbs to provide the major contours of the narrative, and this structure provides the basic framework for viewing a variety of literary features. These literary features consist of: 1) a recurrence of key words and motifs that are highly concentrated within the passage and give it a particular flavor; 2) an *inclusio* of εὐαγγέλιον that provides a frame for

---

69. deSilva, *X Marks the Spot*, 346.
70. Thomson, *Chiasmus in the Pauline Letters*, 14.
71. deSilva, *X Marks the Spot*, 346.
72. Ibid.

the passage; 3) parallelism between John and Jesus, specifically centered on the pivotal moment of 1:8–9; 4) a linear set of temporal markers that provide a past-present-future trajectory to the passage; 5) a clear break with 1:16–20 in terms of emphasis; and 6) a convergence of the preceding five features to create a chiastic structure for the narrative in which John decreases as Jesus increases.

These formal considerations do not answer every question, and in some cases, they raise some. For instance: Does 1:1 relate to the whole of the Gospel or exclusively to the prologue (as I have proposed)? Are the variants υἱοῦ θεοῦ in 1:1 and ὁ in 1:4 to be taken as original or as emendations? Has Mark erred in his citation of Isaiah in 1:2? If the passage functions chiastically, how so, and to what effect? These and other questions will be taken up as we continue our study.

3

Rhetorical Context

IN THE LAST CHAPTER, I attempted to demonstrate on the basis of a number of literary features that Mark 1:1–15 is a well-formed textual unit. That examination was a decidedly *within the text* approach. In this chapter, I shift to a *behind the text* approach by means of which I characterize the milieu within which Mark operated. Said differently, I am moving from questions of how Mark is *seen now* to questions of how Mark *was heard then*. Despite my commitment to treating the text itself first (and with a clear privileging of the text over historical or reader-oriented methods), I in no way intend to discount the necessity of reading Mark within his socio-historical context. The Gospel of Mark does not exist in a vacuum, nor should it be read as such.

The approach to this chapter will consist of five movements. First, I will very briefly describe the aural nature of the NT world, specifically noting that *reading* in the first century must be understood as a practice that happened *aurally* as much as—if not more than—*visually*. Second, I will characterize the nature and role of rhetoric within the first-century Greco-Roman world. The sketch here will be brief, but will (I trust) capture a sense of the discipline as it was practiced in the NT context. I will examine the scope of *macro*-rhetoric (rhetoric that shapes works as wholes), but in terms of *micro*-rhetoric my engagement will be limited to its more elementary aspects. Two reasons warrant this move: first, space does not allow a full engagement with the depth and range of rhetoric as it was practiced; and second, Mark's rhetoric (as I will later show) is of the more basic variety. Third, I will offer a brief overview of the educational training that was in place during the time of Mark's writing and the central role of rhetoric as an academic discipline. Fourth, I will draw some inferences about Mark and his writing in light of his social, rhetorical, and educational milieu.

Finally, I will examine several instances of Mark's employment of rhetorical devices—first in his Gospel at large, and then in the prologue specifically.

"Hearing" the New Testament[1]

Works supporting the aural nature of the NT world abound.[2] I do not intend to make a case that has already been made. Therefore, my focus in this opening section will deal more with the way aural reading functions in practice than with defending the aural character of the first century. My specific interest lies rather in the interface between that aural world and Mark as a written enterprise. In my estimation, Joanna Dewey proceeds along the right line of questioning with regard to the written and aural dimensions of Mark. She asks, for example, if it is reasonable to maintain a clear distinction between written and oral discourse.

> [T]o assert a clear difference between oral and written composition for popular literature in the first century C.E. seems out of place. For even if a work was written, it was meant to be read aloud and to be heard. Most of those who became acquainted with the gospel of Mark undoubtedly heard it read. Thus the distinction between oral and written techniques does not appear applicable from the point of view of the audience.[3]

Christopher Bryan has also made a case for the aural texture of Mark, despite its written nature. He suggests,

> For Jew and Gentile alike in the first Christian century, to read anything regarded as "literature" was normally to read aloud. [. . .] Most of those who experienced the poets or the Scriptures would experience them in performance: in theatre, hall, or synagogue, or perhaps in the family. To read aloud effectively from the unpunctuated texts of the period was a skill, moreover, requiring preparation and considerable familiarity [. . .] therefore most writers wrote to be *heard* (emphasis his).[4]

---

1. Here I acknowledge the work of my former professor to whom I owe a large debt of gratitude for his initial encouragement of my pursuit of postgraduate studies; Green, *Hearing the New Testament*.

2. For example, Kelber, *The Oral and the Written Gospel*; Horsley et al., *Performing the Gospel*; Ong, *Orality and Literacy*; Shiner, *Proclaiming the Gospel*; *Follow Me*.

3. Dewey, *Markan Public Debate*, 29–30.

4. Bryan, *A Preface to Mark*, 69.

Bryan suggests that the size of Mark makes it suitable for public reading. "Mark fits well. It could have been read to a group at one sitting in slightly under two hours [. . . it is] a performance in three 'acts,' the first of about fifty minutes, the second of about twenty, and the last of about forty-five, with short intervals between."[5]

Perhaps no single feature more saliently characterizes the nature of oral composition and aural *reading* than its linearity. Unlike modern texts that are read visually (where one can skip to the end, find out how the story concludes, then read the text in light of that ending), ancient readers could only *read* at the pace at which the text was dispensed. Like a speech, oral composition tends to be "linear and cumulative, and any context in it can only be perceived in contrast to what has gone before, though a very able speaker lays the ground for what he intends to say later and has a total unity in mind when he first begins to speak."[6]

Bryan goes on to identify a number of additional features that are characteristic of oral composition. One of these is *hyperbole*.[7] Within an aural circumstance, hyperbole assigns a certain *gravitos* to the narrative in a dramatic way, emphasizing a point the author wishes to make. It is an attention-getting device. As a feature of oral composition, this feature would not necessarily discount the validity of the statement as much as it would accentuate the impact the author wishes to make. For example, to say about a prominent social engagement (in today's parlance) that "everyone was there" is not to suggest that literally every person was there, but rather that the attendance of the event was remarkably large, inclusive of not only *all* persons, but perhaps even *all kinds* of persons (young/old, rich/poor, popular/notorious, etc.). The significance of the attendance then buttresses the significance of the event. We see evidence of this type of rhetorical flourish in Mark's characterization of the scope of the crowds that gather at the Jordan for baptism: "And were going out to him *all* the Judean countryside and *all* the Jerusalemites" (Mark 1:5, emphasis and translation mine).[8]

---

5. Ibid., 56; observe especially Nepos's comment, "No one at a dinner-party of [Atticus's] heard anything but a reader, which is the most agreeable form of entertainment, at least in my opinion; and dinner was never served at this house without reading of some kind, so that his guests enjoyed the gratification of the mind as well as of the appetite" (*Cornelius Nepos*, 14.1, Rolfe).

6. Kennedy, *New Testament Interpretation through Rhetorical Criticism*, 5.

7. Bryan, *A Preface to Mark*, 73.

8. Note the parallel in Matt 3:5, which also provides language of inclusive, totalizing scope.

Another feature is *parataxis*. Bryan explains the aural impact of scenes set "side by side" in this way: because writings such as Mark's were meant to be memorable, their plots tended to be fairly simple.⁹ Paratactic construction provides the means for a sequential string of events that can be readily retained and recalled. In Mark's opening unit, we see—or *hear*—a number of short scenes joined together to form a tidy sequence in ways that are consistent with oral composition. Witherington observes that εὐθύς is often employed by Mark to create a continuity of motion (e.g., "next") through paratactic chains more so than urgency (*cf.* "immediately").¹⁰ A quick survey of the first few episodes of Mark following the prologue reflects this paratactic nature. In fact, each of five initial episodes¹¹ is conjoined to the previous scene by a paratactic use of καί.¹² The Gospel as a whole follows this pattern.¹³

A third feature is that of *formula*.¹⁴ By this Bryan means narrative structure. We might equate formula (as it is employed here) to an organizing principle that gives shape to a whole. Such formulae include *alternation*

---

9. Bryan, *A Preface to Mark*, 74.

10. Witherington III, *New Testament Rhetoric*, 28.

11. See the call of the first disciples (1:16–20); the exorcism of the unclean spirit (1:21–28); the healings at Simon Peter's house (1:29–34); Jesus' attempt to pray alone (1:35–39); and the cleansing of the leper (1:40–45).

12. As shown in chapter 2, the sub-units of the prologue are also paratactically conjoined by καί, the only exception being 1:14, which—as I argued—is introduced by the climactic marker μετὰ δέ.

13. It is not immediately apparent to me what Tolbert means when she claims, "The kai-paratactic style itself, coupled especially with Mark's fondness of participles, drives the narrative at a relentless rate, as if events were taking place so fast that one had no leisure to fashion full sentences but had, instead, to tumble phrases out on top of each other." Tolbert, *Sowing the Gospel*, 117. First, it should be noted (as Witherington has already suggested above) that the use of εὐθύς is not always or even necessarily to be understood as assigning a measure of urgency to a matter, but rather is a marker of scene connections in most instances, especially early in Mark. One need only note the awkwardness such a reading produces when rendering εὐθύς woodenly as "immediately" in every instance. Further, the claim that Mark has a "fondness for using participles" cannot be maintained statistically. A quick assessment of the frequency of participles per chapter among the narrative books of the NT reveals the following approximations: Matthew=16; Mark=22; John=23; Luke=27; Acts=29. Such suggestions press Mark into a mold for which it may not be suited.

14. For a taxonomy of similar structures in written texts, see Bauer and Traina, *Inductive Bible Study*, 94–122.

(ABC/A'B'C'/A"B"C"/and so on),[15] *inclusio* (ABA'),[16] and *chiasm* (with either a double center [ABCC'B'A'] or single center [ABCB'A']).[17] With regard to the latter, the point to which the listeners return is both the same and different. Such is the desired effect of such a compositional structure on an aural audience, especially as such a structure creates a mechanism for mental retention. Bryan[18] conveys this spirit precisely in his reference of remarks made by Eric Havelock:

> the basic method for assisting the memory to retain a series of distinct meanings is to frame the first of them in a way which will suggest or forecast a later meaning which will recall the first without being identical with it. What is to be said and remembered later is cast in the form of an echo of something said already; the future is encoded in the present. All oral narrative is in structure continually both prophetic and retrospective ... [T]he narrative is not linear but turns back on itself in order to assist the memory to reach the end by having it anticipated somehow in the beginning ...[19]

Having assessed the aural nature of composition in the ancient world as a means of communication, we now move toward the content of communication.

Rhetoric in the Hellenized World

If our third-millennial context might be characterized by a preoccupation with social media, so too might the first-century context be characterized by a preoccupation with rhetoric. Rhetoric was the staple for entertainment, legislation, and literary arts. No sphere of public life would be exempt from the influence of rhetoric. Kennedy defines it as "that quality in a discourse by which a speaker or writer seeks to accomplish his purposes."[20] He goes

---

15. Bryan, *A Preface to Mark*, 76; an example of such alternation is Delilah's repeated and escalating attempts to persuade Samson to reveal the secret of his strength in Judg 16:6–20.

16. Ibid., 77.

17. Ibid., 76–77.

18. Ibid., 78.

19. Havelock, *Oral Composition*, 183; it should be noted here that in referencing the *linear* nature of an oral text, Havelock likely means in an absolute sense. All oral composition is linear insofar as there is no "rewind button."

20. Kennedy, *New Testament Interpretation through Rhetorical Criticism*, 3.

on to declare that the "ultimate goal of rhetorical analysis, briefly put, is the discovery of the author's intent and of how that is transmitted through a text to an audience."[21]

At its basis, rhetoric is a tool of persuasion. In contrast to modern senses that understand the term either as propaganda or polemic, rhetoric in a classical sense is the discipline of crafting an argument so as to win over one's audience. Whether trying to absolve (or convict) a criminal, deciding about a future course of action, or praising (or defaming) an individual, rhetoric offers the tools and strategies appropriate to the task. It must be said from the outset that approaching the NT from a rhetorical perspective (i.e., as a tool of persuasion) in no way minimizes or undermines the historical verisimilitude of a work. As Craig Keener relates,

> Claiming that historical writers used sources [. . .] and were concerned about genuine historical information does not mean that they did not place their own "twist" on the material. To the contrary, it was customary for writers to do so, and the more rhetorically sophisticated the expected audience, the greater the expectations of such displays of rhetorical prowess.[22]

While Keener's larger task is to examine the Gospels as examples of ancient historiography, he engages the issue of authorial *perspective* as an important component of that task, specifically addressing the relationship between ancient historiography and rhetoric. He goes on to say that, "All historians, ancient and modern, write from some systems of values and perspectives, whether these systems reflect the larger culture, conventions of their guild, minority values, or idiosyncratic perspectives."[23] This challenges the modern, Western notion of an objective, neutral, value-free, or unbiased reporting of an event, for any reporting will be selective not only in what it chooses to include, but also in what it intentionally excludes. At some level, all history-writing comes from a perspective. The problem lies less with authors who write from a perspectival slant and more with those who claim to be free of such slant. The aim of historiography is to persuade one's audience that some events, figures, and circumstances are significant while others are less so, and to convince one's audience that the writer's presentation of that history is not only plausible, but preferable to competing presentations. The Gospels, regardless of the degree to which

21. Ibid., 12.
22. Keener, *The Historical Jesus of the Gospels*, 112.
23. Ibid., 117.

one identifies them as historiography, are persuasive documents designed to advance the gospel message.

Rhetoric understood in this way is a trans-cultural phenomenon in terms of its basic processes. Although it varies with respect to style, rhetorical theory can be applied universally insofar as the principles are constant.[24] Witherington has written a concise, readily-accessible volume on ancient rhetoric in the NT world.[25] What follows in this section is highly indebted to that work.

Macro-Rhetoric

In the wake of the rather unsatisfying results of the form- and redaction-critical efforts of the previous century, some recent scholarship has turned its attention away from a preoccupation with the alleged editorial work of NT writers as compilers and arrangers, and toward study grounded in the ancient arts of rhetoric and oratory. Recognizing that the first-century world of the NT was largely characterized by aurality, works such as those by Kennedy and Hans Dieter Betz have helped pave the way for new readings of the NT in light of the rhetorical nature of first-century communication.[26]

Arguing that communication during the NT era was largely ordered around principles of persuasion, Witherington builds on the aural nature of the biblical world as characterized in my preceding section, particularly noting how discourse was undertaken in a society where writing materials were limited, the production of texts was expensive, and literate scribes were in short supply. In the absence of textual clues (such as punctuation and paragraph breaks), authors and speakers relied on different communication strategies to accomplish their rhetorical aims. These strategies became standardized within the educational curriculum of students of that era so much so that various elements of a discourse can now be analyzed with respect to their intended objectives.[27]

---

24. Kennedy, *New Testament Interpretation through Rhetorical Criticism*, 10.

25. Witherington III, *New Testament Rhetoric*; see esp. 1–21. For a fine application of the kinds of principles in view here, see Young, *Whoever Has Ears to Hear*.

26. Kennedy, *New Testament Interpretation through Rhetorical Criticism*; Betz, *Galatians*.

27. For more on the educational structures of the day, refer to the next section of this chapter.

Although some recent trends in rhetorical criticism have attempted to read NT authors through the lens of modern rhetorical categories,[28] others have sought to study the NT authors in light of their adaptation of then-contemporary practices "for their Christian purposes of communication."[29] Betz's work on Galatians[30] and Margaret Mitchell's work on 1 Corinthians[31] are indicative of such macro-rhetorical approaches.

Although it may seem like something of a digression, I want to expound for a moment upon the general features of macro-rhetoric, for these features will provide a pool from which we will be able to draw various inferences later. Although many of these features are primarily characteristic of speech discourse, they all have—at their essence—a capacity to *persuade*. It will be argued later in this study not only that the Gospel of Mark is a *persuasive* document (insofar as it has persuasion as its aim), but also that it exhibits a number of features typical of rhetorical practice. Thus, it will perhaps be helpful to review. Of particular concern for my thesis will be the arguments that: 1) Mark's prologue represents a rhetorical stage rather analogous to an *exordium*; 2) within the prologue, a number of features are suggestive of the rhetorical species of *epideictic* that highlight the authority of divine characters (which is not to suggest that such features characterize the whole of Mark); and 3) the purpose of the prologue serves to evoke *pathos* on the part of the listening audience.[32] In making these initial observations, I in no way mean to suggest that Mark is following such conventions slavishly; rather, I simply mean to suggest that certain elements are likely

---

28. See, for example, Kennedy's critique of the modern approach taken by Frye, *The Great Code*, in Kennedy, *New Testament Interpretation through Rhetorical Criticism*, 5: "Frye's stance throughout is that of a twentieth-century literary critic. He views the Bible in terms of language and myth as understood in our times; he has less interest in the intent of the biblical writers, more interest in how the Bible was read by great literary geniuses of other times, Dante, Milton, and Blake among them. All of this is immensely interesting, but it is distinct from my goal, which is the more historical one of reading the Bible as it would be read by an early Christian, by an inhabitant of the Greek-speaking world in which rhetoric was the core subject of formal education and in which even those without formal education necessarily developed cultural preconceptions about appropriate discourse."

29. Witherington III, *New Testament Rhetoric*, 6.

30. Betz, *Galatians*.

31. Mitchell, *Paul and the Rhetoric of Reconciliation*.

32. As will be seen, the rhetorical phase of *pathos* normally occurs last during most Greco-Roman speeches. However, in the case of Mark's prologue (which, I am arguing, is situated as a discrete unit), the final movement does suggest an emotive appeal.

to be relatively universal among various cultures, and Mark seems to be accomplishing a number of rhetorical aims that at least suggest his familiarity with such functions, if not precise forms. As Kennedy says,

> Rhetoric is a historical phenomenon and differs somewhat from culture to culture, more in matters of arrangement and style than in basic types of invention. The New Testament lies on the cusp between Jewish and Greek culture; the life and religious traditions it depicts are Jewish, its language is Greek.[33]

Macro-rhetoric can be grouped by species.[34] *Forensic* rhetoric, for example, is the language of the law court. It is arguably the most prevalent species of rhetoric in the NT era. Forensic rhetoric is the language of attack and defense and has as its focus events located in past time. As one might guess, forensic rhetoric is the language of the courtroom. *Deliberative* rhetoric, on the other hand, is the language of the assembly (ἐκκλησία). It is the rhetoric of advice and consent, primarily focused on future courses of action. The proceedings of a legislative body illustrate this type of rhetoric. The climactic conclusion to the Markan prologue indicates how Jesus' program was a call to repentance and belief. That the call is issued in a two-part imperative structure clearly locates Jesus' ministry (and the aims of Mark) within a deliberative circumstance.

A third species of rhetoric is *epideictic*, which has as its typical venue a funeral or celebration. It is the language of praise and blame and concerns itself with present matters. Political campaigns often reflect this type of rhetoric, especially as opponents seek to cast doubts upon the character of one another. *Epideictic* rhetoric often employs the devices of *ekphrasis* (vivid description) and *synkrisis* (comparison),[35] two elements that I address below and that will figure prominently in my more detailed exploration of the function of the prologue (chapter 5). While more than one species of rhetoric may be discernible in a given written work, such a work will typically have a preponderance of features that locate it within one species over against the others.

Macro-rhetoric comes in various styles and moves through emotional phases as it is employed.[36] In terms of styles,

---

33. Kennedy, *New Testament Interpretation through Rhetorical Criticism*, 8.

34. Witherington III, *New Testament Rhetoric*, 13–15; see also Kennedy, *New Testament Interpretation*, 19, noting that Kennedy uses *judicial* for *forensic*.

35. Kennedy, *New Testament Interpretation through Rhetorical Criticism*, 24.

36. Witherington III, *New Testament Rhetoric*, 15–16.

[t]wo opposed phenomena may be distinguished: Asianism and the koine. Asianism is a highly artificial, self-conscious search for striking expression in diction, sentence structure, and rhythm. It deliberately goes to almost any possible extreme. Koine, in contrast, is neither artificial nor very self-conscious and results from the use of Greek as a medium of communication throughout the Near East by persons without deep roots in Greek culture. In contrast to both, grammarians and rhetoricians sought to teach Atticism, which is the use of Greek literary prose of the fifth and fourth centuries before Christ as models for imitation in diction and composition.[37]

In terms of emotional phases,[38] macro-rhetoric can be seen to move through three, each of which appeals to one aspect of the human person. *Ethos* seeks to establish rapport with an audience, and is typically the first phase of oration. As such, it appeals to the social self. Following *ethos* is the phase of *logos*, which has as its aim the internal logic that makes an argument. Not surprisingly, *logos* appeals to the intellectual self. Third, *pathos* seeks in the final phase to appeal to the deeper human emotions, and is thus directed toward the affective self. These *emotional phases* comport with Aristotle's theory of three modes of proof: the ethical, the logical, and the pathetic (*Rhetoric*, 1.2.1356a). They are also reflected in Cicero's duties of the orator, which are to *please*, to *teach*, and to *move*, respectively (*Orator*, 69).[39] As will be argued later, the conclusion to Mark's prologue (1:14–15) positions Jesus as the champion over adversarial forces (1:12–13), thus stirring the audience to be more inclined to hear and heed Jesus' climactic summons.

The remaining aspect of macro-rhetoric pertains to its structure.[40] Though not mechanically bound to these components, rhetorical discourse generally consisted of five elements. The first element is the *exordium*. Typically found at the beginning of a discourse, the *exordium* was the means by which *ethos* was established. The *exordium* functioned as the "warm up" to the presentation. Its purpose was enculturation, striving to build rapport with the audience. It is here that a rhetor would attempt to gain the confi-

---

37. Kennedy, *New Testament Interpretation through Rhetorical Criticism*, 31–32.

38. See also ibid., 15–16.

39. Ibid., 18; Robbins extends this framework to identify the focus of ethos as the speaker, that of logos the speech, and that of pathos the audience, in his contribution to Black and Watson, *Words Well Spoken*, 82.

40. Witherington III, *New Testament Rhetoric*, 16.

dence or favor of that audience through acts of hospitality, expressions of comradery, or comments that elicited laughter. It is also here that a rhetor would establish a basic grammar for communication, thought, and reasoning. Klauck observes that this process can be a bit challenging as the writer seeks to bring the reader into alignment with the writer's protocols: „Damit hebt auch das Spiel an zwischen dem Autor, der listenreich das Publikum in seinen Bann zu ziehen versucht, und dem Leser, der ihm halb widerstrebend, halb wißbegierig ins Garn geht."[41]

The second element is the *narratio* in which the basic issues are stated. Although this element is frequently absent, when present it serves to give the audience a summary of the essential matters to be discussed. The *narratio* functioned, in essence, as a "preview of coming attractions."[42] Some have suggested that Mark's opening unit functions in this way, serving as something of an *overture* in which samplings of Markan themes are introduced.[43] Eugene Boring argues that, "Like the overture of an opera, the introduction introduces the main themes that recur in the body of the narrative. There are five main themes which are all elements of the one primary Christological theme as Mark understands Christology. *All* these occur in the introductory section 1:1–15 [. . .] (emphasis his)."[44] The themes he identifies are the *power* of Christ as a manifestation of the *power* of God; the *story* of Christ as the climax of God's mighty acts; the *weakness* of Christ representing the weakness of humanity and thus the power of God; the *secrecy* of Christ as Mark's means of holding divine power and human weakness in tension; and the *disciples* as the messianic people of God. Boring's evidence to support his first two themes are rather self-apparent; the other three, however, require the reader to share the same Christological lens that Boring assumes in order to make these rather tenuous connections.

Following the *narratio* comes the *propositio*. This is the thesis statement. It could also function as a program statement by conveying the essential gist of the argumentation or presentation in summary. My argument will be that the first words of Jesus in the Second Gospel (1:15) serve such a purpose.[45] The *propositio* is an indispensable element of any rhetorical discourse and provides a logical segue into the *probatio*, or arguments

---

41. Klauck, *Vorspiel im Himmel*, 13, citing Miller, *Der empfindsame Erzähler*, 10.
42. Witherington III, *New Testament Rhetoric*, 20.
43. For example, see Mansfield, *Spirit and Gospel in Mark*, 15.
44. Boring, *Mark 1:1–15*, 63.
45. On this, see Klauck, *Vorspiel im Himmel*, 34–35.

"for" the *propositio*. In some cases, the *probatio* may be accompanied by a *refutatio*, or series of counter-arguments. To list and refute the opponent's potential counter-arguments was a sign of highly effective rhetoric. In sum, the *narratio*, *propositio*, and *refutatio* function to advance the *logos* phase of discourse.

At the close of a rhetorical presentation is the *peroratio*, which is aimed at summing up the central argument and making a final, emotive appeal. As such, it facilitates the phase of *pathos*. An obvious Markan problem is the ending, therefore it is a challenge of the first order to confidently assess Mark's movement into such a phase at a macro-rhetorical level.

It would be an error to think of these various attributes of rhetoric in isolation from one another. Instead, these attributes function organically to create a system of thought and action. As I indicated in my introduction, the cohesiveness of the Markan prologue combined with the intrinsic relationship between matters of form and function make it extremely difficult to address Markan features in isolation from one another. An appeal to one typically involves an appeal to another (or more). Although the following table would seem to suggest that its various components are discrete entities, in reality it is meant to present a schematic for understanding the system *and the relationships between its various elements*:

Styles		Venue	Application	Focus
Attic ↑	Forensic	law court	attack/defense	past
	Deliberative	assembly *ekklesia*	advice/consent	future
Asiatic ↓	Epideictic	forum/funeral	praise/blame	present

Phases: Ethos — Logos — Pathos

Exordium   Narratio   Propositio   Probatio   Refutatio   Peroratio

Micro-Rhetoric

Whereas macro-rhetorical concerns relate to the whole of a work, micro-rhetoric is a function of the smaller units or movements within the whole. They include devices such as "rhetorical questions, dramatic hyperbole, personification, amplification, irony, enthymemes (i.e., incomplete syllogisms), and the like."[46] In the Synoptics, for instance, we see a large number of parables put forward by Jesus. These are elementary, inferential devices that closely parallel the parabolē, fable, or *mythos* (Theon, *Progymnasmata* 72) in form and function: for example, "The kingdom of heaven *is like* treasure hidden in a field, which a man found and covered up; then in his joy he goes and sells all that he has and buys that field" (Matt 13:44; emphasis added). The Gospels as a whole are also indicative of widespread use of the *enthymeme*, or ἐνθύμημα, which is a deductive device that provides the cause or basis for an action or saying.[47] These are typically introduced by conjunctions such as γάρ and ὅτι, as in, "Blessed are the poor in spirit, *for* theirs is the kingdom of heaven" (Matt 5:3; emphasis again added). Enthymemes can also characterize utterances where one premise of a syllogism is implied.

Another example of a micro-rhetorical device is that of *synkrisis*, or comparison, which is often found in encomiastic rhetoric. The account of Lazarus in Luke 16, for instance, offers a *synkrisis* of Lazarus and the rich man. A device we find consistently in the Gospels and Acts is that of *narrative* (Theon, *Progymnasmata* 78–96), which can be understood as either individual units (διήγημα) or as extended discourse comprised of multiple units (διήγησις).[48] *Narrative* can be distinguished from *fable* in this way: whereas *fable* is patently fictive, *narrative* is a description of things that actually happen. Its elements (στοιχεῖα) provide the "flesh-and-blood" particularity of the historical past. All elements are required of proper *narrative*, and include person (πρόσωπον),[49] action,[50] place, time, manner, and cause. Effective *narrative* must also exhibit the virtues of clarity, conciseness,[51] and

---

46. Witherington III, *New Testament Rhetoric*, 7.

47. Kennedy, *New Testament Interpretation through Rhetorical Criticism*, 16.

48. On this, compare Ezek 17:2 to Luke 1:1.

49. The *person* of the narrative is conveyed by origin, nature, training, disposition, age, fortune, morality, action, speech, manner of death, and event following death.

50. That is, whether the person's actions are great or small, just or unjust, honorable or dishonorable, etc.

51. Although conciseness is particularly important when conveying something

credibility. While chronology matters for *narrative*, rhetors are free to rearrange their accounts as suits their needs. "It is possible to begin in the middle and run back to the beginning, then to jump to the end, which Homer did in *Odyssey* [. . .]. But it is also possible to begin from the end and go to events in the middle and thus to come down to the beginning" (Theon, *Progymnasmata* 86, Kennedy). The device can be seen throughout the Markan materials.

Of particular significance among this array of micro-rhetorical devices, however, is the *chreia*.[52] This device appears as a concise statement that captures, in distilled form, the essence of an historical particularity. In biography, that particularity typically relates directly to the figure in view and serves to reveal something about that figure's character or nature. More often than not, the character-revealing incident or saying is shortened to bring it into conformity with the virtue of brevity (Theon, *Progymnasmata* 79–80). In this way, the device can be seen to epitomize the action or saying. *Chreiae* are most effective when crafted in such a way as to be memorable. The capacity of *chreiae* to be recalled by the listener afterwards is directly related to the device's success in bringing the short statement to a fitting or climactic conclusion. I will say more about this micro-rhetorical device and others in the next section pertaining to education in the Greco-Roman world.

Education in the Hellenized World

Parts of Rhetoric

The Greco-Roman educational system in place during the NT era remained largely intact for centuries. The Jewish world did not escape its influence, for Jewish schools of rhetoric are attested,[53] as are prominent Palestinian and Syrian rhetoricians, including Theodorus, Caecilius, and Hermogenes.[54]

In fact, the basic *trivium* of grammar, logic, and rhetoric funded primary instruction well into the nineteenth century.[55] Academic work at this

---

potentially distressful to the audience (e.g., "Patroclus lies dead"), the *narrative* can extend if the material is particularly pleasing to the audience.

52. For his foundational work in this regard, see Taylor, *The Groundwork of the Gospels*.

53. Witherington III, *New Testament Rhetoric*, 23.

54. Kennedy, *New Testament Interpretation through Rhetorical Criticism*, 9.

55. Witherington laments the decline, noting that—in the wake of declining commitments to classical education—biblical interpretation has largely suffered. See

level was largely aimed at preparing students for the rigors of declamation in their subsequent studies,[56] which were grounded on the foundation of rhetoric. There were five parts to rhetoric as it was taught: invention, arrangement, style, memory, and delivery.[57] *Invention* relates to the planning and deployment of arguments used in the discourse; *arrangement*, the composing of parts into wholes; *style*, word choice, formation of sentences, and the use of figures; *memory*, the preparation for delivery; and *delivery*, such features as the control of one's voice, the use of gestures, and so forth.

Invention will become a significant factor later in this study, for it is here that we begin to get a sense of how Mark's account evinces rhetorical strategies and how those strategies resemble and differ from prevalent works from his era. *Invention* can be characterized as coming in two varieties: one based on external (inartificial) proofs, and the other based on internal (artistic) proofs. Whereas internal proofs originate in the mind of the rhetor (here, "invented" in a conventional sense), external proofs are independent of the rhetor. In the NT, such proofs include the quotation of Scripture, the evidence of miracles, and the naming of witnesses. Paul likely alludes to the difference between these two types of invention when he asserts, "For Jews demand signs and Greeks seek wisdom" (1 Cor 1:22).

In addition to *invention*, classical rhetoric addresses *arrangement*, specifically in regard to the way arguments are assembled into a cohesive whole. Kennedy conveys Plato's view on arrangement in the *Phaedrus*: "Every discourse should be like a living body in which the parts cohere like limbs."[58] Sometimes authors and rhetors make use of section headings (*kephalaia*) to help guide the audience.[59] The opening verse of Mark's Gospel likely functions in such a capacity with respect to the prologue.

The third part of rhetorical instruction relates to *style*. Cicero in his *Orator* was then followed by Augustine in *On Christian Doctrine*, each of whom associated appropriate styles with the duties of the orator. For instance, the duty of teaching (*logos*) was best served by a "plain" style; the duty of "moving" (*pathos*) by a "grand" style; and that of "pleasing" by a "middle" style. Regardless of one's approach, however, two primary

---

Witherington III, *New Testament Rhetoric*, 214–15.

56. Rhetoric was the exclusive subject of secondary education; on this, see Kennedy, *New Testament Interpretation through Rhetorical Criticism*, 9.

57. Ibid., 13–14.

58. Ibid., 23.

59. Ibid., 24.

components constituted style: lexis and synthesis. *Lexis* (or diction) relates to word choice.[60] G. B. Caird has produced an instructive volume on *lexis* as it relates to biblical texts.[61] *Synthesis*, on the other hand, pertains to the arrangement of materials, specifically noting figures of speech or thought and the use of hypotactic or paratactic sentence structure.[62]

The remaining two parts (*memory* and *delivery*) tend to apply more to speech discourse and will not receive further mention at this point.

Aelius Theon's *Progymnasmata*

We are fortunate to have access to some of the basic textbooks for instruction, and these come to us through such works as the *progymnasmata* ("preliminary exercises") of Aelius Theon, whose text was likely developed within a century of the life of Jesus.[63] This makes his exercises relevant to a survey of education in the NT context since it gives us a direct look at the principles and activities students of elementary education would engage.

The exercises are introduced to students in a progression from simple to more complex. At the foundation of rhetorical training is the *chreia*. "A chreia (*khreia*) is a brief saying or action making a point, attributed to some specified person or something corresponding to a person, and maxim (*gnômê*) and reminiscence (*apomnêmoneuma*) are connected with it."[64] The following table illustrates the points of contact and divergence between *chreiae*, maxims, and reminiscences.

	Chreiae	Maxims	Reminiscences
Attributed to a Person?	Always	Sometimes	Never
Universal, or Particular?	Either	Universal	Universal
Useful for Life?	Sometimes	Always	Always
Action, or Saying?	Either	Saying	Either
Length?	Brief	Brief	Brief or Extended

Theon goes on to refer to this device as the χρεία ("needful thing") *par excellence*, and this seems evident especially in light of the fact that Theon

---

60. Ibid., 26–27.
61. Caird, *The Language and Imagery of the Bible*.
62. Kennedy, *New Testament Interpretation through Rhetorical Criticism*, 27.
63. Kennedy, *Progymnasmata*, 1.
64. Theon in ibid., 96. On the discussion of *chreiai*, see ibid., 96–106.

places this as the first exercise among his *progymnasmata*, whereas subsequent versions (those of Hermogenes, Aphthonius, and Nicolaus) locate it only after *fable* (μῦθος) and διήγημα/διήγησις.[65]

As mentioned in the previous section, *chreiae* are short, anecdotal stories that focus on a word or deed of Jesus. Formally, they share a resemblance with a pronouncement story. Theon observes two general categories of *chreiae*: verbal (λόγιχαι) and actional (πράχτιχαι). Verbal *chreiae* convey their authority through words rather than action. Species include *declarative* (ἀποφάντιχον) and *responsive* (ἀποχρίτιχον). Among declarative verbal *chreiae* are statements voluntarily made by a speaker or writer and statements causally made in response to a circumstance. Among responsive verbal *chreiae* are responses: to a question (ἐρωτήσις, or closed-ended questions that require a simple yes or no reply); to an inquiry (πύσμα, or open-ended questions that invite extended answers); giving cause for an answer (usually by means of γάρ or ὅτι); and that are offered apocritically (as a rejoinder). It is possible for a single *chreia* to be comprised of smaller *chreiae* in varied combinations.

Actional chreiae, on the other hand, reveal meaning without speech. Such actional *chreiae* can be either *active* (in which case the subject is the actant or agent), or *passive* (in which case the subject is being acted upon). *Chreiae*, because of their essential and ubiquitous role in rhetorical discourse, are highly dynamic and can adapt to a variety of circumstances. It is possible, for instance, to see a construction that features both verbal and actional *chreiae* where a verbal question is posed, but a non-verbal response is offered. Theon offers this:

> Mixed chreias are those that partake of both the verbal and the actional but have the meaning in the action; for example, "Pythagoras the philosopher, having been asked how long is the life of men, going up onto the roof, peeped out briefly, by this making clear that life was short." And further, "A Laconian, when someone asked him where the Lacedaimonians set the limits of their land, showed his spear." (Theon, *Progymnasmata* 99; Kennedy)

This survey of the most elementary aspects of micro-rhetoric (along with a more general survey of macro-rhetoric) sets the stage for our exploration of Mark's engagement with the discipline.

---

65. Kennedy provides a very helpful chart that lists the sequences of each curriculum; ibid., xiii.

RHETORICAL CONTEXT

Mark in the Hellenized World

The Practice of Rhetorical Criticism

That Mark comes to us in Greek suggests that he has been in some way shaped by Greek grammatical education. Because basic rhetorical training accompanied grammar as part of the *trivium* of studies at the elementary level, we can assume that Mark was likewise exposed at some level to basic rhetoric. The style of Mark's Greek writing is clear, but simple. He speaks largely in paratactic constructions and tends to avoid more complex grammatical forms as seen in the comparatively higher Greek of Luke and Hebrews, for example. What, though, can we surmise regarding his rhetorical abilities and intentions? To address that question, I will return to Kennedy's description of rhetoric as it was conceived and practiced in antiquity.

> From this somewhat theoretical background we may turn now to the various stages involved in the practice of rhetorical criticism. These stages are set forth below as a sequence, but it is better to view them as a circular process, for the detailed analysis of later stages may in fact reveal aspects of the rhetorical problem or a definition of the species or stasis which was not obvious on first approaching a passage.[66]

It is to these stages that we now turn.

The Rhetorical Unit

The first task in the method is to define the rhetorical unit.[67] This understanding of *unit* comports with the pericope of form criticism. It requires a beginning, a middle, and an end, and must have some magnitude—five to six verses minimally (in most cases). The aim of my second chapter was to establish the veracity of Mark 1:1–15 as a *literary* unit, but we may re-examine this in light of Kennedy's methodology so as to highlight the nature of the passage as a *rhetorical* unit.

In terms of characterizing the broad pattern of 1:1–15, Boring's analysis of the symmetry between 1:2–8 and 1:9–15 can hardly be improved upon. Mark 1:2–3 serves as a fitting beginning insofar as it provides the necessary background for the unit's main character (John), 1:7–8

---

66. Kennedy, *New Testament Interpretation through Rhetorical Criticism*, 33.
67. Ibid., 33–34.

culminates the pericope by way of John's proclamation, and 1:4–6 gives us the vivid description (*ekphrasis*) of the main character of this unit. Weighing in at seven verses, it meets the minimal size requirements. Likewise, 1:9–15 has an appropriate beginning in which Jesus appears on the scene from Galilee. Like 1:2–8, it also culminates with a proclamation by the main character of the pericope. The space between is another vivid description, this time of Jesus. It, too, fits the minimal size requirements for a rhetorical unit, and—with 1:2–8—establishes a *synkrisis* of the characters that is made explicit in 1:8.

The *inclusio* of εὐαγγέλιον in 1:1 and 1:14–15 stitches the bi-partite unit into a whole, thus providing a more robust unit but still within size proportions, still with a beginning (ἀρχή in 1:1), and still with a fitting conclusion in 1:15 with the climactic announcement that the time has been fulfilled and the kingdom of God has approached. Pesch finds no difficulty in assuming that 1:1–8 is a traditional unit, as is 1:9–15. Mark has brought the two traditions together, and his editorial activity is at the edges with a climax at the conclusion: "Der Höhepunkt des Anfangs des Evangeliums (1, 1) ist damit gegeben, daß nun Jesus selbst zu Wort kommt „verkündigend das Evangelium Gottes"."[68]

The Rhetorical Situation

This stage of rhetorical analysis asks questions about persons (especially the audience), events, objects, relations, time, and place.[69] It is the *exigence* of the work[70] and might be inferred from the whole.

In the case of Mark, Jesus is the πρόσωπον[71] of the narrative. Joining him are his forerunner, his disciples, his opponents, and a large cast of maimed, blind, and disenfranchised persons. The audience is likely an amalgam of Jews and Gentiles. The events center upon the last year(s) of Jesus' life with disproportionate attention given to his crucifixion in Jerusalem under the governance of Pontius Pilate and Herod Antipas. Mark is telling the story from a post-Easter perspective.

---

68. Pesch, *Anfang des Evangeliums Jesu Christi*, 314.
69. Kennedy, *New Testament Interpretation through Rhetorical Criticism*, 34–35.
70. Bitzer, *The Rhetorical Situation*.
71. Note the use of the exact term in Mark 1:2 as it applies to an assumed Jesus.

RHETORICAL CONTEXT

The Rhetorical Problem

The *rhetorical problem*, argues Kennedy, is usually visible at the beginning of the rhetorical unit.[72] It is the *raison d'etre* for the work. The *problem* can be stated explicitly, but can also be insinuated through indirect portraiture, especially if the problem is a difficult one. In Mark, the *rhetorical problem* is one of definition: Who is Jesus? Time and time again, Jesus is revealed not through direct claims but rather through his actions and indirect portraiture. Mark answers the rhetorical problem through his portrayal of Jesus' words and deeds without comment, but allows characters within the narrative to identify Jesus explicitly—often in unexpected ways.

The identity questions come in a variety of forms, and for Witherington, constitute the overall structure of Mark as a whole.[73] Mark 1:1—8:27 conveys the "Who?" and "Why?" questions about Jesus' teaching and ministry. Peter answers the "Who?" question with his declaration in 8:27–30 that Jesus is the Christ. A series of statements occurring at 8:31, 9:31, and 10:32 ask and answer questions related to the mission of Jesus (and his disciples): it is (and will be) a mission of *suffering*. The rhetorical problem then finds resolution in chapters 11–16; although Jesus does in fact suffer, the fulfillment of his mission makes it possible for the Gentile centurion to proclaim Jesus as the Son of God (15:39). This declaration by perhaps the most unlikely person parallels the textual variant of υἱοῦ θεοῦ, thus plausibly establishing the *rhetorical problem* at the beginning of the work.

The Arrangement of Material

This brings us to the fourth and final stage of our initial rhetorical analysis of Mark, which is an exploration of the way Mark arranges his material.[74] Drawing on our foregoing discussion, it would seem that Mark follows—at least in elementary ways—the prescriptions of ancient Greco-Roman rhetorical practices. A sounding of Mark's use of rhetorical devices indicates a shallow but consistent employment of the most basic ones: *narrative* (both διήγημα and διήγησις) and *chreiae* (including maxims and reminiscences).

Theon suggests one's opening material (*prooemion*) should differ from the *chreiae* employed elsewhere in the work. "After the prooemion one

---

72. Kennedy, *New Testament Interpretation through Rhetorical Criticism*, 36.
73. Witherington III, *The Gospel of Mark*, 37–38.
74. Kennedy, *New Testament Interpretation through Rhetorical Criticism*, 37.

should state the chreia, then next the supporting arguments. One should here also use whatever amplification and digression and characterization is possible."[75] Assuming 1:15 signals the end of Mark's opening, we find in 1:16–20 a pair of narrations reflecting remarkable symmetry; but for a number of reasons, the nature and shape of the double call narrative deviates significantly from what comes before it. Further, it sets the stage for Jesus' ministry in Capernaum which begins with the healing of the synagogue demoniac.

The Use of Rhetoric in Mark

I have already alluded to a number of aspects of macro-rhetoric that may be at play in Mark's prologue—at least in some measure (e.g., *exordium*, *pathos*, *epideictic*). To attempt to provide a full-scale examination of Mark's use of rhetoric throughout his Gospel would grossly exceed the limits and scope of this project. However, I would like to provide some further soundings with regard to instances of micro-rhetoric at work in Mark's Gospel as a whole. Specifically, I will highlight instances of narrative, *chreia*, and parable.

The Gospel as a Whole

The Chreia

Witherington has provided a concise demonstration of how Mark employs the devices of *chreia*.[76] He cites Mark 6:1–6 as a classic example of a *chreia*, one which he claims meets "all the necessary rhetorical requirements."[77] In this passage, Jesus begins to teach in the synagogue on a Sabbath. Questions immediately arise concerning the source of his wisdom and mighty works. People acknowledge that Jesus is the τέκτων, further identified as the son of Mary and the brother of James, Joseph, Judas, as well as unnamed sisters. Jesus then famously reports that, "A prophet is not without honor, except in his own country, and among his own kin, and in his own house" (6:4). The scene closes in irony: Jesus marvels at their failure to recognize and accept his role as a divinely appointed agent in fulfillment of Scripture. Not even

---

75. Theon in Kennedy, *Progymnasmata*, 105–6.
76. Witherington III, *New Testament Rhetoric*, 28–33.
77. Ibid., 28.

the mighty works—done in full view of the public—can persuade them otherwise. Except for a few healings, Jesus does no mighty works there, but leaves them and continues his teaching from village to village.

This *chreia* reflects a number of traits common to the device: with brevity, it suggests an historical event distilled to its essence; it climaxes with a maxim of Jesus (possibly influenced by a more traditional maxim; see Gospel of Thomas 31, for example); and it relates a circumstance that demonstrates historical veracity. With respect to this last point, Witherington indicates how the unflattering depiction of Jesus' family, his identification as "son of Mary," and his rejection by his own people are unlikely to have been concocted by the author.[78] What is particularly noteworthy about this *chreia* in light of Mark's entire Gospel is its positioning as one of a number of revelatory moments that point to Jesus' ultimate rejection and passion. This helps to highlight the bitter irony of Mark's Gospel.

Another example of a *chreia* is found in Mark 2:14-17, where Jesus calls Levi away from his tax table, and then is reported as having dinner at Levi's house with tax collectors and sinners. Not only is the crowd sizeable, but in this scene we also see that members of the religious establishment are on hand. The challenge they pose is an early one in Mark's account, and is offered to his disciples rather than to Jesus himself. The scribes of the Pharisees, upon witnessing Jesus at table with and in the company of questionable characters, ask Jesus' disciples why Jesus dines with tax collectors and sinners. Jesus, who apparently overhears or perceives the question, declares that, "Those who are well have no need of a physician, but those who are sick; I came not to call the righteous, but sinners" (Mark 2:17).

Once again, we can apply the criteria required for a *chreia*. First, we are dealing with a very concise statement of narration. Only the essentials are provided, and the scene largely lacks any elaboration or vivid detail. For instance, we have no sense of how the invitation to dinner was offered (in fact, the narrative jumps rather abruptly from Levi's abandonment of his station directly to the supper scene), we do not know how or why sinners and tax collectors are numbered among the attendees, and we do not get any sense of how Jesus came to discern the question posed to the disciples. Certainly, had Mark been interested in "boiling up" his narrative, he would have had ample opportunities here. Instead, we get the basic gist of the event with only enough detail to set Jesus up for his climactic utterance about his role and—by extension—his identity. This statement

78. Ibid.

serves to support Mark's program of systematically revealing Jesus' identity throughout his Gospel.

A third example of a *chreia* follows closely on the heels of the preceding episode, and continues the barrage of confrontations between the religious leaders and Jesus. In Mark 2:23–28, Jesus is reported to be passing through grain fields. The Pharisees now pose the challenge directly to Jesus rather than indirectly through his disciples. They ask why his disciples are violating the Sabbath. Jesus answers their challenge by means of an appeal to and short exegesis of Scripture: David did what was seemingly unlawful, yet Scripture does not condemn it. Jesus' unstated inference is that the Pharisees therefore should not be concerned with the action. He then concludes the episode with a climactic utterance: "The sabbath was made for man, not man for the sabbath; so the Son of man is lord even of the sabbath" (Mark 2:27–28).

As with the previous *chreiai*, the narrative has been extremely condensed. We do not have any transition from the prior scene at Levi's house to the current scene; rather, Jesus and his disciples simply appear in the middle of a grain field. Nor do we have any sense of how or why Pharisees are in the midst. However, two crucial details *are* provided in this account: 1) Mark reports that the scene occurs on a Sabbath; and 2) Jesus' disciples begin to harvest grain by hand. Like the episodes involving Jesus' family in Mark 6 and his "sinner dinner" in the previous passage, this narrative moment represents an unlikely account in some regards for a biographical narrative that seeks to extol the virtues of its subject. One might wonder how such episodes, in an honor-and-shame culture, would serve the purpose of casting the main character in a positive light insofar as these episodes set Jesus at odds with the brokers of honor and shame currency. Said differently, it would seem unlikely *a priori* that the biography of a virtuous character would include continuous scenes of Jesus in confrontation with the social and religious exemplars of the day. This is highly suggestive of the likelihood that we are dealing with historical realities that have been summarized for the purpose of revealing the character (and identity) of the subject: Jesus is Lord, even of the Sabbath.

Once again, had Mark hoped to amplify his narrative, he clearly missed opportunities with the preceding two *chreiai*. In addition, the placement of these latter two helps to advance Mark's ongoing program of identifying Jesus as the Son of God. However, the bitter irony of Mark 6:1–16 has its roots in the controversy episodes of Mark 2, controversies that will eventually lead to the arrest and execution of Jesus.

The Parabolē

The *parabolē* (or simply, "parable")[79] in modern vernacular is most frequently associated with the short, moral-pointing fables of Aesop. Characteristic of such fables are their unified nature, their narrative form, and their literary autonomy.[80] Young challenges this notion as representative of all parabolic devices, arguing instead that NT parables employed for a *rhetorical purpose* tend to take shape and function a bit differently. "They are brief comparative proverbs or general analogies drawn from everyday life, serving contextually as stylistic and inductive support for Jesus' discoursive point."[81]

Aristotle considered the parable as a distinct form of a comparison, or *paradeigma* (*Rhetorica* 2.20.1). Thus, the core of a parabolic discourse when employed rhetorically is the comparison and contrast of two or more persons or things. On the lips of Jesus, that comparison usually amounts to contrasting portraits of Jesus and those who will not acknowledge his divine authority. In my view, the parable *par excellence* of Mark's Gospel is that of the wicked tenants in Mark 12. Most likely drawing on the shared presuppositional pool of Isa 5, Jesus presses back against the religious leadership by pointing out their recalcitrance in the face of ongoing representatives dispatched by God. The parable is short and vividly contrasts the dutiful messengers and the special status of the son with the violent and conniving disposition of the tenants. Unlike the fable (or, *mythos*), this parable points to historical, particular reality. The OT is replete with the work of prophets as dispatched agents on behalf of God. (In recent memory of the context of the telling of the parable in Mark 12, John the Baptizer has been "wounded in the head."[82]) Further, the parable—with the vineyard as its basis—is readily understood by the listening audience—it is indeed a short narrative drawn from daily life and told in plain language.

---

79. On *parable*, I draw on the very helpful work of Young, *Whoever Has Ears to Hear*, especially his Excursus, 115–46.

80. Ibid., 115.

81. Ibid.

82. Here, I want to exercise caution so as not to press too hard on possible one-to-one analogies; nevertheless, John's decapitation certainly does come to mind.

A final point about the parable is this: it culminates in a discursive statement by Jesus in which the wicked tenants are expelled and the vineyard turned over to a new cadre of surprising tenants: Gentiles. This not only furthers the *Leitmotif* of Mark's identifying Jesus as the Son of God, but also highlights the Isaian prophecy that God's Anointed One would be rejected by God's own people.

Taken as a unit, the parable of the wicked tenant is a more fully developed device akin to the parable of the sower in Mark 4.[83] It clearly reflects a narrative structure. By contrast, Mark is equally comfortable employing more basic *paraboloi* for his rhetorical purposes. Returning to Mark 2, we observe three *paraboloi* given in rapid succession. The first provides a brief story or analogy about wedding guests. So long as the bridegroom remains, fasting is inappropriate. However, and as would be commonly known, the bridegroom will not tarry forever. The point of his departure will mark the time to resume fasting (2:19–20). And just as with the wedding guests and fasting, questions of suitability can be drawn from simple, ordinary circumstances such as mending garments and storing wine (2:21–22). What is noteworthy about these three instances is that each contains an explicit contrast (fasting during and after the wedding feast; attaching new cloth to old; and storing new wine in old skins); each is succinctly narrated; each is told in concrete particularity using examples from daily life; and each is conveyed in plain language. Most importantly, however, each is specifically shaped to convey the message Jesus is trying to convey.

One of the key advantages of a parable is its intrinsic ability to circumnavigate a direct allegation. In the case of the parable of the wicked tenants, for instance, Jesus never condemns the religious leaders directly. Rather, he uses the inferential capacity of the parable to do that work for him. Apparently, he used it with effect, for the establishment "perceived that he had told the parable against them; so they left him and went away" (Mark 12:12).

---

83. I concur with Young in his dissent from Tolbert, who suggests that the soil types of the sower parable are by their nature unchangeable. This perhaps misses the rhetorical point of the parable, which is to ask a deliberative question in two parts: 1) What kind of soil am I? and 2) How do I become good soil? If there is no potential for soil remediation, the parable serves no purpose. See Tolbert, *Sowing the Gospel*, 160–64; and Young, "Whoever Has Ears to Hear," 208, 98.

RHETORICAL CONTEXT

The Diēgēma

The *diēgēma*, or "narrative," funds the essential plotline of a work. It is "language descriptive of things that have happened or as though they had happened" (Theon, *Progymnasmata* 78, Kennedy). As already mentioned, effective narrative must exhibit the virtues of clarity, conciseness, and credibility, but for Theon, credibility is the most important criterion. "One should always keep to what is credible in the narration, for this is its most special feature. If it does not have credibility, the more clear and concise it is, all the more unconvincing it seems to the hearers" (Theon, *Progymnasmata* 79, Kennedy).

A notable feature of the Second Gospel is Mark's fidelity to Theon's prescription for proper narrative; indeed, most if not all of the required elements are accounted for in Mark's narration: person, action, place, time, manner, and cause (on these, see above). The first such episode I have in mind specifically is an early one in Mark: the Capernaum demoniac in 1:21–28. The essential elements are all in place. Jesus is center stage as having already demonstrated his capacity to teach with unprecedented authority; he is established as a *person*. His *action* in exorcising the demon performs a restorative function for the demonized man. The narrative takes *place* in the Capernaum synagogue at the *time* of the Sabbath. His *manner* is characterized as demonstrating authority, and the *cause* is the outcry of the demon, an entity that must be silenced.

Another notable feature of Mark is his inclusion of narrative details that lend credibility to the narrative account without compromising or overplaying clarity and conciseness. Returning to Mark 1:21–28, the episode depicts what would seem perhaps like any ordinary Sabbath, except that—in the midst of Jesus' teaching—a man with an unclean spirit disrupts the service. Rebuking the spirit, Jesus exorcizes it. The unclean spirit convulses and gives a loud cry, leaving the man presumably in wholeness. Mark then includes this brief narration:

> And the unclean spirit, convulsing him and crying with a loud voice, came out of him. *And they were all amazed*, so that *they questioned among themselves,* saying, "What is this? A new teaching! With authority he commands even the unclean spirits, and they obey him." And *at once his fame spread everywhere* throughout all the surrounding region of Galilee." (Mark 1:26–28; emphasis mine)

Of particular significance here is the material I have taken the liberty to highlight. In a fictional world, strange things are commonplace. That Winnie the Pooh's extraordinary appetite for honey is more remarkable within the narrative than the fact that he is a talking bear underscores the "fabulous" nature of fiction. In a non-fictional world, though, a talking bear would generate headlines; it would, in fact, be *noteworthy*. Similarly, that Jesus demonstrates the ability to rebuke and exorcise a demon is a noteworthy fact. Mark captures with realism the kind of response one would expect: *all* are amazed, questions arise, and his fame spreads *immediately* and *everywhere*. Notice again how a simple infusion of realism serves to lend credibility to Mark's narration. In the healing of the paralytic in Mark 2:1–12, Jesus' fame had spread to an extent that it was difficult—if not nearly impossible—to gain access to him because of the crowds (a credible circumstance in its own right and in light of Jesus' prior miracles). When friends of a paralytic arrive on the scene, they are denied access. In their desperation, they literally tear the roof off the house in order to place the paralytic before Jesus. After a discussion about Jesus' authority to forgive sins, Jesus commands the paralytic to rise and walk. "And he rose, and immediately took up the pallet and went out before them all; so that they were all amazed and glorified God, saying, 'We never saw anything like this!'" (Mark 2:12). Again, Mark provides, in measured form, a short narrative statement that lends credibility to a seemingly incredible circumstance.

The Prologue

Within the short space of Mark's opening unit we observe a small but significant use of micro-rhetorical devices. As already argued, the prologue takes shape largely in two movements: the ministry of John (1:2–8) and the ministry of Jesus (1:9–15). In each, we see *chreiai* at work.

In John's case, we note an historical particularity,[84] the substance of which has been reduced to its essence (1:4). The conclusion of the *chreia* is John's climactic announcement of his unworthiness relative to the stronger One to come. Once it has been announced that Jesus will baptize with Holy Spirit (in contrast to John's water baptism), nothing is left to be said by John. Mark leaves him silent from this point forward (except for the retrospective moment of Mark 6 which narrates John's demise at the

---

84. On the historical basis of John's baptizing ministry, see, for example, Keener, *The Spirit in the Gospels and Acts*, 53; see also Schweizer, *Good News according to Mark*, 37.

hands of Herod). Mark has cast this summarization of John's message in a short, memorable way.

However, two important verses stand between the summary of John's ministry in 1:4 and the summary of his message in 1:7–8. In 1:5, we are privy to a ground-level perspective of what was taking place during John's ministry. As already mentioned, the scope of the response was inclusive and totalizing in rhetorical force. Further, John is identified as wearing a garment made from the hairs of a camel and a leather belt around his waist. His diet is insects and undomesticated honey. Collectively, these suggest that John was widely recognized by his contemporaries as donning the garb of a prophet. The vivid characterization represents *ekphrasis*. Bart Bruehler suggests that such a moment serves to highlight divine activity in a positive way. He says that, "Ekphrasis is the exercise that prepares the rhetorical student to continue writing a narrative with clarity but bend the rule of conciseness with vivid description in order to achieve greater credibility."[85]

In a similar way, the introduction of Jesus to the narrative begins with a simple moment of narration in 1:9 that then climaxes in 1:14–15. Jesus' announcement of the advent of the kingdom and the fulfillment of the appointed time represents the warrant for his summons to his hearers to "repent and believe in the gospel." As will be explicated in greater detail later in this study, Mark's attribution of these words to Jesus likely represents an attempt on Mark's part to summarize the essential message of Jesus in a way that is memorable, is presented authoritatively, and prepares the reader for the explication of the message in the remainder of the Gospel.

The space between the simple introduction and baptism of Jesus and Jesus' climactic utterance in 1:15 is—once again—space that Mark uses for *ekphrasis*. The vivid details of both Jesus' baptism and his wilderness temptation serve to underscore and intensify divine activity in a positive way.[86] The addition of these details serves to amplify the narrative. The parallel accounts of John and Jesus thus form the basis for a *synkrisis* of their two characters, a point on which I will refrain from expounding for the moment.

The manner and degree to which Mark accomplishes his rhetorical aims here will be subject to much closer study in chapter 5. In particular,

---

85. Bruehler, *Patterns of Ekphrasis in Luke-Acts*, 6.

86. Bruehler in fact cites the Lukan parallel to Jesus' baptism as an example of *ekphrasis*, ibid., 13–14; on the other hand, Keener is much more cautious in attributing ekphrastic embellishment to Luke; see his *The Historical Jesus of the Gospels*, 116.

that chapter will provide the occasion to more fully explore how Mark's Gospel functions as a rhetorically adept narrative. For now, I am interested only in introducing the essential concepts which may be operative within Mark's narration.

Summary

Although a written document, Mark's audience would likely have *read* his Gospel aurally. Such *reading* requires the author to compose his work in such a way that an oral presentation of it will provide the necessary structure to guide the audience in their listening. Mark demonstrates not only the ability to create discourse that lends itself to oral presentation, but also bears the hallmarks of classical Greco-Roman education, especially training in the rudiments of rhetoric. Mark also demonstrates the use of deliberative rhetoric throughout.

Let us assume, for the moment, that Mark's prologue as I have defined it functions as an *exordium* in which Mark establishes the credibility of his main character, Jesus. Let us also assume that the prologue is capstoned by a *propositio* in 1:14–15 in which the basic gist of Jesus' ministry is captured by the idea of proclaiming the good news of God. Let us further assume that the *propositio* concludes with a two-fold imperative to repent and believe. Given these assumptions (none of which are in any way implausible in my estimation), Mark's prologue would be highly suggestive of deliberative rhetoric. Where his work deviates from established norms of his Hellenistic milieu will be discussed in chapter 5. The task at hand, though, is to turn to chapter 4 for an investigation of the forms and functions of prologues in antiquity.

4

Prologues in Antiquity

IN MY SECOND CHAPTER, I made a case for Mark 1:1–15 as an integrated whole based on various formal features. In my third chapter, I explored the context of Mark in light of ancient Greco-Roman rhetorical conventions. Whereas the former was a *within the text* analysis, and the latter a *behind the text* analysis, this fourth chapter will offer a comparative analysis that might rightly be called a *beside the text* approach. The aim will be to situate Mark alongside a selection of ancient works with the hope that doing so will shed light not only on formal questions related to Mark's opening materials, but on functional concerns, as well.

The immediate challenge, however, is the selection of works with which to compare Mark. Richard Burridge has argued that Mark demonstrates a number of features that are consistent with ancient Greco-Roman βίοι.[1] In making his case, Burridge selected ten βίοι that represent a range of ancient biographies—five originating prior to the time of the Gospels, and five originating afterwards. Although he does not specify the precise criteria he used in selecting these particular works, they nevertheless represent a range of types and styles. Despite the great diversity of these works, the common denominator among them is a primary focus on a single individual. Because Mark also has a primary focus on a single individual, it seems that Burridge's study is a reasonable place to begin a comparative analysis.

In this chapter, I will provide a brief summary of each of the works used in Burridge's study, and then I will compare them with one another in regard to their common and dissonant features. I will follow that analysis with a comparison of Mark with Burridge's chosen corpus, again looking for similarities and differences. My hope is that such an approach

---

1. Burridge, *What Are the Gospels?*; for a work that builds on Burridge's model, see Guijarro, *Why Does the Gospel of Mark*, 29–30.

will provide further traction for understanding both the form and the function of Mark 1:1–15.

The Corpus for Comparison

For his study, Burridge chose the following works: from the earlier period, Isocrates's *Evagoras*, Xenophon's *Agesilaus*, Satyrus's *Euripides*, Nepos's *Atticus*, and Philo's *Moses*;[2] from the later, Tacitus's *Agricola*, Plutarch's *Cato Minor*, Suetonius' *Lives of the Caesars*, Lucian's *Demonax*, and Philostratus's *Apollonius of Tyana*.[3] With regard to Suetonius's *Lives*, Burridge focuses primarily on those of Julius Caesar and Augustus. However, and because of the fragmentary nature of *Julius Caesar* (the beginning is in fact lost), we will limit our examination to the life of Augustus. Likewise, the beginning of *Euripides* is lost; in its place, I propose to look at Josephus's *The Life of Flavius Josephus*.

Isocrates's *Evagoras*

The occasion of the *Evagoras* is the death of the Cyprian king, Evagoras, probably in the vicinity of 374 BC. As such, it is the oldest member of our corpus under review.[4] The work is the third oration of three written by Isocrates to Nicocles (son of Evagoras). In the first, Isocrates addresses Nicocles as to how a king should relate to his subjects. In the second, he goes on to advise Nicocles in the ways subjects should relate to their king. The third oration is a funeral encomium shortly after the death of the king. Although Aristotle reports that Evagoras was murdered, Isocrates tactfully avoids that issue.

Isocrates laments the fact that he does not have the same latitude as poets in using effusive language (although that does not seem to prevent him from doing so at times). Of overarching concern to Isocrates is the demonstration of Evagoras' fine character and the opportunity for Nicocles to emulate that character as he prepares to assume the throne vacated by the untimely death of his father:

---

2. Burridge, *What Are the Gospels?*, 125–28.
3. Ibid., 151–55.
4. The order in which the works are listed in the preceding is roughly chronological.

> It is my task, therefore, and that of your other friends, to speak and to write in such fashion as may be likely to incite you to strive eagerly after those things which even now you do in fact desire; and you it behooves not to be negligent, but as at present so in the future to pay heed to yourself and to discipline your mind that you may be worthy of your father and of all your ancestors. (Isocrates, *Evagoras*, 207.80; Van Hook)

The work thus functions as epideictic βίος. On one hand, it seeks to extol the virtues of Evagoras; on the other, it evinces a strongly deliberative attempt to positively influence the behavior of Nicocles.

Evagoras begins with a preface by Isocrates in which he addresses Nicocles, then moves into establishing the context in which Evagoras became king. The bulk of the remaining narrative is a testament to the king's virtues; the narration of Evagoras's deeds provides the proof[5] for those virtues. Although the narration is indeed biographical, it seems to serve as a secondary mechanism for Isocrates' primary purpose: the commemoration and imitation of Evagoras's virtues. "For my part, Nicocles, I think that while effigies of the body are fine memorials, yet likenesses of deeds and of the character are of far greater value" (Isocrates, *Evagoras*, 204.73; Van Hook).

Xenophon's *Agesilaus*

Xenophon considered Agesilaus to be the ideal Spartan king. Assuming the throne jointly in 398 BC, he reigned for nearly forty years after having already served an illustrious career as a field commander. The *Agesilaus* is a tribute to the deceased king and, as such, is encomiastic.

The shape of the work is rather unique in that it is ordered around two different presentations: the first is an historical recollection of the king's life and military exploits; the second, however, is a systematic treatment of the king's various virtues. Those virtues are then summarized and restated following a eulogistic epilogue. Like the *Evagoras*, the overarching purpose is to extol the virtues of the king and to encourage imitation. The proof of one's character likewise lies in his deeds: "Actions like these need no proofs; the mere mention of them is enough and they command belief immediately" (Xenophon, *Agesilaus*, 3.1; Marchant).

---

5. Compare σημεῖον (190.8) with τεκμήριον (200.58) for "proof."

Nepos's *Atticus*

Our third work is likewise an encomium, but unique in that it is written for a living person. In fact, the *praefatio* is addressed to the biographical subject: Atticus. Written in a plain style with limited vocabulary and short sentences, Nepos drafted his tribute to Atticus in an effort to entertain popular, non-scholarly audiences and to point a moral.[6] As such, it is somewhat paraenetic in purpose. Burridge states that this is the "first surviving example of Roman biography" and shows a strong familiarity with the *Evagoras* and *Agesilaus*.[7]

Most likely written just before the death of Atticus in 32 BC, the *Atticus* is part of a larger series by Nepos on the *Great Generals of Foreign Nations*. A few years following its first promulgation, the series was expanded to include subjects outside the sphere of Greeks and Romans.[8] In his preface, Nepos refers to the challenges of writing amid differing cultural customs:

> If these men can be made to understand that not all peoples look upon the same acts as honourable or base, but that they judge them all in the light of the usage of their forefathers, they will not be surprised that I, in giving an account of the merits of Greeks, have borne in mind the usage of that nation. [. . .] On the other hand, many actions are seemly according to our code which the Greeks look upon as shameful. (Nepos, *Praefatio* 3, 6; Rolfe)

Philo's *Moses*

In his preface, Philo refers to his subject as "the greatest and most perfect man that ever lived" (Philo, *Moses* 1.1, Yonge). His purpose is to present Moses to the Greek world, a world which has largely neglected its intellectual capacities by failing to include the life of Moses among its biographies:

> [T]he historians who have flourished among the Greeks have not chosen to think him worthy of mention, the greater part of whom have both in their poems and also in their prose writings, disparaged or defaced the powers which they have received through education, composing comedies and works full of Sybaritish profligacy and licentiousness to their everlasting shame, while they

---

6. Rolfe, trans., *Nepos*, xi.
7. Burridge, *What Are the Gospels?*, 128.
8. Rolfe, trans., *Nepos*, xi.

ought rather to have employed their natural endowments and abilities in preserving a record of virtuous men and praiseworthy lives[. . .]. (Philo, *Moses* 1.2–3; Yonge)

As with the *Atticus*, Philo illustrates the expansion of βίοι to other cultures (in this case, Alexandrian Judaism).[9]

Blending his primary sources of Scripture and the teachings of Jewish elders, Philo conveys his account in two volumes. The first relates the events surrounding the life of Moses, while the second focuses on his traits (and in this way his structure is not entirely different from the *Agesilaus*). Chief among those traits are Moses's exemplary performance of roles as king, law-giver, priest and prophet.

Josephus's *Life*

One might object to the inclusion here of an autobiography on the grounds that it does not precisely fit the category of βίος. I think two reasons will support my move. First, although autobiography as a genre may not perfectly fit that of biography, I believe it is fair to say that autobiography—as a subset or species of biography—fits *within* it. Second, given the diversity of the works included in Burridge's corpus, Josephus's *Life* is not so different as to be beyond comparison (as will be shown below).

The *Sitz* of Josephus's *Life* was originally as an appendix to the *Antiquities*. Its purpose was to vindicate Josephus against the allegedly inaccurate accounts of him in the writings of a competing historian, Justus of Tiberias.[10] He begins his account by recounting his heritage, most notably his connection to the Hasmonean line of descent. As such, he claims status within both priestly and royal lineages. He goes on to explain his investigation of the three sects (Pharisees, Sadducees, and Essenes), choosing to spend three years in the wilderness under the tutelage of the ascetic, Banus.

Josephus's works are of interest for my study especially in regard to his well-structured prefaces, not just in his *Life*, but also in his introductions to the *Antiquities* and *Wars*. That Josephus is writing from a Jewish perspective and with time spent in first-century Galilee makes him of special concern for the forms and functions of prefatory materials in the NT era.

---

9. Burridge, *What Are the Gospels?*, 128.
10. Ibid., ix.

Tacitus's *Agricola*

Agricola was sent by the Roman Empire to Britain in order to facilitate the suppression of resistance from Wales. The aim was to establish sustainable occupation of the British colony. Probably written shortly after his death in AD 93, the *Agricola* is a testament to the military and diplomatic genius of a leader trying to reconcile two very different cultures.

> A kind, honest, judicious man himself, he appreciated the virtues of the British people and at the same time valued the benefits of Roman civilisation. He tried not to destroy the native way of life but to blend it with Roman institutions, so that a civilized, educated, and decent society should flourish in Britain just as it flourished in his own Gallia Narbonensis. It was this vision, a vision which only a provincial by origin and education like himself could fully experience, which inspired Agricola's life.[11]

The shape of the work reflects Agricola's diplomatic posture. It begins with a formal introduction, and then moves into a brief history of his career prior to his British deployment. Following these accounts, Tacitus provides an innovative ethnographic description of the British people, providing essential background for the main episode of his father-in-law's biography,[12] which is the narration of Agricola's time and efforts in Britain. The work closes as it opens: with a rhetorical defense and celebration of the virtues of Agricola.

The dominant theme of the work is the tension that Agricola experienced between the unchecked liberty of the Britons (which can only lead to chaos) and the absolute power of Rome (which can only lead to moral degradation, loss of self-respect, and fear).[13] His life, then, is an example of moderation demonstrated as early as his youth:

> [H]e was shielded from the snares of sinners not merely by his own good and upright nature but because from the outset of his childhood the home and the guide of his studies was Massilia, a blend and happy combination of Greek refinement and provincial simplicity. I remember how he used himself to tell that in early life he was inclined to drink more deeply of philosophy than is permitted to a Roman and a Senator, had not his mother's discretion imposed a check upon his enkindled and glowing imagination:

---

11. Hutton, trans., *Tacitus*, 1:15.
12. Ibid., 1:17.
13. Ibid., 1:20.

no doubt his soaring and ambitious temper craved the beauty and splendour of high and exalted ideals with more ardour and prudence. *Soon came reason and years to cool his blood: he achieved the rarest of feats; he was a student, yet preserved a sense of proportion.* (Tactius, *Agricola* 4.2–3; Hutton; emphasis added)

As with our preceding authors, the *Agricola* contains a strong element of paraenesis and maintains the axiom that one's actions are confirmed by one's deeds (Tacitus, *Agricola* 46.1–4). Unlike the preceding, however, Tacitus reserves biographical information concerning Agricola's birth, death, physical appearance, and family for the very end of the work.

Plutarch's *Cato Minor*

Plutarch writes amid the ascendancy of Rome to its second golden age. Whereas Tacitus rebuked and wrote in opposition to the excesses of Domitian, Plutarch lived and wrote during the revival of Roman nationalism that reached its peak under Hadrian. The life of Cato Minor, as with Plutarch's other *Lives*, is broadly historical, but nevertheless contains a strong ethical tone as seen in his *Moralia*. As with his *Lives*, Plutarch has paired a Greek figure with a Roman one. In this case, Cato is the parallel for Phocion.

Plutarch says about Cato as a youth that he was difficult to persuade, making him a sluggish student. Plutarch is quick to find redemption for this quality by suggesting euphemistically that,

> Cato's reluctance to be persuaded made his learning [of] anything more laborious. For, to learn is simply to allow something to be done to you, and to be quickly persuaded is natural for those who are less able to offer resistance. Therefore young men are more easily persuaded than old men, and sick folk, than those who are well, and, in a word, where the power to raise objections is weakest, the act of submission is easiest. (Plutarch, *Cato Minor* 1.4; Perrin)

The opening materials of the work feature a further description of Cato's character, including his uncommon ferocity (which was slow to awaken; 1.2) and his abiding love for his brother, Caepio (3.5). The closing materials provide a detailed description of Cato's suicide (68–70), about which Plutarch writes, "Before one would have thought that all in the house could learn of the event, the three hundred were at the door, and a littler later the people of Utica assembled. With one voice they called Cato their saviour and benefactor [. . .]." (Plutarch, *Cato Minor* 71.1; Perrin)

Suetonius's *Augustus*

Suetonius's *Lives of the Caesars* represents an early commitment to writing a detached, objective account of a life. J. C. Rolfe suggests that they are not biography in the strict sense, since "no ideal life is presented, to inspire imitation and point a moral, and no attempt is made to trace the development of character as influenced by heredity, education, and environment."[14] Neither can it be said about them that they are pure history-writing, for "[g]reat historical events, such as Caesar's campaigns in Gaul, are dismissed in a brief chapter, or with a casual allusion, like the defeat of Varus. The acts of the senate and people, and the edicts of the emperors, receive fuller attention, but are wholly subordinate to the personal element."[15] As such, the style of the writing gives "the thoughtful reader abundant opportunity for the reflexions and deductions which the writer has omitted."[16] Thus, authorial intrusions are minimal, and the identification of the subject's virtues and vices are both listed, albeit separately.

The broad organization of the work features the personal background of Augustus, including a mention of the Octavian legacy; his birth, infancy, and youth; and a summary of his life. The account then transitions to a narrative of his public life in civic and military affairs followed by a narrative of his private life and domestic relations. The presentation is topical, in keeping with the general pattern of the *Lives*, with chronology being followed only with respect to the subject's early years and death.

Lucian's *Demonax*

As we introduce the *Demonax*, we cannot help but notice that the pendulum swings rather quickly. Whereas the life of Augustus represents a dispassionate account of the life of its subject, the *Demonax* is an unapologetic celebration of the life of a beloved philosopher. Lucian's aim is not to reform society, but rather to amuse it. He is serious only in his desire to please his readers, and his work thus represents epideictic discourse.[17]

> It is now fitting to tell of Demonax for two reasons—that he may be retained in memory by men of culture as far as I can bring it

---

14. Rolfe, trans., *Suetonius*, 1:xvii.
15. Ibid.
16. Ibid.
17. Harmon, *Lucian*, 1:x.

about, and that young men of good instincts who aspire to philosophy may not have to shape themselves by ancient precedents alone, but may be able to set themselves a pattern from our modern world and to copy that man, the best of all the philosophers whom I know about. (Lucian, *Demonax* 2; Harmon)

Demonax (as portrayed by Lucian) is an eclectic blend of philosophies and schools of thought. He demonstrated a forgiving disposition (7), and his character was kind, gentle, and cheerful (9). Lucian seems to most appreciate the witticisms of Demonax. In fact, the biography lacks any real narrative; it consists almost entirely of character attributes (1–11) and a listing of pithy statements and dialogues that reveal the endearing charm of Demonax (12–62). The work concludes with a brief look at his passing, the manner of which was fully in keeping with his character (63–67).

Philostratus's *Apollonius*[18]

By far the largest individual work in our corpus, the *Apollonius* is based on memoirs composed by a disciple and companion of Apollonius named Damis (Philostratus, *Apollonius* 3). It was likely published sometime after AD 217 for the purpose of rehabilitating the reputation of Apollonius who had been accused of wizardry. The work thus bears a forensic element.

The opening of the work is comparatively complex by the standards of our previous biographies. This may be attributed to the overall scale of the *Apollonius*. The opening materials are a mixture of biographical information concerning the subject, discussion of selection and use of sources, and comparisons of Apollonius with ancient figures (such as Pythagoras and Proteus). The work in large measure features a number of striking parallels with the Gospels in general, and Mark in particular. So striking are the parallels that it has been suggested that the *Apollonius* was designed to provide an alternative to the Jesus of Christianity.[19] Just a few of these similarities include the following: a mystical announcement to Apollonius's mother prior to his birth (4); portents accompanying his birth (5); and the use of water in confession and repentance (6). Most notable are his mighty acts and miracles that dot the narrative landscape.

An additional similarity relates to an external matter: just as the life of Apollonius is attributed to Lucian through Damis, so also is the life of Jesus

18. Conybeare, trans., *Philostratus*.
19. Ibid., 1:xiii–xiv.

attributed to Mark through Peter. Such matters make the *Apollonius* quite significant for the present study.

Analysis of the Corpus

This brief depiction of the various works indicates a general unity in terms of biographical focus. Burridge highlights two primary factors that contribute to the identification of a biographical subject: 1) analysis of verbs in which the biographical subject is the grammatical subject; and 2) the allocation of space to that biographical subject.[20] In each instance above, the featured subject is preeminent. The works begin to differentiate, however, when one moves beyond a simple examination of the treatment of the subject. This is especially true of their opening materials. The following analysis will build upon and enlarge Burridge's concise treatment of the opening features (which he particularizes as the title of the work and the opening formula, prologue, or preface of each work); but before doing so, it will be helpful to do a brief survey of some of the general features of the works.

General Features

We observe that the corpus represents an extraordinary amount of diversity with respect to a number of general features. One such feature is size. Burridge has selected his corpus to function as something of a control group for comparison with the Gospels. As such, the works comprising the corpus should share an affinity for one another in important ways. One of the attributes of the works is *size* (understood here as word count). The range of the works in terms of size is remarkable. For instance, *Demonax* weighs in at just over 3,000 words, while *Apollonius* breaks the scales at 82,000 words. From a rhetorical perspective, all species are present, whether it is the forensic nature of *Josephus* or *Apollonius* (in defense of the subject), the deliberative nature of *Evagoras* or *Atticus* (with respect to the emulation of virtue), or the epideictic nature of *Agesilaus* or *Moses* (celebrating the character and impact of an individual). We see equal diversity among the various styles, ranging from the "judicial coldness"[21] of Suetonius to the

---

20. Burridge, *What Are the Gospels?*, 110–12.
21. Rolfe, trans., *Suetonius*, 1:xix.

warmth and witticisms of the *Demonax*, and from the embellishments of *Evagoras* to the simplicity of *Atticus*.

We observe further diversity in terms of narration. Most works employ direct discourse ("quoted" material) in scant measure; *Demonax* and *Apollonius* make heavy use of it. Also, some works faithfully follow the chronologies of their subject's lives (*Josephus* and *Cato Minor*), some separate chronology from systematic (topical) treatment (*Agesilaus*), and some blend the two (*Evagoras* and *Suetonius*).

Title

Although a title of a work can and often does give a fairly clear indication of a work's genre (in some cases as understood by early librarians rather than the authors themselves), the tendency for a title to be altered makes such titles a bit difficult to assess. The problem is compounded by transmission issues where titles are most likely to experience physical alteration. Despite these factors, we can observe some common tendencies among the works. More often than not, the name of the subject appears in the title. A typical formulation is for the word *life* to appear, accompanied by the name of the subject in the genitive case, as with *De Vita Mosis*, Ἰωσήπου βίος, *De Vita Iulii Agricolae*,[22] and βίος Δημώνακτος.[23] Where a work appears as part of a series, the series title may convey such indications (e.g., *De Vita Caesarum* in the case of Augustus, or Πλουτάρχου βίοι Παραλλήνοι in the case of Cato Minor).

Opening Formulae

THE PREFACE

Once we move beyond the title, matters became increasingly complex with regard to the manner in which authors introduce their works. Dennis Smith has provided a brief but very helpful taxonomy of the various ways ancient works could begin.[24] One way was by means of a preface (προοίμιον

---

22. Burridge gives the full title as "Cornelii Taciti de Vita Iulii Agricolae liber incipit," per the Aesinas Codex; Burridge, *What Are the Gospels?*, 156.

23. On this, see Houston, *Inside Roman Libraries*, about which I will say more in the following chapter.

24. Smith, *Narrative Beginnings*.

or φροίμιον) in which the author would state his intentions for his work.[25] Aristotle felt that the most critical function of the preface is to clarify the main purpose of the work (Aristotle, *Rhetoric* 3.14.6). Such devices can be found (in accordance with their respective conventions) in historical, literary, and scientific writings.[26] A survey of the opening units of the works we have in mind reveals some common trends. For instance, it is typical for an author to insert himself by means of first-person discourse. Nowhere is this more prevalent than in association with statements of purpose or the occasion for the writing. In fact, all of the works show strong evidence of a first-person preface, with the exception of Plutarch and Suetonius. Although Josephus lacks a formal preface, his account is entirely in the first person. Further, his work as a whole could be considered a preface in terms of function as it relates to his *Antiquities*. In each of the cases where such first-person insertions are evident, a fairly apparent statement of purpose is either expressed or implied. Such purposes include commemorating and advocating the virtues of the subject (*Evagoras*, *Agesilaus*, and *Demonax*), chronicling the life of a noteworthy figure (*Moses* and *Agricola*), and defending the figure against false or inadequate presentation (*Josephus* and *Apollonius*).

It is common for authors to discuss in their prefaces the obstacles or challenges they face in their tasks. Isocrates, for instance, says that,

> I am fully aware that what I propose to do is difficult—to eulogize in prose the virtues of a man. The best proof is this: Those who devote themselves to philosophy venture to speak on many subjects of every kind, but no one of them has ever attempted to compose a discourse on such a theme. And I can make much allowance for them. For to the poets is granted the use of many embellishments of language [. . .] not only in conventional expressions, but in words now exotic, now newly coined, and now in figures of speech, neglecting none, but using every kind with which to embroider their poesy. Orators, on the contrary, are not permitted the use of such devices [. . .]. (Isocrates, *Evagoras* 190.8–9; Van Hook)

Similarly, Xenophon writes, "I know how difficult it is to write an appreciation of Agesilaus that shall be worthy of his virtue and glory" (Xenophon, *Agesilaus* 1.1; Marchant). For Nepos, the challenge was to bridge cultural customs at variance between Greeks and Romans; for Philo, it was the

---

25. Ibid., 1–3.
26. Ibid., 1.

seeming obstinacy of Greek historians to consider a subject as ancient as Moses. In Tacitus' case, eulogizing Agricola carried with it an implicit indictment against the Empire, making his task not only difficult, but dangerous. Such an appreciation for the exigence of the *Agricola* can only be inferred through direct engagement with the social and political milieu from which the work originates.

It is also common for authors to discuss their personal connection to the subject (Tacitus, *Agricola* 3.3; Lucian, *Demonax* 1.1) and their use of sources in their prefatory remarks (Philo, *Moses* 1.1.4; Philostratus, *Apollonius* 1.3). Taken together, these features are tightly woven into units that may be read as prefaces. In most cases, these units are clearly defined:

	Prefatory Unit
Evagoras	189.1–11
Agesilaus	1.1
Atticus	*Praef.* 1–8
Moses	1.1.1–1.2.5; 2.2.1
Josephus	arguably, "the whole"
Agricola	1.1—3.3
Cato Minor	
Augustus	
Demonax	1–2
Apollonius	1–3

Among the Gospels, Luke is the only writer to employ a device that comports with a preface in this sense by using a first-person insertion, a statement of purpose, and a mention of sources. We do get glimpses of similar first person insertions in John's Gospel (20:30–31; 21:24–25), but these are clearly not a part of the opening materials.

The Prologue

The second type of opening formula that Smith discusses is the prologue.[27] Two types are attested. On one hand, the *dramatic prologue* functioned in ways similar to a preface in that the author would address the reader through first person discourse, defend himself against the attacks of his opponents, or cultivate favor among the readership. More important for

---

27. Ibid., 3–4.

our study, though, is the *expository prologue* in which the author situates the narrative action within a contextual framework or against a contextual background.

With our corpus in view, it is readily apparent that Greek, Roman, and Jewish authors made use of the expository prologue. Since biographies have as their primary focus the life of an individual, details related to the individual's ancestry, birth, childhood, youth, and education all fund the contextual background. In some cases, that background points to the source or origin of the individual's virtuous character (*Evagoras* and *Agesilaus*, for instance); in other cases, the background serves to explain the significance or timelessness of an individual's contribution (e.g., *Agricola*). In yet other cases, signs and portents accompanying the birth of the individual hint at the destiny of the individual (as with *Apollonius*).

All of the specimens in view include a direct reference to the subject's ancestry. Likewise, all of the specimens discuss the subject's youth. Nearly all mention details regarding the birth of the subject (the exceptions are the *Atticus*, *Josephus*, and *Cato Minor*), and nearly all of them mention the subject's parents and their formative role in shaping the character of the subject. The vast majority of references related to ancestry, birth, childhood, youth, and education occur at the beginning of the work in what appears to be an expository prologue. In most cases, such a prologue can be readily delineated, though at times the boundaries are less than clear. Here is a listing of those units:

	Prologic Unit
Evagoras	191.12—193.21
Agesilaus	1.2–6
Atticus	1.1—3.3
Moses	1.1.5–7
Josephus	arguably, "the whole"
Agricola	4.1–3
Cato Minor	
Augustus	1–9
Demonax	3–4
Apollonius	4–12

The Incipit

Smith describes the *incipit* as a short text string that identifies the work,[28] often occurring as the first line or sentence of that work.[29] He suggests that the opening of the *Gospel of Thomas* is indicative of this device. Alternatively, the incipit might be understood as the title of a work. Over time, scroll tags (*sillybos* or *titulos*) were employed to identify the author and the work. This likely provides the basis for the "Gospel according to" superscriptions associated with the canonical Gospels.[30] W. D. Davies and D. C. Allison have argued that Matt 1:1 is just such an incipit.[31]

The "Virtual Preface"

Smith reports a fourth type of opening for an ancient work that Lucian dubbed the *virtual preface* (or προοίμιον δυνάμαι).[32] The *virtual preface* is an implied device that lies embedded in a narrative that begins *in media res*. The author assumes that the flow of the narrative will perform the necessary indoctrination for the reader. In reality, the *virtual preface* cannot be formally identified but nevertheless serves a function, leading Smith to describe Lucian's concept as "lame but ingenious."[33] It might be argued that Plutarch and Suetonius are the only members of our corpus who might have employed this device.

In sum, our sampling of works indeed exhibits a very wide range of features. The features that are absolutely consistent among the works are the primary focus on the main character as the subject and the mention of the subject's ancestry and youth. Features that are mostly consistent are the appearance of either a prologue that conveys contextual information supporting the narrative, or a preface that addresses matters related to the author. In some cases, both are present. Also generally consistent among the works are a preference for third-person narration over direct discourse and some mention of the subject's parents and birth. Beyond

---

28. An *incipit* can serve multiple purposes; e.g., it can function internally as a title of a whole work or as a section heading, and externally as a cataloguing device.
29. Smith, *Narrative Beginnings*, 4–6.
30. On this, see Hengel, *Studies in the Gospel of Mark*, 64–84.
31. Davies and Allison, *A Critical and Exegetical Commentary on Matthew*, 149–60.
32. Smith, *Narrative Beginnings*, 6–7.
33. Ibid., 7.

these, the works are incredibly diverse with respect to size, purpose, style, and commitment to chronology.

The Corpus and Mark

In light of the preceding analysis, how does Mark compare? I would like to say from the start that scholars are not at all united in their views of Mark's relationship to ancient Greco-Roman βίοι. D. Dormeyer finds Mark's prologue, for example, completely at home within a Hellenistic biographical classification: "Mk 1,1–15 läßt sich in die hellenistische Biographieliteratur einordnen. Der archaische Prologbeginn wird narrativ mit den Topoi der hellenistischen Philosophen- und Gründerbiographie aufgefüllt."[34] Conversely, S. Guijarro says, "Mark's Gospel does not follow the rules of Hellenistic 'lives,' which usually began by praising the ancestry and education of the main character."[35] J. B. Gabler and C. B. Wheeler contend that, "The gospels were not written as biographies of Jesus, nor can a biography be extracted from them,"[36] while L. T. Johnson counters that, "The form of the Gospels most closely resembles that of Hellenistic biographies."[37] What, then, can be said about Mark in light of its Greco-Roman counterparts?

It might be the case that divided opinions are based on the fact that Mark is both *like* and *unlike* ancient biographies of the Greco-Roman world. Where Mark resembles such biographies, it resembles them strongly; but where it differs, it differs just as strongly. In terms of size, Mark is a little over 11,000 words, making it very representative of the mid-sized works in Burridge's corpus.[38] The following table illustrates the span:

---

34. Dormeyer, *Mk 1,1–15 als Prolog*, 202.

35. Guijarro, *Why Does the Gospel of Mark*, 28; it should be noted, however, that despite Mark's lack of formal correspondence to Hellenistic biography, Santiago claims that Mark does manage to accomplish the same purpose of those biographies. "Mark did not begin his gospel talking about Jesus' origin and education because the available data were not suited to reveal his ascribed honor. Mark, nonetheless, did not abandon this goal, so important in Hellenistic lives; he tried to reach it through another route," 36–37.

36. Gabel and Wheeler, *The Bible as Literature*, 185.

37. Johnson, *The Writings of the New Testament*, 145; for this and the preceding quote by Gabel and Wheeler I am indebted to Burridge, *What Are the Gospels*, 185.

38. Burridge, *What Are the Gospels*, 134–35, 164–65, 194.

3,000–4,999 words	5,000–9,999 words	10,000–19,999 words	20,000–79,999 words	More than 80,000 words
Demonax *Atticus*	*Evagoras* *Agesilaus* *Agricola*	*Gospel of Mark* *Cato Minor* *Augustus* *Josephus*	*Moses*	*Apollonius*

Beyond Mark's normal size, it clearly features a single individual as the main focus of the whole, in keeping with the corpus.

> Jesus himself is the subject of about a quarter of the verbs (24.4%) and a further fifth occur on his lips, in his teaching or parables (20.2%). These results are very close to Satyrus' where Euripedes was the subject of 25.8%, with 17.5% occurring in quotations from his plays. We have the same concentration on the subject: no other individual scores above 1%.[39]

Alongside a handful of works, Mark can be seen to be "normal" once again:

Agesilaus	18%
Agricola	18%
Gospel of Mark	24%
Euripedes	26%
Demonax	34%

Thus, judging by the standards set by other biographies, Mark's placement of Jesus as the grammatical and narrative subject clearly identifies his Gospel with Greco-Roman βίοι. We can further note that Mark, like the ancient βίοι, follows a broadly chronological framework, but is not opposed to interrupting his narrative in order to explain cultural customs (compare Mark 7 on the Pharisees with *Agricola* 10–17 on the Britons) or insert speech material (compare Jesus' apocalyptic discourse in Mark 13 to *Agricola*'s inspiring battle speech in 33–34).

Here, however, the strong similarities cease. Whereas each of the Greek and Latin works covers the lifespan of the subject, Mark's treatment is likely only one to three years,[40] including the ministry of John the

---

39. Ibid., 190.

40. This depends, of course, upon whether one assumes Synoptic or Johannine chronology.

Baptizer. Whereas the Greek and Latin βίοι feature first-person insertions in dedicated prefatory material (and elsewhere, as well), Mark features no such insertions. Whereas *all* the Greek and Latin βίοι speak in some measure of the subject's lineage, birth, and youth, Mark offers *nothing* in regard to Jesus' life prior to his appearance as an adult in Mark 1:9. Whereas the Greek and Latin βίοι mostly tend to avoid the use of direct discourse, such is a staple for Mark.

In light of these strong differences, what can we surmise regarding the function of Mark's opening material? It may be the case that this comparative analysis raises more questions than it answers, and those may in fact be the questions that we need to be asking. For example, we have seen works in which the primary thrust of the narrative is biographical, but the authorial purpose is expressly stated in forensic terms. We see this quite clearly in the *Apollonius* where Philostratus seeks to defend Apollonius from accusations of wizardry. To capture a glimpse of this rhetorical aim, I offer the following extended excerpt from Philostratus' opening remarks:

> [S]ome, because he had interviews with the wizards of Babylon and with the Brahmans of India, and with the nude ascetics of Egypt, put him down as a wizard, and spread the calumny that he was a sage of an illegitimate kind, judging of him ill. For Empedocles and Pythagoras himself and Democritus consorted with wizards and uttered many supernatural truths, yet never stooped to the black art; and Plato went to Egypt and mingled with his own discourses much of what he heard from the prophets and priests there; and though, like a painter, he laid his own colours on to their rough sketches, yet he never passed for a wizard, although envied above all mankind for his wisdom. For the circumstance that Apollonius foresaw and foreknew so many things does not in the least justify us in imputing to him this kind of wisdom [. . .]. (Philostratus, *Apollonius* 1.2; Conybeare)

What this demonstrates is this: while a work may be *quantitatively*[41] *biographical* in *form*, the very same work may be *qualitatively rhetorical* in *function*. Biographies are forms— they have no intrinsic function apart from simply chronicling a life. Those functions are assigned to them. Said differently, biographies do not exist apart from a purpose. They exist to praise, to blame, to enjoy, to imitate, or to commemorate. That only some lives are chronicled (while the vast majority are not) indicates the *purpose*

---

41. By *quantitatively* I simply mean the amount of space allocated to the life of the main character.

underlying the biography.[42] More often than not, the purpose is rhetorical in the sense of attempting to *persuade*: to *persuade* the readers that the subject was a noble character worth emulating; to *persuade* the reader that the subject was misunderstood or innocent of unjust charges; or to *persuade* the reader that the subject made a contribution to society and is worth commemorating.

In the same way that a discourse can be sandwiched between epistolary devices (as with so many NT letters), so too can a biography be sandwiched between rhetorical devices. Put differently, a biographical work can—and typically does—reflect rhetorical features and purposes throughout. A quick review of the works under consideration reveals a variety of forms in which the opening—and in some cases, the closing—materials reveal such functions. For Philo, his biography of the life of Moses was epideictic, aimed at honoring and praising the ancient law-giver. Josephus, like Philostratus, was interested in vindication (of himself, in this case), and thus his autobiography served a similarly forensic function as Philostratus'. Nepos, in chronicling the life of Atticus, was most interested in advancing Atticus as an exemplar, thus establishing a deliberative rhetorical aim with regard to the future conduct of those to follow.

As we have already observed, Mark offers no explicit mention of his purpose; but as I have just shown, biographies do not exist without purpose. If Mark is a biography (as Burridge has attempted to demonstrate), logic requires us therefore to ask: what was Mark's purpose? In light of the preceding analysis of ancient Greco-Roman βίοι, I suggest that the answer will lie in Mark's opening remarks. Our comparative analysis in this chapter (along with our literary and rhetorical analyses in the preceding chapters) has helped frame the task. The challenge before us, then, is to infer from his opening remarks what that purpose is. This is indeed a challenge for at least two reasons. First, Mark has given us no expressed statement of purpose or intent through explicit, first-person remarks—the Gospel of Mark has no preface. Second, the opening material that Mark does provide (if it can be considered a prologue, which Burridge disputes[43]) deviates in significant ways from the prologues of Greco-Roman βίοι. One of the most significant differences between Mark's Gospel and the Greco-Roman biographies surveyed above is this: Mark provides us with no identification of Jesus'

---

42. As I argued in the previous chapter, all historical works reflect some degree of *Tendenz*. I refer once again to Keener, *The Historical Jesus of the Gospels*, 117–23.

43. Burridge, *What Are the Gospels?*, 188.

ancestry, birth, parents, youth, training, or education. If such matters were of central concern in establishing the virtues and capacities of Greek and Roman individuals worth remembering, what explains the absence of such matters in Mark's opening materials? As will be shown below, Mark appeals to conventions more suited *in some measure* for a Jewish than a Hellenistic audience. As will be more fully established toward the conclusion of this study, Mark seeks to legitimate Jesus as the duly authorized representative of God on earth. Mark presents Jesus as *the Son* of God. Given the pro-logic nature of Mark's opening, it stands to reason that one part of Mark's purpose would be to establish Jesus' credentials or to legitimate him with a miraculous sign at birth, yet Mark does not provide us with a birth narrative as do Matthew and Luke. William Abbott proposes that,

> In many ways, Matthew and Luke use their infancy narratives to provide the credentials of Jesus. Each give him a theological identity card that introduces us to who it is that proclaims the good news that is the gospel of God. Mark, for his part, does not utilize the infancy narrative approach. [. . .Yet] while Mark omits any infancy account, that does not mean he fails to accomplish in his own way what Matthew and Luke do with their much longer and more elaborate introductions to Jesus.[44]

Abbott strikes upon something important here, namely that Mark may be establishing Jesus' credentials through an alternate means. Guijarro maintains that Mark begins the way he does because Mark is interested in presenting the introduction of Jesus as a *status transformation ritual*.[45] In the absence of a genealogy to properly *ascribe* nobility or honor to Jesus, the only way for Jesus to obtain honor would be to *acquire* it through his actions.[46] This presents a quandary, though, since Jesus is portrayed almost entirely as a passive character in the prologue.

I propose that Mark *does* in fact provide this seemingly missing element in his expository prologue, but does so in ways that would appeal more to a sectarian audience than one under the dominant influence of Hellenism. Keener has highlighted the role of the Spirit in the Gospels, specifically noting a concentration of activity by the Spirit in Mark's opening unit. Although Keener acknowledges the relative paucity of the Spirit's

---

44. Abbott, *What Happened to Mark's Infancy Story?*, 203–4.

45. Guijarro, *Why Does the Gospel of Mark*, 34–35.

46. Ibid., 32–34; for studies related to honor and shame, also see Malina, *The New Testament World*; and deSilva, *Honor, Patronage, Kinship & Purity*.

appearance in Mark (mainly in 3:29; 12:36; and 13:11), it is perhaps instructive that the Spirit is explicitly identified three times within the span of five verses in Mark's prologue (1:8, 10, 12). Keener takes this to mean that, "Mark gives his primary lesson on pneumatology up front, in the introduction, one of the most critical sections of his Gospel."[47]

He suggests that a proper understanding of Markan pneumatology should come from the literary context of Mark itself, that Mark is in fact "our earliest extant narrative interpreter of Jesus as the Spirit-bringer, and provides a natural exegetical starting point for the discussion."[48] Using the other instances in which the Spirit plays an explicit role in Mark, Keener surmises that in contrast to the Q material (which relates Spirit and fire baptism, ostensibly to emphasize purification), Mark's presentation of the Spirit in connection to Jesus' baptism emphasizes prophetic empowerment. That Spirit empowered David to envision One whose enemies would become his footstool—One who would in fact sit at the right hand of God (Mark 12:36, referencing Ps 110:1). That Spirit also stands by to empower followers of Jesus with a ready defense when those followers are delivered up to trial (Mark 13:11).

Mark's means of establishing Jesus' credentials does not come through human means (i.e., by means of ancestry and upbringing); rather, Jesus' legitimation happens pneumatologically. It is *the Spirit* that authorizes and empowers Jesus for his divinely appointed mission.[49] That Jesus is divinely legitimized is clearly and repeatedly indicated in the prologue; one need only note the transcendent conversation of 1:2–3, John's role as "the messenger" in heralding the advent of Jesus, the descent of the Spirit onto Jesus in 1:10, the affirmation by the voice in 1:11, the guiding role of the Spirit in 1:12, and the sustaining role of the angels in 1:13. In fact, Jesus' legitimation through divine agents is the prime concern of Mark's prologue.

Summary

We have seen in the preceding analysis that two primary means were used by Greco-Roman biographers to introduce their works. In some cases, writers would provide first-person insertions indicating their aims or the

---

47. Keener, *The Spirit in the Gospels and Acts*, 50.
48. Ibid.
49. It is not my intent here to enter a theological debate over trinitarian matters. By "Spirit" I simply mean divine agency.

exigence of their writing. I will refer to these as *prefaces*. In other cases, writers would provide the necessary contextual background for understanding or appreciating the significance of the biographical subject. A common denominator among those works surveyed reflects a strong consistency with regard to the inclusion of background information related to the subject's ancestry, family, and/or birth. I will refer to these as *prologues*. Of course, writers could and certainly did blend these devices in any number of creative ways, at times also adding to their work a short, introductory text-string that identified that work (an *incipit*).

What we see with Mark, though, is both strong comportment with and deviation from common introductory practices. While Mark's opening exhibits many features that are common to the expository prologues of Greco-Roman βίοι, it nevertheless lacks the standard inclusion of a statement of the subject's ancestry, birth, or youth. I submit that, despite the lack of such an element, Mark pneumatologically ascribes to Jesus the honor necessary to warrant Jesus' proclamation of a new era of salvation history.

5

The Function of Mark 1:1–15

THIS CHAPTER MAKES THE transition from matters of form to matters of function. The preceding chapters have been nudging us in this direction, for the bridge from form to function is built on the apparatus of context. The question before us is this: if Mark 1:1–15 is a formal unit, what purpose does it serve?

Our previous chapters have been an attempt to establish a context for a first-century reading of Mark. I have made that attempt by appealing to four methodologies: *comparison* with literature roughly contemporary to Mark (chapter 4); *contextualization* of Mark within a rhetorically-saturated milieu (chapter 3); *formal analysis* of the visible, literary features of Mark (chapter 2); and *conversation* with recent interpreters of Mark, each of whom helps give shape in some way to a theoretical framework for interpreting Mark (chapter 1). In this present chapter, I will analyze the various internal elements of Mark's prologue, specifically noting the functional aspects of smaller units and their relationships to one another.

Because the opening materials of any written work are crucial in establishing the parameters for the reading experience, and because the more significant scholarly issues pertaining to Mark are concentrated in the first three or four verses, it is here that I will spill the most ink. If we are to arrive at a destination proximate to that which Mark intended, it is imperative that we embark on an accurate initial course heading.

Mark 1:1

In addressing the function of Mark's opening verse, two primary issues confront us. First, is υἱοῦ θεοῦ original to Mark's Gospel? Second, what is the extent of "the beginning" of the Gospel? Neither of these is a new issue, and each deserves another look in light of our preceding work.

The first question is a horizontal question: How far does 1:1 extend as we read from left-to-right? Specifically, should it extend so far as to include υἱοῦ θεοῦ? Before answering, it will be helpful to revisit the earlier suggestion that Mark's opening is the result of editorial emendation. Clayton Croy has advanced the claim that Mark has experienced frontal damage.[1] I have already mentioned his position by indicating that his is a minority view built almost entirely on conjecture.[2] Perhaps one thing is worth considering, however. He claims that the range of attested variants for 1:1 suggests emendation. I am inclined to think, however, that the evidence he offers actually tends to confirm the opposite—the originality of 1:1, perhaps even inclusive of υἱοῦ θεοῦ. Croy offers the following list of variants:[3]

1. Ἀρχὴ τοῦ εὐαγγελίου (Irenaeus, Epiphanius)
2. Ἀρχὴ τοῦ εὐαγγελίου Ἰησοῦ (Codex 28)
3. Ἀρχὴ τοῦ εὐαγγελίου Ἰησοῦ Χριστοῦ (Codices a and Θ, some Coptic, Armenian, and Georgian MSS, Origen, Jerome, and others)
4. Ἀρχὴ τοῦ εὐαγγελίου Ἰησοῦ Χριστοῦ υἱοῦ θεοῦ (a corrector of Codex a, Codices B, D, L, W, and 2427)
5. Ἀρχὴ τοῦ εὐαγγελίου Ἰησοῦ Χριστοῦ υἱοῦ τοῦ θεοῦ (Codex A and a very large number of other Greek MSS, some Ethiopic, Georgian, and Slavic MSS)
6. Ἀρχὴ τοῦ εὐαγγελίου Ἰησοῦ Χριστοῦ υἱοῦ τοῦ κυρίου (1241)

In addition to these he offers the following:

7. *Initium evagnelii domini nostril Iesu Christi filii dei* (three Vulgate MSS)
8. Εὐαγγέλιον τοῦ κυρίου Ἰησοῦ Χριστοῦ (Palestinian Syriac version)
9. Ἀρχὴ τοῦ εὐαγγελίου Ἰησοῦ τοῦ υἱοῦ τοῦ θεοῦ τοῦ ζῶντος (a single Arabic MSS)

Tommy Wasserman has offered a decisive critique of Croy's proposal on the basis of textual evidence.[4] What becomes evident, *contra* Croy's

---

1. Croy, *The Mutilation of Mark's Gospel*, 113–36.
2. Decker goes so far as to say that "in the absence of any external evidence whatsoever, such a conclusion remains very speculative and unproven," in *Mark 1–8*, 1.
3. Croy, *The Mutilation of Mark's Gospel*, 115.
4. Wasserman, *The Son of God*, 22–23.

proposal, is the remarkable consistency of the variants, especially when one eliminates—per Wasserman's suggestion—those readings that are "unattested in Greek MSS and represent typical adaptions by Fathers and versions."[5] Unlike the wide variations of readings for the Markan *ending*,[6] the variants for the Markan *beginning* are remarkably consistent. If Mark 1:1 functions as a heading in some sense (see below), then it may very well be the case that subsequent scribes and archivists took the liberty to move the opening verse to the outside of the scroll where it would be subject to alteration, especially shortening (by accident or intention). George Houston provides a fascinating look into the process of "tagging" scrolls, here quoted at length:

> In the case of both end titles and initial titles, the author's name and the title of the work would be hidden once the papyrus was rolled up. In a few known cases, the title and author were written also on the verso, that is, on the outside of the roll, so that the volume could be identified without being unrolled. More commonly, it seems, manuscripts were provided with a title tag, or *sillybon*. This was a strip of papyrus or parchment, roughly 3 by 8 cm, on which were written the author and title. It was glued to the edge of the roll but extended out from the edge so that, when the papyrus was rolled up, the *sillybon* protruded from one end of it, thus enabling the reader to identify the contents of the roll. It is not known how common *sillyba* were. In the absence of an external title or *sillybon*, and if the previous reader had rerolled the volume after use (or had a slave roll it back up), the reader would need to unroll the first twenty or thirty centimeters of the papyrus and identify the text from the initial title or the opening lines.[7]

The remarkable consistency of the variants thus suggests scribal trimming rather than scribal fabrication. Thus, the balance of probability suggests, on the basis of textual evidence, that υἱοῦ θεοῦ is original. The *Son of God* language in 1:1 (as we will see) is in fact programmatic for the entire Gospel.

The second question related to Mark 1:1 is a logical continuation of the first and moves through the vertical axis: how far down the page does "the beginning" extend? To put it another way, what is the τέλος of ἀρχή?

---

5. Ibid., 22.

6. Sapaugh, "An Appraisal."

7. Houston, *Inside Roman Libraries*, 9–10; see also Hengel, *Studies in the Gospel of Mark*, 64–84.

The word ἀρχή is governed by temporal/logical concerns: if there is a *beginning*, it logically follows that a point will be reached in which the beginning ceases and the main part of the narrative ensues. If so, what marks the terminus of ἀρχή? Does 1:8 serve that end, or 1:13, or 1:15, or does ἀρχή govern the entire Gospel? In this study, I have proposed that the terminus of the opening unit is 1:15, but to answer the question with regard to the precise *end* of the *beginning* requires the proper identification of a terminal clue. Once we have identified that clue, I suspect that we will have found the *end*; and with the end identified, we will be in a position to make an educated guess about the antecedent of ἀρχή.[8]

It is safe to dismiss suggestions that Mark's *beginning* is meant to apply exclusively to the whole of the Gospel.[9] Gerhard Arnold has undertaken the task of examining relevant ancient works, specifically noting opening materials that feature ἀρχή and its cognates. Surveying prophetic, didactic, and apocalyptic writings of the OT, as well as an array of extra-biblical writings (including Philo, Josephus, Isocrates, and Tacitus, among others), Arnold has determined that—when ἀρχή occurs in the opening materials of a work—the term identifies an opening section of the work rather than the entire work itself.[10]

Further, we have already noted that much of the material in the closing bracket of Mark's inclusio (1:14–15) is paralleled in the opening verse, creating a concrete connection between the two. This suggests that the extent of the *beginning* is the prologue proper. In addition, Mark's insertion of μετὰ δὲ τὸ παραδοθῆναι τὸν Ἰωάννην in 1:14 provides the transitional clue that marks the *end* of the *beginning*. The reference to John's arrest is not essential to the flow of the logic *per se*, but serves as a parenthetical insertion, the effect of which is to identify the terminus of John's ministry. The insertion is essential to the flow of the *narrative* nevertheless, for it provides the necessary moment of closure to John's ministry that allows Jesus to take center stage. Given that the prologue "begins" and "ends" with the ministry

---

8. I say "antecedent" here because the opening verse is a verbless clause. It makes no explicit grammatical assertion; however, there is certainly an implied assertion that "[this is] the beginning of the good news . . ." Thus, we are, in reality, seeking the antecedent of "this." What (or who), then, is "this"? Although it is unusual for a NT writer to begin with an undefined pronoun (here, by implication), it is not unattested. Most notably, we see this in the opening of 1 John.

9. For this view, see Boring, *Mark*, 29; and Donahue and Harrington, *The Gospel of Mark*, 59–60.

10. Arnold, *Mk 1:1 und Eröffnungswendungen*, 123–27.

of John, we can surmise that the antecedent of ἀρχή is in fact John's season of ministry, a season which comes to an end in 1:14. Therefore, the extent of ἀρχή is the extent of the prologue, which terminates at 1:15.

We have thus addressed the two key questions related to Mark 1:1. The *Son of God* variant is likely original, and the terminus of Mark's *beginning* is 1:15. The remaining question is this: how does 1:1 then function? In my previous chapter dealing with ancient prologues, we considered Dennis Smith's short taxonomy of "narrative beginnings."[11] A re-examination of those types immediately rules out three of his four. Because 1:1 exhibits none of the features typically characteristic of a *preface* (first-person insertion, statement of purpose, mention of sources, etc.), that is an unlikely option. Likewise, with only a handful of words 1:1 provides little if any of the contextual background we customarily see with a *prologue*. Third, and because we have an explicit statement, any suggestion that it may be a *virtual preface* is untenable. This leaves us with the *incipit*, which—as Smith has characterized it—performs a function for which 1:1 seems ideally suited. In this case, 1:1 is to be understood as the heading (or *kephalaion*) of Mark's prologue, and as such, it sets the essential agenda for the prologue.

Two main things can be said about the function of 1:1. First, it would appear as though Mark has affixed a short, descriptive heading to his prologue, probably to indicate that the prologue is meant to be read discretely from the Gospel proper. To demonstrate how this was probably meant to work, I will call upon a contemporary illustration. Anyone familiar with the *Star Wars* movies knows that each episode begins with an introductory prologue that scrolls across the screen. I will use the original *Star Wars* movie (1977) as a case in point. The function of that prologue is to situate this particular episode within the broader context of the saga.

> It is a period of civil war. Rebel spaceships, striking from a hidden base, have won their first victory against the evil Galactic Empire. During the battle, Rebel spies managed to steal secret plans to the Empire's ultimate weapon, the DEATH STAR, an armored space station with enough power to destroy an entire planet. Pursued by the Empire's sinister agents, Princess Leia races home aboard her starship, custodian of the stolen plans that can save her people and restore freedom to the galaxy . . .[12]

---

11. Smith, *Narrative Beginnings*.
12. Lucas, *Star Wars*.

This prologue immediately follows a short heading: "Episode IV: A New Hope." The narrative of the prologue certainly alludes to "a new hope," but its primary function is to provide necessary background information as to how this particular "hope" is "new."

This heading is distinct from the title of the whole movie, which is, of course, *Star Wars*. Formally, however, the "Episode IV" heading belongs to the prologue specifically insofar as it is text that "crawls" across the screen with the prologue: it is part of the unit clearly defined as the prologue. I make no attempt here to offer this illustration as a perfect analogy with what we see in Mark. I do, however, bring this to light to indicate that such a tactic makes sense when an "episode" (such as Mark's narration of the life and ministry of Jesus) fits within an epic narrative whose past runs deep. Just as the identification of a "new" hope requires an explanation of what lies before, so too does the "beginning" of the gospel warrant a short explanation of the events leading up to the gospel moment.

The second observation about the function of 1:1 follows from Houston's depiction of cataloguing techniques in ancient libraries. Hengel specifies the kinds of circumstances that would require a work such as Mark's to have some sort of title. Whether for reading Scripture as part of worship, or simply for identifying works in community libraries and book-chests, works like Mark's—when brought into circulation within a public domain—required some sort of identifying label.[13] For the Second Gospel, that label is 1:1. Only later was the superscription KATA MAPKON added as a title of the whole work, most certainly to distinguish it from the other Gospel accounts.

Mark 1:2–8

The seven verses following the *incipit* feature John as the primary subject focus. The Isaian citation in vv. 2–3 provides the prophetic expectation for John's role as messenger, the vivid description of John's ministry in vv. 4–6 conveys both the scope of his impact and the nature of his office, and the discourse in vv. 7–8 conveys his relationship to the One to come. In this passage, we are primarily interested in one critical matter: what explains Mark's attribution of 1:2 to Isaiah? Before undertaking this question, though, we must first account for the formulaic expression of καθὼς γέγραπται.

---

13. Hengel, *Studies in the Gospel of Mark*, 74–81.

My efforts in chapter 3 brought to view the rhetorically-saturated milieu in which Mark likely lived and wrote. Central to the rhetorical practices of that day was the employment of internal, artificial (or "artistic") proofs to substantiate claims. These proofs often (if not typically) took the form of *enthymemes* which served to provide cause-and-effect relationships. By use of enthymatic statements linked in logical succession, rhetors could "invent" or develop sustained treatises for purposes of argumentation. The devices that connect these enthymatic statements are typically the causal conjunctions γάρ and ὅτι.[14]

Mark's employment of the καθὼς γέγραπται phrase is a significant indication that he is deviating in some way from standard practices of Greek rhetorical composition. In fact, nowhere in Mark's prologue does either term, γάρ or ὅτι, appear; the first appearance of a causal conjunction of any kind is not until 1:16.[15] His use of the *just as it has been written* formula indicates that Mark is operating under a somewhat different set of rhetorical standards. His appeal to a sacred text is an appeal to an external or *inartificial* proof, one that stands self-evident, outside of and beyond the machinations of the rhetor. Ernesto Grassi characterizes this type of rhetoric (or, the rhetoric of "sacred language") as demonstrating a handful of features: 1) it is purely revelatory rather than demonstrative, pointing to truth authoritatively rather than inferentially; 2) it has an immediacy that lacks supporting rationale; 3) it ascribes to sensory experiences new meaning through metaphorical interpretation and re-imagining; 4) what it asserts has an absolute claim to authority; and 5) its claims are atemporal.[16] George Kennedy refers to such a claim or doctrine that "is purely proclaimed and not couched in enthymemes" as "*radical Christian rhetoric* [. . .] which is characteristic not only of some individual pericopes, but of entire books as the Gospel of Mark."[17] Kennedy goes on to identify at least three ways in which NT authors employ external, inartificial proofs to support their claims: citations of Scripture, the evidence of miracles, and the naming of witnesses.[18]

---

14. See Beale et al., *An Interpretive Lexicon of New Testament Greek*, 33, 75.

15. Although ὅτι does appear in 1:15, it is clearly being used as a marker of discourse rather than in a causal sense.

16. Grassi, *Rhetoric as Philosophy*, 103–4; see also Kennedy, *New Testament Interpretation through Rhetorical Criticism*, 6.

17. Kennedy, *New Testament Interpretation through Rhetorical Criticism*, 7.

18. Ibid., 14.

Mark's appeal to an Isaian citation explicitly points to a use of Scripture as an inartificial proof for a claim. The claim here is that John's appearance in the wilderness is to be understood in view of the Isaian prophecy. Although Mark is operating here within a *radical Christian rhetoric* paradigm, such does not negate the possibility that he has more common Greco-Roman rhetorical practices and/or tactics in mind, as well. What I mean to suggest here is that Mark need not be understood as operating exclusively within one and only one paradigm; rather, we must fully appreciate the eclectic dimension of his work and the way in which multiple rhetorical influences are shaping that work.

This segues into our examination of Mark's attribution of 1:2 to Isaiah. Bearing in mind that Grassi's third point above suggests that rhetoricians of sacred language have the freedom to re-imagine sensory experiences, we must be careful to avoid projecting Western (past and present) categories of expectation onto Mark's appropriation of Isaiah; or, to put it differently, to expect Mark to appropriate an OT text *verbatim* may be an unrealistic expectation.

This question of Mark's attribution of 1:2 to Isaiah is a thorny one and deserves significant attention. An error at this point will in all likelihood result in a major impact on our destination. In the following sections, I will offer a survey of various proposed solutions along with my own proposal. As my readers will see, my proposed solution will not only address the issue of Mark's citation, but will also provide the basis for the larger question of this chapter: how does Mark's prologue function?

Mark 1:2–3

Mark 1:2: A Survey of Proposals

> O Apostle Peter, your son Mark, son in the Spirit not in the flesh, expert in spiritual matters, has made a mistake here.[19]

In so many ways, this comment by Jerome concerning the seeming incongruence of Mark's allusion to Isaiah and the composite nature of the citation captures the spirit and angst of its interpretation throughout history. On the one hand are those who sheepishly apologize for the "mistake," seeking alternative explanations for the phenomenon. The rationale is that Scripture, as an inspired text, is inviolate to such quibbling. On the other

---

19. Kealy, *A History of Mark*, 1:24.

are those who point to this seeming "error" as yet another example of the human fallibility in Scripture writing. The task of the interpreter, so goes the argument, is to distill from the written account either the larger theological "truth" or the historical reality underlying the written text: a text undeniably smudged by human fingerprints.

What is not particularly remarkable is the latter portion of the citation (Mark 1:3), given that each of the other three Gospel writers employs it as a means of identifying the nature and role of John the Baptizer. What *is* noteworthy is the fact that Mark, while ascribing it to Isaiah, appears to be drawing upon a passage foreign to Isaiah in Mark 1:2. This issue has befuddled scholars for millennia.

There is no lack of proposed explanations for the issue, and the range of such explanations is broad. I will briefly address six of these proposals, highlighting representative voices to typify each. These consist of the following: 1) Mark made a mistake; 2) the first three verses are not original to Mark's Gospel; 3) consistent with Jewish practices, the lead author (here, Isaiah) was cited; 4) the text is a conflation of multiple texts; 5) the text represents typical Jewish midrash; and, 6) the text reflects an underlying source of *testimonia*.

The first proposal assumes that the Gospel writer has made a mistake in his citation. As far back as the dawn of the Middle Ages, we note Jerome's angst with regard to Mark's "error." Jerome here represents one interpretive stance that sees this as a mistake on Mark's part, and one which must somehow be explained or corrected. In the same vein, we noted in chapter 2 a textual tradition that seems to have attempted an emendation of the text itself to iron out the wrinkle. Although this idea that Mark may have made a mistake is a plausible one perhaps, the evidence nevertheless suggests that the essence (if not the exact words) of Mark 1:2 can in fact be found in Isaiah. This point will be made later.

A second approach (and a clear minority view among scholarship) is the postulation that Mark's opening verses as we have them today are not original to Mark, but are in fact redactional.[20] J. K. Elliott argues that the original material of Mark 1 has been lost, and he proposes an imaginative scheme whereby subsequent redactors have supplied, in various stages, Mark's present opening.[21] This proposal, though certainly innovative, can be summarily dismissed for the simple reason that it lacks evidence en-

---

20. We have already covered the position of Croy in this regard.
21. Elliott, *Mark 1:1–3*.

tirely. In fact, Elliott himself offers evidence contrary to his own proposal by noting that, "[e]ven though our earliest Greek manuscript witnesses of Mark are fourth century, versional and patristic evidence that vv. 1–3 were an integral part of copies of Mark's Gospel is firmly established for the preceding era."[22] He goes on to note that all "surviving texts of Mark's Gospel (excluding, of course, fragmentary manuscripts) begin with 1:1; none begins at v. 4."[23] The grounds for his position are thinly based on stylistic features of the Gospel, and the evidence he offers is of a type I would at best describe as conjecture.

A third approach identifies a lead author of a composite citation, consistent with extant Jewish practices. Robert Gundry proposes that Mark, although incorporating Mal 3:1, is actually ascribing it to Isaiah. He bases his position on a common rabbinical practice whereby one could and would "quote various persons under one name if a similarity existed between the characters or actions of the persons."[24] He then supports this on the basis of Z. H. Chajes' work, which argues that the Rabbis adopted as standard practice the identifying of different persons by the same name where and when similarities (good or ill) were noted in either their character or their actions.[25] He further explains that the basis of rabbinic exegetical exposition was the praising of the virtuous and the denigration of the wicked.

Gundry attempts to establish Mark's tactic here as one consistent with rabbinic practices, but such a move falters on at least four grounds. First, we have no evidence that Mark adopted such rabbinic practices. Second, and an extension of the previous, such rabbinic practices likely post-date the Markan composition. Third, there is no seeming praise/blame identification between the text of Mark 1:2 and 1:3; rather, Isaiah and (perhaps) Malachi seem simply to serve as instruments in the divine drama, rather than exemplars of character or virtue in their own right. Fourth, it is not at all clear that Malachi is even in focus here. I will expound on this for a moment.

New Testament scholars seem rather evenly divided as to whether Mark 1:2 is a direct citation of Mal 3:1 or Exod 23:20. At this point, a textual exploration is in order. A first step is to assess the plausibility of arguments

---

22. Ibid., 586.
23. Ibid.
24. Gundry, *Use of the Old Testament in Matthew*, 125; also see Gundry, *Mark*, 1:35.
25. Chajes, *The Student's Guide through the Talmud*, 172.

that situate Mark 1:2 alongside a Mal 3:1[26] or Exod 23:20[27] source. From a purely textual standpoint, one must ask what standard exists, if any, to identify a given OT passage as the basis of a NT citation. Said more practically, to what degree must a NT citation comport with an OT text in order to establish the latter as the basis of the former? Must the text be a *verbatim* appropriation? If not, what tolerance for divergence exists? Further, must a text consist of a certain number of words or letters to warrant the allusion? Although such a question may seem pedantic, it is in fact central to the definition of a "piece of scripture" capable of "defiling the hands," at least according to John Barton.[28] He maintains that a collateral text string consisting of a number of letters less than a prescribed standard could be a coincidental matter. According to Jewish interpretive tradition, in order to attain reliable correspondence between passages, or to exist as a *sepher*, a text string must contain at least eighty-five letters. With such, "there can scarcely be any doubt: the likelihood of that many words merely coinciding accidentally with a passage of scripture is minimal."[29] Interestingly, the text string of Mark 1:2 contains just sixty-four letters, only three-fourths of the quantity required to be reliable as a definable text string under this rubric. Thus, it may simply be coincidental that these two passages have such high comportment. Further, the correspondence of Mark 1:2 to Mal 3:1 is not one-to-one. Several differences exist between the Markan citation and the Septuagint text of Mal 3:1. The table below will illustrate the differences:

Mal 3:1	Mar 1:2
ἰδοὺ	ἰδοὺ
ἐγὼ	(1)
ἐξαποστέλλω	ἀποστέλλω (2)
τὸν ἄγγελόν μου	τὸν ἄγγελόν μου
	πρὸ προσώπου σου (3)
καὶ ἐπιβλέψεται ὁδὸν	ὃς κατασκευάσει τὴν ὁδόν σου (4)
πρὸ προσώπου μου	

26. France, *The Gospel of Mark*, 63. It should be noted here that France and Marcus (see below) are listed as merely illustrative of their respective positions.
27. Marcus, *Mark 1–8*, 142.
28. Barton, *What Is a Book?*, 2.
29. Ibid.

Four features are noteworthy if Mark has appropriated Malachi. At (1), Mark has omitted the explicit first-person personal pronoun. At (2), he has opted for a non-prefixed form of the verb. At (3), he has repositioned the phrase. At (4), he has made a very generous emendation to the text, although remaining within the essential contours of it. Thus, on the basis of the relatively short text-string and the differences in the texts, one wonders if Mark is in fact pointing to Mal 3:1 at all.[30] Such doubts are especially well-placed when one likewise considers the alternate view that Mark is not appropriating Malachi, but Exodus. Here again, however, we encounter similar difficulties:

Exod 23:20	Mar 1:2
καὶ ἰδοὺ	ἰδοὺ (1)
ἐγὼ	(2)
ἀποστέλλω	ἀποστέλλω
τὸν ἄγγελόν μου	τὸν ἄγγελόν μου
πρὸ προσώπου μου	πρὸ προσώπου σου
	ὃς κατασκευάσει τὴν ὁδόν σου (3)

In this instance, the comportment is perhaps even greater than with Mal 3:1. Specifically, I observe the following (and assuming a Markan appropriation of Exodus): at (1), Mark omits the conjunction, but this may not bear high significance; at (2), Mark once again omits the explicit first-person personal pronoun, but he does retain the same verb form as found in Exodus; at (3), Mark has supplied a text-string that is alien to Exodus. On the basis of this analysis, then, it seems premature to adopt a position like Gundry's.

This brings us to a fourth option, and one closely related to the previous one: namely, that Mark has conflated the text. In his commentary on Mark, Eugene Boring argues that the *de facto* merging of both Malachi and Exodus is not an innovation on Mark's part, but rather a longstanding practice consistent with Jewish exegesis.[31] In effect, Mark locates a series of texts that, when stitched together, highlight a trajectory of divine intent and action. Beginning with Exodus, we observe God's redemptive posture

---

30. Of course, it is entirely possible that Mark was so saturated with the OT that its text formed the warp-and-woof of Mark's narrative thought world. In such a case, it would be very difficult at times to differentiate a direct scriptural citation from a mere appropriation of or allusion to an older text.

31. Boring, *Mark*, 35; for related concerns, also see his *Mark 1:1–15*.

alongside his chosen people, effectively sending Moses as God's agent to prepare a path in the wilderness for the Exodus. Malachi continues to narrate God's posture through Malachi's oracle of 3:1. A typological messenger will indeed—and again—prepare the way for God's people to experience liberation from captivity. The shape of that messenger finds actualization in Elijah *redivivus* as John the Baptizer in Mark 1. Thus, Mark is simply highlighting an ongoing thread of God's work on behalf of his people at various mileposts along the way.

This proposal actually has much to commend it, specifically in that it avoids the trap of necessitating one OT text over another, and it remains faithful to the interpretive trajectory of Mark's discourse. (I would especially note here the resonance such a theory would maintain with Mark's deployment and placement of the parable of the wicked tenants in Mark 12.)

A fifth proposal is that Mark is operating in typical midrashic fashion. Although he does not comment specifically on our passage under investigation, Michael Fishbane establishes a basis for Jewish thought around two poles: biblical *language* and biblical *speech*.[32] With regard to *language*, he explains that the closed canon of Jewish Scripture essentially provides the material background for the contextualization of God's word and will. In this way, Scripture possesses the intrinsic potency (or, as Fishbane employs Saussure's terminology, *langue*) to accommodate and adapt to any concrete historical situation through its kinetic properties (or *parole*). In this way, generations of Jewish interpreters are able to enliven and re-animate the word of God for any given context and occasion.

Whether or not such a premise is sustainable in Mark's case is debatable. We once again have to assess the degree to which Mark was influenced by and operating under traditional rabbinic or pre-rabbinic practices. This in itself will be a most difficult task. A distinctive feature of midrashic exegesis in this sense is its artistry, and by that I mean something other than the objectivity and empirical certainty of modern, Western methods and epistemologies.[33]

This brings us to our sixth and final proposal. John Donahue and Daniel Harrington have suggested that Mark is employing a parcel of a

---

32. Fishbane, *The Exegetical Imagination*, 9–21; see also his *Biblical Interpretation in Ancient Israel*, 18.

33. Casey is instructive here; see his *Aramaic Sources of Mark's Gospel*.

testimonia collection.³⁴ Witherington,³⁵ drawing on the work of C. H. Dodd,³⁶ has made a similar suggestion. This hypothesis has its origin in the pioneering work of Rendel Harris,³⁷ who argued that evidence abounds in the NT in support of an unknown collection of summary statements that circulated in the earliest Christian periods. In effect, Harris argues, a common tradition among pre-Christian Jewish interpreters was to extract and re-formulate dense portions of Scripture that could then be deployed apologetically in defense of Judaism. These nuggets functioned as a primer for Jewish thought and practice and operated in a vein similar to creedal formulations. During the earliest part of the Christian era (and preceding the writing of the NT manuscripts), the Church continued the practice, only in this case in defense of Christianity *against* Judaism. Harris argues that these pieces were eventually collected and disseminated, thus providing the basis for much of what is common among various NT documents. He suggests that Mark 1:2 is evidence of such.

This view also has much to commend it. However, it seems that Harris in his particular approach may be creating a scenario not on the basis of the actual evidence, but perhaps rather on his desire to defend his high view of the received text tradition. He suggests that the error inherent with Mark's 1:2 citation lies with a corrupt, pre-Markan *testimonium*. With regard to this discrepancy between the Western text type and the earliest codices (discussed in my second chapter), he simply asserts that the "revised text is therefore wrong in fact but right in tradition."³⁸

Language of "Dispatch" in Isaiah

We thus have before us at least six proposals to account for the phenomenon we see in Mark 1:2, and two or three of these proposals legitimately demonstrate explanatory power. At this point, it would be easy to become derailed from our immediate task, which is to assess the function of the unit defined by Mark 1:2–8. While the matter of 1:2 remains yet unsolved, I wonder if this is really such a difficulty. In my view, the larger question is

---

34. Donahue and Harrington, *The Gospel of Mark*, 35, 61; see also Albl, *And Scripture Cannot Be Broken*.

35. Witherington III, *The Gospel of Mark*, 71.

36. Dodd, *According to the Scriptures*, 28–60.

37. Harris and Burch, *Testimonies*, 1–20.

38. Ibid., 22.

not how Mark came to equate the text-string of 1:2 to Isaiah, but whether or not the text-string of 1:2 can be found in Isaiah. Perhaps an appeal to a modern phenomenon might be of use.

If asked about the legal basis for America's separation of church and state, most of its citizens would (I hope!) rightly point to the First Amendment to the Constitution. The problem is this: *nowhere* in the First Amendment do the words *church*, *state*, or *separation* occur. The relevant portion of the amendment reads as follows: "Congress shall make no law respecting an establishment of religion, or prohibiting the free exercise thereof." So how, then, can a *separation of church and state* be attributed to the First Amendment of the Constitution? We seem to have two poles: that of the historical Bill of Rights, and that of today's understanding of those Rights. Between the two poles lies a precipitating event, namely the judicial decision rendered in regard to *Everson v. Board of Education* (1947) in which Supreme Court justices interpreted the First Amendment so as to effect a "wall of separation" between government and religion. This explains the matter and fills the gap. Absent such an explanation, however, one unfamiliar with the American process could be truly confounded by the phenomenon.

I think in the same way we are confounded by Mark's move in 1:2. We have the textual reality of Isaiah at one pole, and we have Mark's rendering of it at the other. We seem to be missing the middle. What explains the process by which Isaiah's *that* became Mark's *this*? Unfortunately, we simply cannot answer the question at present. What we can answer, though, is a question regarding the conceptual relationship between Mark 1:2 and Isaiah. Can the substance of 1:2 be found there? I think it indeed can. Unlike the example of the First Amendment (in which none of the words *separation*, *church*, or *state* can be found in connection to religion and government), the actual words of Mark 1:2 will be our heuristic guide.

The first word of note in the Mark 1:2 citation is ἀποστέλλω, and this word arguably sets the agenda for the citation. In Isaiah, the word and its cognate ἐξαποστέλλω are well attested, occurring thirty times. As with Mark 1:2, a number of these instances feature the Lord as the sending agent.[39] In every single instance where the Lord also appears as the first-person subject of the verb, the verb occurs in the future tense,[40] foretelling

---

39. Isa 6:6, 8 (*bis*); 9:8; 10:6, 16; 16:1; 19:20; 43:14; 48:16; 61:1. On *the Lord* as the sending agent of Mark 1:2, see below.

40. Isa 6:8; 10:6; 16:1; 43:14.

judgment on the wicked or vindication to the oppressed. A number of the passages resonate strongly with Mark 1:2. For example, Isa 19:20 conveys the idea that the Lord will send someone to save his people through an act of divine justice. Isaiah 48:16 likewise conveys the notion that the Lord has sent Isaiah (in the Spirit of the Lord) to proclaim good news to the afflicted. This not only provides a direct point of contact with the *good news* of Mark 1:1, but also underscores the pneumatological kinship between holders of the prophetic office. Perhaps nowhere else, however, do we find a stronger parallel between Mark 1:2 and Isaiah than in Isa 6:8.

τίνα ἀποστείλω καὶ τίς πορεύσεται πρὸς τὸν λαὸν τοῦτον καὶ εἶπα ἰδού εἰμι ἐγώ ἀπόστειλόν με (Isa 6:8)

ἰδοὺ ἀποστέλλω τὸν ἄγγελόν μου πρὸ προσώπου σου, ὃς κατασκευάσει τὴν ὁδόν σου (Mar 1:2)

Several things are worth mentioning about this text. First, Isa 6:8 can arguably be read as part of a programmatic passage for Isaiah. It not only represents the account of Isaiah's commissioning, but also represents the first time God speaks in Isaiah.[41] It is depicted as a call narrative, and positioned at the end of Isaiah's initial oracle in chapters 1–5 (which, for John Oswalt, function as an introduction).[42] Second, the co-text shows strong affinities with Mark's Gospel as a whole and the Markan prologue in particular. Isaiah 6:7 tells of the purification of Isaiah's lips so as to prepare him for service as an agent of God. The act has the effect of pardoning Isaiah's lawlessness and cleansing his sins. This is strongly suggestive of the baptizing ministry of John, which specifically involved John proclaiming a baptism of repentance leading to the pardoning of sins. Isaiah 6:9–10 describes the inability of the people to see and hear, to perceive and understand—a significant theme in Mark (e.g., 4:11–12; 8:17–18).

In sum, then, the following aspects can be found in both Mark 1:2 and Isa 6:8: 1) the Lord as a first-person, sending agent; 2) the enlistment of a human subject as the bearer of the message; 3) the necessity of remission of sin as preparation either for service to or reception of the Lord; and 4) the subsequent refusal of (some of) the people to receive the Lord. If one follows to its logical conclusion each narrative event, then the passion narrative of

---

41. Oswalt, *The Book of Isaiah, Chapters 1–39*, 185.

42. Ibid., 54. It is interesting not only that Mark's opening verse ("The beginning of the good news of Jesus Christ, son of God") closely parallels that of Isaiah ("The vision of Isaiah, son of Amoz") but also that Isaiah features a first-person call narrative following his prologue, as does Mark (assuming that the call narrative in Mark comes from a first-person Petrine source).

Mark 14-15 falls into alignment with the Suffering Servant motif of Isa 52-53. Although there is far from a one-to-one correspondence between the two passages, the conceptual framework is nevertheless evident.

While it may seem singularly unsatisfying to some to leave the issue unresolved, it remains the case that Mark has, for whatever reason, attributed both parts of the citation to Isaiah. The first part of the citation resembles Mal 3:1, but it is not a perfect match; if it is Malachi, it has been modified by Mark (or a tradition standing between Malachi and Mark). In the same way, Mark 1:2 resembles Exod 23:20, but here again, it appears to be re-touched.

I have just attempted to demonstrate that the substance of Mark 1:2 can in fact be found in Isaiah, in spirit if not in letter. However, one more stone deserves to be turned. As indicated, Isaiah contains a large number of instances in which the Lord dispatches a representative either to rebuke the wicked or to vindicate the oppressed. These occurrences dot the Isaian landscape, beginning with Isaiah's call in Isa 6,

> Then flew one of the seraphim to me, having in his hand a burning coal which he had taken with tongs from the altar. And he touched my mouth, and said: "Behold, this has touched your lips; your guilt is taken away, and your sin forgiven." And I heard the voice of the Lord saying, "Whom shall I send, and who will go for us?" Then I said, "Here am I! Send me." And he said, "Go, and say to this people: 'Hear and hear, but do not understand; see and see, but do not perceive.' Make the heart of this people fat, and their ears heavy, and shut their eyes; lest they see with their eyes, and hear with their ears, and understand with their hearts, and turn and be healed." (Isa 6:6-10)

and culminating in Isa 61,

> The Spirit of the Lord GOD is upon me, because the LORD has anointed me to bring good tidings to the afflicted; he has sent me to bind up the brokenhearted, to proclaim liberty to the captives, and the opening of the prison to those who are bound; to proclaim the year of the LORD's favor, and the day of vengeance of our God; to comfort all who mourn; to grant to those who mourn in Zion—to give them a garland instead of ashes, the oil of gladness instead of mourning, the mantle of praise instead of a faint spirit; that they may be called oaks of righteousness, the planting of the LORD, that he may be glorified. (Isa 61:1-3)

With the exception of chapters 36–39 in which a number of instances of *dispatch* are indicated with respect to diplomatic correspondence between kings, military commanders, and Isaiah himself, language of *divine dispatch* punctuates the Isaian corpus with regularity; indeed, *sending* language is depicted prominently in each of the three Isaian movements of chs. 1–39, 40–55, and 56–66.

That dispatch language can be found throughout Isaiah, and in prominent positions, is a clue with regard to Mark's *modus operandi*. Another clue can be found at the end of the Markan prologue. Just as the last page of a mystery novel often holds the interpretive key to the entire plot, I suggest that the last verse of the prologue holds the key to understanding Mark's work in 1:2.

Ipsissima Vox or Verba of Jesus?

As I have previously argued, 1:14–15 appears to be the climax of Mark's opening unit, both in terms of the way it is structured and the content of Jesus' proclamation. The *end* of the *beginning* is the arrest of John and the initial summary proclamation of Jesus in 1:14–15. An important question emerges at this point, however: are the words of Jesus in v. 15 the *actual words of Jesus*? Said differently, does Mark 1:15 quote Jesus *ipsissima verba* ("in the very words") of Jesus, or does the quote come *ipsissima vox* ("in the very voice") of Jesus? Clearly, Jesus had more to say during his Galilean ministry than merely what is reported in 1:15. Mark appears to have distilled the words of Jesus. However, to even suggest this possibility invites a possible firestorm of controversy, as has been seen in recent years among members of the Evangelical Theological Society (ETS).[43] Maintaining a high commitment to scriptural inerrancy, some ETS members hold a very narrow view of *ipsissima vox*,[44] arguing that the "red letters" of the Bible are in fact the very words of Jesus, and only under certain circumstances (non-red letters) do the words come to us via paraphrase.[45] Other ETS members embrace a broader view, suggesting that at various points we have the gist or essence of Jesus' words, but not necessarily the exact

---

43. For a brief overview of the "firestorm," see Osborne, *Historical Criticism: A Response*, 113–17.

44. The view is so narrow as to really be an *ipsissima verba* view.

45. Green, *Evangelicals and Ipsissima Vox*, 49–68; Wilkin, *Toward a Narrow View of Ipsissima Vox*; Thomas, *Historical Criticism: Another View*, 97–111.

words he used.⁴⁶ Much more could be said on this matter, but it will suffice to characterize the issue using Darrell Bock's rhetoric of "live, jive or Memorex?"⁴⁷ Writing for a popular audience, Bock lays the issue out this way. Some view the words of Jesus in the NT as "Memorex"⁴⁸ in that they reproduce, in transcript fashion, the exact words uttered by the mouth of Jesus. Thus, the words as we have them in the NT go back directly to Jesus himself. On the other hand, others presume that much of the NT discourse concerning Jesus' speech is reproduced through and conditioned by oral tradition. Thus, what we observe in the NT in many cases are approximations or theologized recensions of Jesus' words. The *Jesus Seminar* is noted for embracing such a view. Bock dubs this the "jive" view.

Alternatively, he makes a case for a "live" view, maintaining that there is in fact some degree of latitude in the NT between what Jesus actually said and what can be reasonably and reliably conferred through the NT authors' paraphrases. Bock characterizes the perspective in this way:

> Each Evangelist retells the living and powerful words of Jesus in a fresh way for his readers, while faithfully and accurately presenting the "gist" of what Jesus said. I call this approach one that recognizes the Jesus tradition as "live" in its dynamic and quality. We clearly hear Jesus, but we must be aware that there is summary and emphasis in the complementary portraits that each Evangelist gives to the founder of the faith.⁴⁹

For Bock, maintaining a broader view of *ipsissma vox* allows the reader to not only navigate what would otherwise seem to be contradictions in the various reports of Jesus' words, but also invites the reader into the theological thought world of the writers and the messages they proclaim.

Moving beyond the mere words, however, results in a more broadbanded approach that "considers the way an author acknowledged dependence on an earlier author or text in a kind of literary imitation, in order to redeploy and recontextualize the older work."⁵⁰ The output of

---

46. Osborne, *Historical Criticism and the Evangelical*, 193–210; see also Wallace, *An Apologia*, to whom I owe a debt of gratitude for sharing his manuscript with me.

47. Bock, *The Words of Jesus in the Gospels*, 73–99.

48. Memorex is a trade name for a company noted in the latter part of the twentieth century for producing audio and video recording media (such as cassettes and data/audio discs). One of the chief marketing slogans was, "Is it live, or is it Memorex?"

49. Bock, *The Words of Jesus in the Gospels*, 77.

50. Arnold, *Deuteronomy as the Ipsissima Vox of Moses*, 71.

this approach is to be distinguished from inner-biblical exegesis. In my treatment of Fishbane's methodology earlier in this work, I referenced his *inner-biblical exegesis* approach, noting it as serving the needs of typical Jewish midrash. What should be noted here is that such an approach relies ultimately upon lemmatic specifics (particular words re-deployed by subsequent authors of Scripture).

Mimesis (or *imitatio*), by contrast, is a programmatic undertaking that has as its raw material not a variety of lemmatic specifics, but rather an individual worthy of emulation. Bill Arnold suggests that the net gain of such a mimetic approach (over against a purely inner-biblical exegesis approach) lies in its great valuation of the "prized tradition of the older text," while simultaneously passing on the tradition to new interpretive communities and contexts. He summarizes this *via media* in this way:

> Deuteronomy is certainly not a fraud—pious *or* irreligious—but rather the result of ancient Israel's method for an evolving *traditio* while respecting the *traditum* of the great lawgiver. And in this way too, the reader avoids the impasse between fideism and skepticism, because one's reading embraces both the figure of Moses and the result of critical investigation.[51]

The challenge in applying this theory to Mark 1:2 is this: given the large periods of time for such a process to unfold, it is unlikely that Isaiah would have come to the Markan shape within the available space of time.

A more recent exploration of the issue comes to us from Richard Hays in a practice he calls, "reading backwards."[52] Perhaps Mark is not the careless secretary that Jerome originally supposed. Perhaps instead he is operating fully within the range of accepted interpretive practices of his day. Hays' perspective on "reading backwards" presupposes that,

> all four canonical Gospels are deeply embedded in a symbolic world shaped by the Old Testament—or, to put the point in a modern critical idiom, that their "encyclopedia of production" is constituted in large measure by Israel's Scripture. (This does not mean that the symbolic world of Greco-Roman pagan antiquity is insignificant for the Gospels, but that it is secondary; the Evangelists' constructive Christological affirmations are derived chiefly

---

51. Ibid., 74.
52. Hays, *Reading Backwards*.

from hermeneutical appropriation and transformation of Israel's sacred texts and traditions.)[53]

In effect, the OT storied world becomes the framework by which Mark's world is both understood and re-shaped.[54] Figural reading seeks to identify meaningful points of contact between the present and the past, to make sense of the *now* by appropriating the *then*, and to re-signify history in light of contemporary realities. Hays draws from and builds upon the work of Erich Auerbach on figural reading, who offers this definition:

> Figural interpretation establishes a connection between two events or persons in such a way that the first signifies not only itself but also the second, while the second involves or fulfills the first. The two poles of a figure are separated in time, but both, being real events or persons, are within temporality. They are both contained in the flowing stream which is historical life, and only the comprehension, the *intellectus spiritualis*, of their interdependence is a spiritual act.[55]

Mark 1:2–3 as Sammelbericht

Having returned to Mark 1:15 and applied these understandings to the climactic proclamation of Jesus in the Markan prologue, it is clear that Mark has put forward the proclamation *ipsissima vox* of Jesus rather than *ipsissima verba*, for as I indicated previously Jesus certainly had more to say than what is indicated in 1:15. Mark has condensed the actual words of Jesus into an essential, summarizing statement that serves to programmatize Jesus' ministry and message. At least three indications confirm this. First, when Jesus speaks in 1:15, we note that there is no audience or object of his address. All we can know is that he made the statement while transitioning into Galilee. The absence of an addressee lends the statement much more of a generalizing than a particularizing quality.[56] Second, the quotation is a

---

53. Ibid., xii.

54. On figural reading as a community forming enterprise, see Dawson, *Christian Figural Reading*.

55. Auerbach, *Mimesis*, 73.

56. It is not at all apparent to me how Mary Ann Tolbert concludes that "Jesus speaks to other characters" in 1:14–15, for no such characters are indicated. The first instance of direct address does not come until 1:17 where a dative pronoun is employed. See her *Sowing the Gospel*, 116.

content clause for the participle λέγων. The present tense form of the participle broadens the bandwidth of the verbal aspect to lend the word a more generalizing quality. The present tense participle κηρύσσων also appears and is compounded with λέγων, further underscoring the internal, "open-ended" dimension of the participles. Third, this precise language occurs nowhere else in the Gospels, except for a possible point of contact with Matt 3:1 and 4:17.

Mark 1:15	"The time is fulfilled, and the kingdom of God is at hand; repent, and believe in the gospel."
Matt 3:1	"Repent, for the kingdom of heaven is at hand." (words of John the Baptist)
Matt 4:17	"Repent, for the kingdom of heaven is at hand." (words of Jesus)

The notion of summarizing material has been raised with regard to Mark, most notably by C. H. Dodd, who argues that Mark's work consists of "short generalizing summaries (*Sammelberichte*) that punctuate the narrative, help the transition from one pericope to another, and remind the reader that the particular incidents narrated in detail are episodes in a widely extended ministry."[57] These *Sammelberichte* are recognizable on the basis of their differences with traditional pericopae. The *Sammelberichte* are less concrete and particular. They are not grounded in an exclusive time-and-space moment. They tend to have a higher frequency of verbs in the imperfect tense. They also serve a linking function between pericopae (Dodd specifically identifies Mark 1:14–15 as a *Sammelbericht*).[58] John Donahue notes that these literary devices, characterized by their ability to "recapitulate the preceding section and anticipate what is to come," constitute "major devices both in the theology and structure of the Gospel [of Mark]."[59] Vincent Taylor even goes so far as to say that 1:14–15 is one of the most significant summaries in Mark.[60]

Applying these criteria to 1:14–15, we note that all are satisfied: no concrete location is given (compare the particularity of "passing along the Sea of Galilee" in 1:16); no concrete time is given (we are simply told that

---

57. Dodd, *The Framework of the Gospel Narrative*, 396; the speech summaries in the second and fourth chapters of Acts are prominent examples.
58. Ibid., 398.
59. Donahue, *Jesus as the Parable of God*, 384.
60. Taylor, *The Gospel according to St. Mark*, 85.

Jesus goes into Galilee sometime "after the arrest of John"); the verb ἦλθεν in 1:14 is qualified by two present tense participles ("proclaiming" and "saying"); and the passage serves a transitional function.[61] Although the imperfect tense does not appear in these two verses, what is more important is the presence of the internal verbal aspect commonly associated with the imperfect tense. As mentioned above, the internal aspect is central to the present tense participles. Dodd's third criterion would thus be better stated by including the present tense along with the imperfect tense, or better yet, by simply referring to verbs that convey internal aspect (including periphrastic participial constructions; see Mark 1:6, 13).

We thus see that Mark 1:14–15 not only satisfies Dodd's criteria for a *Sammelbericht*, but also includes within it a statement *ipsissima vox* of Jesus.[62] However, the final verses of the prologue are not the only instance in which a *Sammelbericht* with an *ipsissima vox* statement appears. In light of Dodd's criteria and the seeming structural similarities between 1:14–15 and 1:7–8,[63] could the suggestion that Mark 1:7–8 is a *Sammelbericht* alongside 1:1–15 withstand scrutiny? Here again, we lack an explicitly identified audience, the content clause is introduced exactly as Jesus' words are (by means of the participle λέγων), and the text string is unique to Mark (*cf.* Matt 4:11 and Luke 3:16 in their variance). At each point, the form and content of 1:7–8 distill John's message to its essence, convey a general rather than a particular quality, and transition material from what precedes to what follows.

This suggestion may hold the key to understanding the nature not just of the *ipsissima vox* of John in 1:7–8 and Jesus in 1:15, but perhaps Isaiah, as well, in 1:2–3. If we assume that Mark has in fact created a summarization of Jesus' words (effectively functioning as a climax to the prologue and serving as a strategic passage for anticipating the material that follows), then we can begin to see how an *ipsissima vox* rendering serves the rhetorical needs of a writer by distilling a message to its essence for purposes of fulfillment and anticipation. Further, it would not be at all beyond reason to assume that

---

61. On the transitional nature of 1:14–15, see Lightfoot, *The Gospel Message of St. Mark*, 20; Hedrick, *The Role of Summary Statements in Mark*, 3; Kingsbury, *The Christology of Mark's Gospel*, 72; Marcus, *Mark 1–8*, 174; and Lambrecht, "John the Baptist and Jesus in Mark 1.1–15," 361.

62. That Jesus most likely spoke in Aramaic only strengthens the case for an *ipsissima vox* understanding of 1:15 and, in fact, for most of his speech in the Gospels.

63. Mark 1:7 essentially reads, "and [John] was proclaiming, saying that . . . ," while 1:14–15 reads "Jesus went into Galilee proclaiming and saying that . . ."

Mark has made the same rhetorical move with regard to the words of John at 1:7-8, also for purposes of fulfillment and anticipation.

Having just suggested that the words of John at Mark 1:7-8 are delivered *ipsissima vox* of John, and that the words of Jesus at Mark 1:15 are delivered *ipsissima vox* of Jesus,[64] we can actually look at the beginning of the prologue with its culmination (1:15) in view. As we saw in the literary structure of 1:1-15, an *inclusio* brackets the text. Verses 2-3 are the opening stanza, vv. 14-15 are the closing stanza, and vv. 7-8 (specifically realized by ἐβαπτίσθη in 1:9) likely serve as a transitional, or *crucial*, stanza. If this is the case (as I have attempted to demonstrate), then it follows that Mark 1:2-3 may likely be given *ipsissima vox* of Isaiah. Such an assumption would explain the minor textual differences between the GNT and the Septuagint at 1:3:

Mar 1:3	φωνὴ βοῶντος	ἐν τῇ ἐρήμῳ	ἑτοιμάσατε τὴν ὁδὸν κυρίου	εὐθείας ποιεῖτε τὰς τρίβους	αὐτοῦ
Isa 40:3	φωνὴ βοῶντος	ἐν τῇ ἐρήμῳ	ἑτοιμάσατε τὴν ὁδὸν κυρίου	εὐθείας ποιεῖτε τὰς τρίβους	τοῦ θεοῦ ἡμῶν

This may provide the necessary clue in understanding what Mark is doing in 1:2. It also helps to explain what may be happening in 1:3 with respect to the change from Isa 40:3 (which reads in part, "make straight the highways *of our God*") to Mark's "make straight *his* highways."[65] Mark has already demonstrated his tendency to summarize larger swaths of narrative material and to distill them into generalizing statements *ipsissima vox* of a character within his narrative. I suggest that he is doing the exact same thing in Mark 1:2-3. He has encapsulated the whole of the Isaian message and re-contextualized it for the purpose of introducing John as the forerunner of Jesus. Mark 1:2-3 can thus be read as a *Sammelbericht ipsissima vox* of Isaiah.

What is most striking (and even perplexing to many) is the way 1:2 evokes either Exod 23:20, Mal 3:1, or both. Is there a strategic purpose behind this? This issue relates to one of our implications for further study

---

64. Guijarro identifies this parallelism between John and Jesus as a literary *diptych*. This device then becomes for him a constituitive device in forming the prologue as a *status transformation ritual*. See *Why Does the Gospel*, 28, 34; see also Klauck, *Vorspiel im Himmel*, 33.

65. Tolbert's suggestion that Mark's change was to create a rhyme with the genitive endings of 1:1 seems unlikely. See *Sowing the Gospel*, 111, 245.

in my final chapter. For now, however, we can simply surmise that Mark has committed no error in 1:2. Instead, he has appropriated the message of Isaiah and distilled it into a summary statement conveyed in the voice of Isaiah. *How* he did it will remain open to debate, but as I have demonstrated, there are a number of plausible explanations. The real issue is *that* he did it, and did so in ways that are consistent with the essential message of Isaiah. The rhetorical effect of this carefully crafted citation is to provide an inartificial proof by means of an appeal to Scripture. The circumstance for which the Isaian citation is proof constitutes the next topic.

Mark 1:4–8

As stated earlier, Mark 1:1 is an *incipit* standing over the prologue, the function of which is to set the agenda for the prologue. We have in the *incipit* an imbedded, partial clue with regard to the closure of the prologue, and that clue is the twice-mentioned *good news* in 1:14–15. Two characters are introduced in the *incipit*: θεός (which I am taking as original to the text of Mark's opening), and his anointed son, Jesus.[66] The "transcendent, offstage"[67] conversation in 1:2–3 is thus between these two characters, and the topic of the conversation is the messenger. This messenger, as we immediately learn, is John.[68]

The points of contact between 1:4 and 1:2–3 are solid. As a messenger sent by God and a voice crying in the wilderness, John appears in the wilderness proclaiming a message of preparation in the form of baptism. His ministry of baptism is in preparation for the personal appearing of the Lord, and such preparation requires confession and baptism for the

---

66. There is arguably a third character introduced in the *incipit*: that of John as the messenger. BDAG lists as a possible lexical sense for ἀρχή, "one with whom a process begins," 1153.2. See Gen 49:3; Col 1:18; Rev 3:14; 21:6; 22:13.

67. Boring, *Mark*, 33.

68. Tolbert attempts to identify Jesus as the messenger rather than John, but to do so she must make a very questionable methodological commitment to discount the synoptic evidence, and to entirely ignore the Johannine evidence in which the Baptizer explicitly identifies himself as the voice crying in the wilderness (John 1:23). See *Sowing the Gospel*, 239–43; Incigneri attempts to defend Tolbert's position by claiming that her opponents have not adequately responded to her objections to the traditional reading. His citing of "opponents," however, is limited to two; see his *The Gospel to the Romans*, 256. This seems hardly representative of what Tolbert herself refers to as the consensus of scholars who "have almost universally understood the Isaiah quotation in Mark 1:2–3 to refer to John the Baptist alone," *Sowing the Gospel*, 240.

remission of sins. The Coming One before whose presence John appears is mightier than John, particularly evidenced by his baptism with Holy Spirit, in contrast to John's baptism of water.

In addition to the καθὼς γέγραπται formula in 1:2, the inclusive scope of the crowds in 1:5 who turn out for John's baptism constitutes a second rhetorical proof: the naming of witnesses. What is of interest about this circumstance is the scope of the witnesses: *all* the Judean countryside and *all* the Jerusalemites—too many, in fact, to be named. Thus, John's baptizing ministry took place in full view of the public, a public who would have implicitly accepted the authority of John presumably on the basis of a common understanding that John was fulfilling the role of the *voice* in Isa 40:3. The vivid description of John's attire and diet further locates him within the prophetic tradition, especially in terms of 2 Kings 1:8, but perhaps also of Zech 13:4. The use of ἐγένετο to introduce John gives the impression that John appears almost as if from thin air. Unlike Jesus, who is said to have come from Galilee, John simply "happens." Although it is a speculative point, it may be the case—especially in view of the strong connection with Elijah—that Mark may bring John onto the stage in this mysterious way to provide continuity with Elijah's being caught up into heaven in 2 Kings 2:11; whereas the Elijah narrative ends with a divine *dis*-appearance, the John narrative begins with a divine *re*-appearance, perhaps as Elijah *redivivus*.

The episode of the Baptizer concludes with his proclamation and anticipation of the Coming One. Here, we note that, like the opening and closing verses of the prologue in 1:2–3 and 1:14–15, John's message and ministry are summarized by means of a *Sammelbericht* conveyed *ipsissima vox* of John. The statement lacks concrete particularity, it exhibits a high concentration of verbs with internal aspect (especially if one includes 1:5–6 as part of Mark's summarization of John's ministry), and it transitions in explicit ways; whereas John has up to this point baptized with water, Jesus will—moving forward—baptize with Holy Spirit. John's direct discourse, as with 1:2–3 and 1:14–15, serves to programmatize his ministry in condensed form.

The text of Mark 1:2–8 thus exhibits a thread of continuity from the prophetic office of Isaiah (and arguably Elijah, Zechariah, and others) to and inclusive of John. Further, Jesus is implicated in that lineage insofar as he is brought to bear by *synkrisis* with John. The result for Mark's listening audience is a presentation that is grounded in two important matters: 1) the authority of the written and spoken word as conveyed through Scripture and the prophetic office (now at work in their recent past); and 2) the potentially corroborating testimonies of a throng of witnesses.

Mark 1:9–15

Mark 1:2–8 reflects a transition in focus from Isaiah to John. However, we must note that the shift is not a linear shift in a scene-*following*-a-scene manner; rather, the John episode is better understood to exist as a scene-*within*-a-scene, for it occurs in logical continuity with and fulfillment of the prophecy of Isaiah. The next unit reflects a shift in focus from John to Jesus. However, we must note again that the shift is not a linear shift in a scene-*following*-a-scene manner; rather, the Jesus episode is also better understood to exist as a scene-*within*-a-scene. The identification of the episode as taking place *in those days* (1:9) locates the episode within a narrower bandwidth of narration, but still within the broader context of John's baptizing ministry. The Jesus scene is a sub-scene of the larger John scene. Note that John is still on hand and an active participant; John is in fact the explicit agent of Jesus' baptism in 1:9–11. Jesus' wilderness experience parallels that of John in many ways, and the Jesus sub-scene concludes simultaneously with the larger John scene—when John's arrest is effected. The relationship between the three nodes of Isaiah, John, and Jesus can be depicted in this way:

The Nested Nature of the Scenes in Mark's Prologue

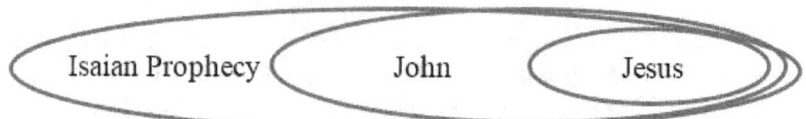

The baptismal scene features a fourth (third in sequence) unit of direct discourse for consideration (1:11). This discourse provides the content of the supernatural manifestation of a voice speaking from the separated heavens as Jesus—coming up out of the water—meets the Spirit—coming down from the sky. The voice declares its pleasure in Jesus in 1:11. Witherington (among others) has suggested that the scene is consistent with visionary experiences, and that "the voice from heaven speaks only to Jesus.

This is a private experience and revelation (*cf.* Matt. 3:16–17). It is only Jesus who is said to see the Spirit coming down."[69] Witherington rightly notes the difference between Mark's account (featuring a second-person address *to* Jesus) and that of Matthew (featuring a third-person address *about* Jesus). He further notes parallels between the theophany of Mark 1:10–11 and the visionary experience of John on the island of Patmos in Rev 1, specifically with regard to the embodying presence of the Spirit, a sound of a great voice, and a vision offered in graphic detail. In sum, he maintains, this scene has the makings of an apocalyptic moment.[70]

As we know, the baptismal scene ends abruptly with Jesus being compelled into the wilderness by the Spirit. Like the wilderness scene in 1:5–6, 1:12–13 is rich with *ekphrasis*: the Spirit *compels* (ἐκβάλλει, internal aspect) Jesus into the wilderness; Jesus *was* (ἦν, internal aspect) in the wilderness forty days; he was *being tempted* (πειραζόμενος, internal aspect) by the Adversary; he *was* (ἦν, internal aspect) with the wild animals; and the angels *were ministering* (διηκόνουν, internal aspect) to him. The presence of the Adversary suggests a third stream of thought with regard to the legitimation of Jesus: while the Baptizer *authorizes* Jesus within an earthly tradition, and while the divine voice *legitmates* Jesus from a heavenly perspective, the presence of the Adversary as an agent of tempting or testing serves to underscore that even the underworld must *acknowledge* that this is no ordinary agent of God.

The vivid description of 1:5–6 and 1:10–13 deserves further attention. As mentioned in chapter 3, such descriptions are catalogued as *ekphrasis* in the *progymnasmata*. Bruehler suggests about Luke's depiction of the baptism of Jesus that Mark

> sets the scene by stating that many others were being baptized. Jesus was then baptized and while praying "the heavens opened" and the Holy Spirit descended on him "in bodily form like a dove." Then a clear voice (another aural element) speaks from heaven affirming Jesus as God's son. The vivid visual (and aural) details of

---

69. Witherington III, *The Gospel of Mark*, 74.

70. Taylor observes, "The rending of the heavens is a common feature of apocalyptic thought, the underlying idea being that of a fixed separation of heaven from earth only to be broken in special circumstances. (Cf. Apoc. Bar. xxii. 1, Test. Levi ii. 6, v. 1, xviii. 6, Test. Jud. xxiv. 2, and in the NT Jn. i. 51, Ac. vii. 56, Apoc. iv. 1, xi. 19, xix. 11.) That the idea is old is shown by Isa. lxiv. 1." Taylor, *The Gospel according to St. Mark*, 160.

this scene help to persuade the audience that God approves of and is actively involved in the ministry of Jesus.[71]

Although there are subtle differences in the accounts of Mark and Luke, the inclusion of such graphic detail as the heavens being opened, the descent of the Spirit, and the voice coming from the heavens are in common. What is of particular interest, as Bruehler notes, is that no such instances of ekprhastic material appear in Q; all occurrences are from either the Markan tradition or Luke's special source.[72]

What we observe with regard to *ekphrasis* in Mark 1 is found in part in copular statements and periphrastic constructions. In 1:5-6 and 1:10-13, we observe the following:

Verse	Subject	Copula	Predication
1:6	John	was	wearing
1:6	(John)	(was)	eating
1:13	(Jesus)	was	in the wilderness
1:13	(Jesus)	(was)	being tempted
1:13	(Jesus)	was	with the wild animals

We also observe, as already noted, a number of internal aspect verbs that give the narrative a dramatic or descriptive hue:[73]

Verse	Subject	Progressive/Descriptive Verb	Verbal Identification
1:5	crowds	were going out	Imperfect Tense
1:5	(crowds)	were being baptized	Imperfect Tense
1:5	(crowds)	(while) confessing	Present Participle
1:7	(John)	was proclaiming	Imperfect Tense
1:10	(Jesus)	(while) coming up	Present Participle
1:10	heavens	(while) being opened	Present Participle
1:10	Spirit	(while) coming down	Present Participle
1:13	angels	were serving	Imperfect Tense

(Although ἐκήρυσσεν occurs in 1:7, it is grammatically tied to the subject of the preceding material.)

---

71. Bruehler, *Patterns of Ekphrasis in Luke-Acts*, 14.
72. Ibid., 9.
73. Wallace, *Greek Grammar beyond the Basics*, 518-19, 543-44.

We can further note a number of graphic visual and aural elements, elements without which the narrative would still move forward (although with immeasurably less impact):

Verse	Subject
1:5	*all*, in the Jordan River
1:6	garment of camel's hair, leather belt, locusts, undomesticated honey
1:10	coming up from the water, the heavens being separated, the spirit descending as a dove
1:11	a voice, the heavens
1:12	into the wilderness
1:13	in the wilderness, forty days, the Adversary, wild beasts, angels

I think it is significant that these two concentrations of ekphrastic depiction (1:5–6 and 1:10–13) are at the same time similar to and different from one another. Baptism as a context, the Jordan River, and time in the wilderness each combine to create a clear link between the episodes of John and Jesus. However, differences nevertheless exist. In the episode of John, his diet and apparel suggest that his needs are somehow being met through non-human sources. The *wild animals* seem to have been used to his advantage: camels, hide-producing animals, bugs, and bees. He seems rather the master of his domain. In addition, his station changes from one of remoteness to one of proximity. By this I mean that he begins his ministry heralding in the wilderness where—presumably—he is alone. In short order, however, throngs of people gather around him to such a degree that the same physical location can no longer be understood as quite so desolate a place.

The Jesus episode works a bit differently. First we note, unlike John, that Jesus is a silent figure who is largely acted upon. His time in the wilderness is a time of being tempted or tested. The trials last an insufferable amount of time for one who is depicted as being subject not only to spiritual forces, but physical forces as well—he was with the wild animals yet no mention is made of his provisioning. Further, Jesus' station changes as well as John's, but in reverse: Jesus moves from a throng of proximity to a place of remoteness. Only at the end of this episode are we told that angels care for him. Of course, in the very next verse, we see an immediate reversal of

THE FUNCTION OF MARK 1:1–15

fortune (so to speak), for John is arrested at the cusp of Jesus' proclamation of the arrival of the kingdom and the fulfillment of the anticipated time.

The contrast in these ekphrastic depictions supports the clear comparison and contrast of 1:7–8, in which John identifies Jesus as coming after John, as being mightier than John, and as baptizing with Holy Spirit rather than merely with water. The two instances of ekphrasis on either side of 1:7–8 thus support the central and crucial *synkrisis* of John and Jesus, captured explicitly in John's proclamation of 1:8. While the vivid detail of John's episode lends credibility to John's role in the divine drama here, the empowerment of Jesus by the Spirit intensifies in a positive way the divine activity being depicted, and thus differentiates Jesus from John in a substantial way.

The Jesus sub-scene closes in climax as Jesus utters his first words in the Markan account. As already noted, those words come to us by means of a final *Sammelbericht*, this time *ipsissima vox* of Jesus. The primary issue for Mark in his opening unit is the legitimation and authorization of Jesus' message and ministry, specifically insofar as Jesus bears the imprimatur of divine sonship. On trial is the legitimacy of Jesus' proclamation in 1:15. The *Anlauf*[74] to this moment has been Mark's marshaling of evidence to support his claim that Jesus is duly authorized as the Anointed Son of God to usher in the Kingdom of God on Earth.

We now are in a position to see how the literary *form* of Mark 1:1–15 (chapter 2) is placed as a *prologue* (chapter 3) and serves to convey a rhetorical *function* (chapter 4). The inversion of character focus reaches its climactic conclusion with the exit of John and the initial utterance of Jesus. The rhetorical shape of the prologue thus can be schematized as follows:[75]

---

74. Klauck, *Vorspiel im Himmel*, 13–15.

75. I have identified in bold the relevant words and phrases that represent each rhetorical device. Note how the *diēgēma* is established by the boldface of those elements indicated as such, while the boldface elements of *ekphrasis* could in theory be omitted without harming the flow of the narrative. This underscores the way in which the ekphrastic elements serve a rhetorical function.

THE FORM AND FUNCTION OF MARK 1:1–15

Verse	Text	Rhetorical Device/Proof
1:1	Ἀρχὴ τοῦ εὐαγγελίου Ἰησοῦ Χριστοῦ υἱοῦ θεοῦ.	*Incipit* of Prologue
1:2–3	Καθὼς γέγραπται ἐν τῷ Ἠσαΐᾳ τῷ προφήτῃ· ἰδοὺ ἀποστέλλω τὸν ἄγγελόν μου πρὸ προσώπου σου, ὃς κατασκευάσει τὴν ὁδόν σου· φωνὴ βοῶντος ἐν τῇ ἐρήμῳ· ἑτοιμάσατε τὴν ὁδὸν κυρίου, εὐθείας ποιεῖτε τὰς τρίβους αὐτοῦ,	Citation of Scripture
1:4	ἐγένετο Ἰωάννης βαπτίζων ἐν τῇ ἐρήμῳ καὶ κηρύσσων βάπτισμα μετανοίας εἰς ἄφεσιν ἁμαρτιῶν.	*diēgēsis*
1:5–6	καὶ ἐξεπορεύετο πρὸς αὐτὸν πᾶσα ἡ Ἰουδαία χώρα καὶ οἱ Ἱεροσολυμῖται πάντες, καὶ ἐβαπτίζοντο ὑπ᾽ αὐτοῦ ἐν τῷ Ἰορδάνῃ ποταμῷ ἐξομολογούμενοι τὰς ἁμαρτίας αὐτῶν. καὶ ἦν ὁ Ἰωάννης ἐνδεδυμένος τρίχας καμήλου καὶ ζώνην δερματίνην περὶ τὴν ὀσφὺν αὐτοῦ καὶ ἐσθίων ἀκρίδας καὶ μέλι ἄγριον.	Testimony of Witnesses; *ekphrasis*
1:7–8	Καὶ ἐκήρυσσεν λέγων· ἔρχεται ὁ ἰσχυρότερός μου ὀπίσω μου, οὗ οὐκ εἰμὶ ἱκανὸς κύψας λῦσαι τὸν ἱμάντα τῶν ὑποδημάτων αὐτοῦ. ἐγὼ ἐβάπτισα ὑμᾶς ὕδατι, αὐτὸς δὲ βαπτίσει ὑμᾶς ἐν πνεύματι ἁγίῳ.	Testimony of Witness; *synkrisis* (John and the Coming One)
1:9	Καὶ ἐγένετο ἐν ἐκείναις ταῖς ἡμέραις ἦλθεν Ἰησοῦς ἀπὸ Ναζαρὲτ τῆς Γαλιλαίας καὶ ἐβαπτίσθη εἰς τὸν Ἰορδάνην ὑπὸ Ἰωάννου.	*diēgēsis*
1:10	καὶ εὐθὺς ἀναβαίνων ἐκ τοῦ ὕδατος εἶδεν σχιζομένους τοὺς οὐρανοὺς καὶ τὸ πνεῦμα ὡς περιστερὰν καταβαῖνον εἰς αὐτόν·	Evidence of Miracle; *ekphrasis*
1:11	καὶ φωνὴ ἐγένετο ἐκ τῶν οὐρανῶν· σὺ εἶ ὁ υἱός μου ὁ ἀγαπητός, ἐν σοὶ εὐδόκησα.	*diēgēsis*; Evidence of Miracle; Testimony of Witness
1:12	Καὶ εὐθὺς τὸ πνεῦμα αὐτὸν ἐκβάλλει εἰς τὴν ἔρημον.	*diēgēsis*
1:13	καὶ ἦν ἐν τῇ ἐρήμῳ τεσσεράκοντα ἡμέρας πειραζόμενος ὑπὸ τοῦ σατανᾶ, καὶ ἦν μετὰ τῶν θηρίων, καὶ οἱ ἄγγελοι διηκόνουν αὐτῷ.	*ekphrasis*
1:14–15	Μετὰ δὲ τὸ παραδοθῆναι τὸν Ἰωάννην ἦλθεν ὁ Ἰησοῦς εἰς τὴν Γαλιλαίαν κηρύσσων τὸ εὐαγγέλιον τοῦ θεοῦ καὶ λέγων ὅτι πεπλήρωται ὁ καιρὸς καὶ ἤγγικεν ἡ βασιλεία τοῦ θεοῦ· μετανοεῖτε καὶ πιστεύετε ἐν τῷ εὐαγγελίῳ.	*diēgēsis*

Promise and Fulfillment

P. J. Sankey has prepared an instructive and compelling case that Mark 1:1–15 should be understood within the context of promise and fulfillment.[76] He maintains that the prologue intentionally establishes a cycle of credible witnesses based on the fulfillment of earlier promises. Although the promises are sometimes fulfilled in unexpected ways, the cycle is nevertheless accomplished. Sankey provides a judicious treatment of Mark from the perspective of reader-response criticism; of special significance is his presupposition that Mark would have been presented aurally by a reader who would have had a fair degree of familiarity with the text, and who would have been able to present the text in such a way as to remind the listening audience of earlier promises. He draws on Elizabeth Struthers Malbon's idea of "echoes and foreshadowings"[77] to demonstrate how readers "constantly make connections between parts of a text, looking back and remembering what has been read (retrospection) whilst speculating as to what will happen (anticipation). The past forms background for the present; the present generates expectations in the light of which the future will be understood."[78]

A literary perspective on the structure further confirms this anticipation/fulfillment scheme. Bauer and Traina specifically point to Mark's opening as indicative of *preparation* and *realization*.

> Mark begins his Gospel with the account of the ministry of John the Baptist (1:2–11[79]). Yet Mark is not finally interested in the ministry of John as such but includes this account only insofar as John's ministry provides background for the real concern of the Gospel of Mark: the ministry of Jesus. The reader of this Gospel, then, is to interpret Mark's narrative of Jesus' ministry according to the background or setting of Mark's account of John's ministry.[80]

---

76. Sankey, "Promise and Fulfillment."
77. Malbon, *Echoes and Foreshadowings in Mark 4–8*, 211.
78. Sankey, "Promise and Fulfillment," 4.
79. As indicated throughout, I would broaden the view of John's ministry to include 1:14–15, where the closure to his ministry is identified.
80. Bauer and Traina, *Inductive Bible Study*, 114.

Arguing that the OT relates to the NT according to this pattern of preparation and realization (when the Bible as a whole is in view),[81] they go on to say that,

> The primary development within the Bible is the progression between the Old Testament and the New Testament. The New Testament concept of *fulfillment* requires that students take seriously the progression from preparation to fulfillment, keeping in mind the combination of continuity and discontinuity that is implicit within the notion of fulfillment. Indeed, this relationship between the Testaments is the central issue in biblical theology (emphasis original).[82]

The relationship between *prediction* and *fulfillment* thus serves as a specific type of *preparation/realization*.[83] In Mark's opening, the OT context of Isaiah's prophetic message as preparation/prediction finds realization/fulfillment in the ministry and message of the Baptizer, which in turn provides the preparation for and prediction of the realization/fulfillment of the ministry and message of Jesus. This structure enables Mark to establish a trajectory along which the crucial moments of Isaiah's prophetic message, John's preparatory ministry, and the advent of Jesus as the Anointed Son are highlighted.

Summary

The Markan prologue is subsumed under the *incipit* of 1:1 and organized in two movements: from the time of Isaiah to John, and from the time of John to Jesus. As indicated above, these movements are not to be understood merely as temporal sequence, but rather as logical fulfillment.

The *incipit* of 1:1 introduces and establishes the parameters and agenda for Mark's opening unit. The *beginning* (alternately, the *basis* or *source*) of the good news from and about Jesus is the prophetic tradition (specifically focalized in John) preceding and anticipating Jesus. That tradition reached its penultimate climax with John's ministry, a ministry which provides the primary context for the prologue. Jesus is not only anointed in his capacity as the fulfillment of messianic expectations, but is also identified as the Son

---

81. Ibid., 298.
82. Ibid., 345.
83. Ibid., 114.

of God. The transcendent conversation in 1:2–3 between the Father and the Son is immanently actualized at the baptism of Jesus in 1:11. The summary statements placed in the voices of Isaiah, John, and Jesus establish the basic programmatic framework for each era of the prophetic tradition, beginning with Isaiah's message of anticipation, transitioning through John's ministry of preparation, and culminating in Jesus' proclamation of the arrival of God's kingdom and the necessity of human response.

Mark's purpose in his prologue is to prove that Jesus' ministry and message were in fulfillment of OT prophecies about him as a bearer of good news. The ministry and message of John the Baptizer likewise confirm Jesus as the Expected One. Mark's aim is to *persuade* his audience that Jesus is indeed the Anointed Son of God through Jesus' role in continuity with and differentiation from the prophetic office. To accomplish his task of persuasion, he provides a mix of rhetorical devices suited for a mixed audience: for Jews, Mark relies upon the inartificial proofs of Scripture, witnesses, and signs; for Gentiles, Mark relies upon conventional, Greco-Roman devices that would be understood by readers/hearers familiar with at least the most elementary devices. What follows the prologue beginning with the call of the first disciples and their reckless abandonment of their lives can only be understood in light of Jesus' identity: "Truly, this man was the Son of God."

Conclusions and Implications

Summary of Conclusions

WE BEGAN THIS STUDY with my statement that an error with regard to Mark's directional heading in his opening material would likely compound itself the further we journeyed into Mark. The results of a compounded error would therefore likely result in our arriving at a destination Mark never intended. I need to say at this point that I have no bright-eyed expectations that we can discern Mark's full intent with complete accuracy. On the other hand, I am not so grounded in an epistemology of skepticism regarding the possibility of approximating his intent that I am willing to concede that multiple interpretations would be consistent with Mark's original purposes. I firmly believe that Mark wrote for a reason, and that reason was to communicate more broadly a series of extraordinary, history-altering events that had taken place within his lifetime. My goal as his reader is to read in ways that demonstrate fidelity to both his content and his cues.

In chapter 1, I conducted a survey of relatively recent scholarship concerning the Gospel of Mark in general, and his opening materials in particular. I indicated how, beginning with the advent of redaction criticism, interpreters have sought to identify the role of Mark as a creative theologian. This new interest in Mark prompted numerous studies that began to focus on the text itself, especially its narrative characteristics, literary qualities, and rhetorical function. Within these methodologies, I gave special attention to those works dealing with matters related to literary prologues and—because of the significance of my identification of 1:14–15 as the terminus to Mark's opening—summary statements. I am grateful to benefit from the work of the scholarly guild in this regard.

In chapter 2, I presented my inductive analysis of 1:1–15 as a literary unit. Here, I made a case for some text-critical issues as a preliminary task,

CONCLUSIONS AND IMPLICATIONS

demonstrating (for example) that the variant υἱοῦ θεοῦ in 1:1 is likely original on the basis of both external and internal evidence. I also presented a syntactic analysis of the passage, specifically giving attention to the way that 1:2–3 should be read in light of the material surrounding it. I determined, based on both standard grammatical patterns and the evidence of similar constructions within and outside of the biblical corpus, that Mark 1:1 should be read apart from 1:2–3, and that 1:4 should be read as the main clause for which 1:2–3 provides subordinate support.

In the bulk and remainder of the chapter, I highlighted several features about 1:1–15 that give it literary coherence as a unit of thought. My primary methodology was inductive analysis, drawing largely on the work of Bauer and Traina.[1] The recurrence of key words and motifs in high concentration within the passage, the role of εὐαγγέλιον as forming an inclusio between 1:1 and 1:14–15, the parallelism and contrast of John and Jesus, the temporal markers leading to climax, the relatively clear break between 1:15 and 1:16, and the overall schematic inversion of character focus all contribute to and confirm the unity of the passage. Further, the structural relationships of preparation and realization provide an interpretive scheme for understanding the relationship between smaller units within the opening.

In chapter 3, I surveyed the rhetorical milieu that likely shaped Mark's writing. Here, I briefly characterized the aural nature of that environment and examined how Greco-Roman rhetoric functioned at macro- and micro-levels. I then presented a sketch of first-century education, particularly noting the role of rhetoric as a basic ingredient of that experience. Kennedy's foundational work on NT rhetoric[2] and Witherington's application of that theory to the NT writings[3] provided the basis for this study. Central to rhetorical training was the acquisition and development of skills in using the various rhetorical devices, and Aelius Theon's *progymnasmata* provided the basic curriculum for that training. I then examined Mark's Gospel in light of its rhetorical milieu, concluding that Mark clearly reflects at least basic facility with regard to the more elementary principles of rhetoric (which he would certainly have attained alongside his acquisition of Greek language and grammar). I determined that, although Mark employs

---

1. Bauer and Traina, *Inductive Bible Study*.

2. Kennedy, *New Testament Interpretation through Rhetorical Criticism*; and Kennedy, *Progymnasmata*.

3. Witherington III, *New Testament Rhetoric*.

basic Greco-Roman rhetorical devices, his work is nevertheless eclectic in its simultaneous use of non-enthymatic, inartificial proofs (which is more characteristic of Jewish rhetoric than Greco-Roman).

In chapter 4, I undertook the task of conducting a survey of samplings from ancient Greco-Roman βίοι in hopes of establishing a basis for understanding ancient prologues. The corpus that served the survey was that used by Richard Burridge in his defense of the Gospels as examples of ancient biography.[4] Building on Burridge's brief observations about the opening materials of each βίος, I attempted to establish some more detailed patterns with respect to the form and function of ancient "beginnings." I determined that opening materials typically feature one or more of the following: first-person authorial insertions that address the purpose or occasion of the work (a *preface*); background information necessary in establishing the biographical figure within his social or political context (an *expository prologue*); and short, introductory text-strings that primarily serve to simply identify or introduce the work (an *incipit*).

I determined that Mark's opening unit fits the pattern of an expository prologue insofar as it provides the necessary information to properly situate its central character (Jesus) in context. However, at least one major difference exists between Mark's prologue and that of ancient Greco-Roman prologues: whereas the latter almost always includes some information about the central character's lineage or family origins, Mark does not. He provides an alternate means of situating his main character in context. By evoking Isaiah and John directly (and Elijah inferentially), Mark locates Jesus within a tradition of the ongoing presence of the Spirit that empowers and equips human agents for divine service. Here again, we see Mark following typical Greco-Roman practices, but doing so in ways that cast a distinctively Jewish hue upon his work.

In chapter 5, I drew upon my findings in my earlier chapters to establish a function for the form of 1:1–15. I began by identifying the opening verse as an *incipit* which serves to identify Mark's opening unit. The opening unit is rhetorically organized around three summary statements *ipsissima vox* of the unit's major figures: Isaiah, John, and Jesus. Collectively, they form the opening, pivot, and climax of the unit. The space between is filled with brief narrative moments (*diēgēsis*) that fund the essential flow of the narrative, vivid description (*ekphrasis*) that intensifies positively the divine activity, and comparison (*synkrisis*) that highlights

---

4. Burridge, *What Are the Gospels?*

the similarities and contrast between John and Jesus. These devices demonstrate Mark's facility with elementary Greco-Roman rhetoric. On the other hand, the use of scriptural citations, the testimony of witnesses, and the evidence of miracles provide inartificial proofs that demonstrate rather conclusively that Mark is equally comfortable working within a Jewish framework of rhetorical discourse. The net effect of the unit is to legitimate Jesus as the Anointed Son of God, and that emphasis can be seen throughout Mark's Gospel as a whole. The initial identification of Jesus as *Christ* and *Son of God* is corroborated and punctuated at multiple points throughout Mark's Gospel, especially at such strategic moments as Peter's declaration in 8:29, the divine confirmation in 9:7, and the pronouncement by the centurion in 15:39.

So the final question is this: how does the Markan prologue prepare readers of the Gospel for the material that follows the prologue? First, it offers a basis for understanding why initially four commercial fishermen (1:16-20), then others (2:13-14; 3:14-19), would simply walk away from their families, their homes, and their livelihoods to follow an itinerant Jewish preacher around the Galilean countryside. The prologue provides the warrant for the extraordinary status of Jesus as the Anointed Son of God; as a result, Mark's readers are not only asked to accept Mark's claims that the first disciples responded to Jesus' call with such vigor, but are implicitly encouraged to do likewise. Second, it declares that the Coming One is indeed mightier: he teaches with unprecedented authority (1:21-22); he exercises dominion over the realm of unclean spirits and liberates those oppressed by them (1:23-28); he heals the sick (e.g., 1:29-24 and 1:40-45) and spreads good news of healing and wholeness (1:38-39). The good news regarding wholeness means one can receive forgiveness of sins as proclaimed in the wilderness by John (*cf.* 1:4-5 to 2:1-12). The prologue establishes the authority of Jesus within an earthly tradition of prophetic ministry *and* by means of a supernatural affirmation of Jesus' special status. That Jesus prevails over a time of temptation in the wilderness at the hands of the Adversary further establishes the potency of his special status. Jesus' mighty works are shown from the beginning to have their basis in divine authority.

Such a proclamation of good news could not escape notice, though. If the establishment would detain (1:14) and execute (6:27-28) John, they would certainly deal likewise with the greater threat of Jesus (3:6). Because Jesus' mission lay in the broader mission of those *sent* before him, Jesus would expect to receive treatment no different from his forebears. Those who reject Jesus' authority are those who may "indeed see but not perceive, and may indeed hear but not understand" (4:10). Jesus knows what is written of him, and he is prepared to pursue that path. His followers, however, struggle to "see" this path. The progressive predictions regarding Jesus' passion (8:31; 9:31; 10:32–34) seem to fall on deaf ears. However, Peter realizes that Jesus is more than John, or Elijah, or the prophets of old (like Isaiah). Although he sees through the glass but dimly, he recognizes that Jesus is fundamentally different—he is, in fact, *the Anointed One* introduced in Mark 1:1, authorized in 1:11, and confirmed to Peter personally in 9:7 at the transfiguration.

The passion narrative that follows seems on the surface to be a storyline that has run tragically afoul. Like John (and so many of the prophets before), Jesus is yet another casualty in the divine dispatch of messengers. The *titulus* above the cross bears witness to the biting irony: "The King of the Jews" (15:26). Nevertheless, the divine drama is unfolding exactly as scripted in the parable of the wicked tenants, and Jesus' passion predictions come to pass. No one expected the *fulfillment of time* and the *approach of the kingdom* (1:15) to involve the death of the Son; yet this was part of the plan since time immemorial. As a result, Mark's readers are guided into a new understarding of the concept of *anointed* (1:1) insofar as Jesus' anointing is not for the purpose of elevated status, but for the purpose of suffering at the hands of human agents.

The penultimate act of this divine drama closes with a glimmer of hope, though. From the most unlikely of corners, a new voice cries out in fulfillment of the promise that the owner would wrest control of the vineyard away from the wicked tenants and give it to others: "Truly this man was the Son of God!" (15:39). The Mightier One has come—and gone; but he has not gone for long, for "he has risen" (16:6). The fullness of time and the approach of the kingdom have been prepared for those who will repent and believe in the good news.

Assuming that Mark wrote to a primarily aural audience, we can surmise that Mark's reader would have had access to a manuscript in advance of the presentation, and would in all likelihood have had the opportunity to rehearse his or her presentation so as to maintain fidelity to the syntactic, literary, and rhetorical cues embedded in the work. That presentation would have made it clear from the onset that Jesus of Nazareth was indeed the anticipated Christ, the Son of God, *just as it has been written*.

CONCLUSIONS AND IMPLICATIONS

Implications for Further Study

This study raises any number of small concerns. For instance, the text-critical issue of the variant article ὁ, in 1:4 remains unresolved, yet will likely not prove to be a significant issue with regard to either the Markan prologue or Mark's overall program. However, I am struck by three primary matters that emerge from this study. One of these issues has a more historical bent, while the other two relate to matters of theology. These issues include Mark's potential role as Peter's hermeneut, the function of Isaiah in Mark (and particularly in the prologue), and the nature of John's baptism as a preparatory rite.

Mark as Peter's Hermeneut

The Papias tradition suggests that Mark was the ἑρμηνευτής of Peter (Eusebius, *Hist. Eccl.* 3.39.14). Taking this evidence at face value, how might the form and function of Mark 1:1–15 challenge or confirm the likelihood that Mark compiled the recollections of Peter's teaching οὐ μέντοι τάξει? Conversely, how does the Papias tradition contribute to our understanding of the form and function of Mark 1:1–15? Addressing the matter from a different perspective, Richard Bauckham has suggested that

> Mark's Gospel not only . . . claims Peter as its main eyewitness source; it also tells the story predominately (though by no means exclusively) from Peter's perspective. This Petrine perspective is deliberately, carefully, and subtly constructed. Mark's Gospel is no mere transcript of Peter's teaching, nor is the Petrine perspective merely an undersigned survival of the way Peter told his stories. While it does correspond to features of Peter's oral narration, Mark has deliberately designed the Gospel in such a way that it incorporates and conveys this Petrine perspective. Several literary features combine to give readers/hearers Peter's "point of view"
> . . . . It is this literary construction of the Petrine perspective that has so far gone almost unnoticed in Markan scholarship.[5]

The approach taken in this present study has been in part a decidedly literary one. In view of the conclusions reached here, how might the need to legitimate Jesus as the Anointed Son of God be found within Peter's teaching?

---

5. Bauckham, *Jesus and the Eyewitnesses*, 179.

Might there have been a specific occasion or circumstance to which Peter's teaching might be directed?

One possible avenue of future research lies in the relationship between Acts 5:31–33 and Mark 1:1–15. In the Acts passage, Peter and the apostles—following their arrest by Jewish authorities, miraculous release by an angel of the Lord, and second arraignment—provide a defense for their teaching. That defense is grounded in several points, not the least of which is the elevation of Jesus as ἀρχηγόν (*cf.* ἀρχή of Mark 1:1) and the giving of μετάνοιαν and ἄφεσιν ἁμαρτιῶν to Israel (*cf.* Mark 1:4, 15). These possible points of contact raise a number of questions. In what ways does Jesus' identification as ἀρχηγόν comport with or deviate from our understanding of the period of John's baptizing ministry as the ἀρχή of the gospel? How might such a claim by Peter and the apostles about Jesus' status elicit the response by the Jewish leadership in Acts 5:33, namely that "they were enraged and wanted to kill them"? How does the term χριστός in Mark 1:1 relate to the immediate persecution of the early Christians following Jesus' death insofar as Mark presents Jesus as one "anointed to suffer" (9:31; 10:33–34; but especially Jesus' corrective understanding of χριστός in 8:29–31)? How might this occasion in some way be suggestive of the impetus (if not the dating) of Mark's Gospel? These questions and others may help to give shape to subsequent studies aimed at understanding Mark's relationship to the Petrine tradition.

John's Baptism in Historical and Theological Context

My second interest lies in the nature and role of baptism as a preparatory event. The Isaian citation in Mark 1:2–3 points to the role of the messenger as one who prepares *the way* of/for the Lord. John's appearance in 1:4 (as I have already shown) is the fulfillment of that prophecy, and his appearance is described as serving the purposes of baptizing and proclaiming: "John appeared [for the purposes of] *baptizing* in the wilderness and *proclaiming* a baptism of repentance for forgiveness of sins." Given the very significant role of baptism in the prologue, how does baptism prepare the way of/for the Lord? Further, how does baptism function in Mark more generally (and here I am thinking specifically of Mark 10:38–39)?

Everett Ferguson has produced a landmark work on baptism in the early centuries of the church.[6] His study would provide the basis for an exploration that seeks to connect a number of dots related to the issue. For example:

- How does the word βαπτίζω and its cognates function in the OT and in extra-canonical works of the first-century era? (Both Philo and Josephus provide a number of fascinating insights into common understandings of the concept, understandings which bear almost no correspondence with modern notions of the word as an initiatory rite.)
- How does the baptism of Mark's prologue relate to the baptism of suffering that Jesus foretells in Mark 10?
- How does baptism of water differ from baptism of Holy Spirit?
- Assuming that participants were fully immersed (a point that would need to be substantiated), how would that experience have functioned as a means of *preparation for the Lord*?
- Why could John's baptism not have been self-administered?
- What connection do *forgiveness* and *confession* (Mark 1:4–5) have to baptism within the theology of the Markan prologue (and Mark's Gospel as a whole)?

My key question is this: when Mark invoked the language of baptism in his prologue, what would that have meant to his readers? My chief concern is that, too often, John's baptism is viewed anachronistically through the lens of later baptismal theology, rather than being read on its own terms within the context of its historical and theological particularity. Two immediate differences that fail to receive sufficient attention with regard to John's practice are: 1) that the act of public confession happens contemporaneous with or—more likely—subsequent to the ritual act;[7] and 2) that the rite performs a preparatory[8] rather than an initiating function (for no specific or identifiable community is prescribed yet, unless one wants to argue abstractly for an eschatological community). As a preparatory rite, John's baptism likely served as a means of readying persons for the Coming

---

6. Ferguson, *Baptism in the Early Church*.

7. The present tense form of the participle ἐξομολογούμενοι is suggestive of this likelihood.

8. Note the language of κατασκευάσει and ἑτοιμάσατε in 1:2–3.

One who would establish an eschatological community, but John's baptism did not constitute such membership.

Mark's Use of Isaiah

Third, I maintain a continued interest in the way Isaiah provides the context for Mark, especially in Mark's prologue. I suspect that Mark is drawing on Isaiah because Isaiah, as a whole, represents the three distinct movements of judgment (Isa 1–39), repentance (40–55), and forgiveness and restoration (56–66). Thus, Isaiah is uniquely poised to convey the essence of this cycle. However, this cycle is hardly represented in Isaiah alone, for it in fact is illustrative of the entire biblical history of God's dealing with his people.

This Isaian theme is central to understanding not only the Markan prologue, but I suspect the whole of Mark, as well. In some cases, interpretations "wide of our Mark" result when insufficient attention is given to Mark's reliance upon an Isaian context.[9] In other cases, conclusions "narrowly miss our Mark" in their appropriation of Isaiah. Rikki Watts is a case in point. Although he gives a thoroughgoing treatment of Mark's use of Isaiah, he makes a subtle error in his initial course heading when he suggests *a priori* that the Exodus is the defining moment in Israel's community identity formation. His study is a critical piece in understanding the overall framework of Mark, and especially of the way the prologue is situated to establish the parameters for understanding the Gospel as a whole. However, I think he stops short of ascertaining the full extent of Mark's OT appropriation.

Rather than reading Isaiah as a new iteration of the Exodus (the event in which—he argues—Israel finds its true identity), I suggest that Mark would understand Isaiah as going even further back into Israel's history. Evidence for such is found in the citation of Isaiah in Mark 1:2, specifically with regard to the present tense form of ἀποστέλλω[10] and the dispatch of an ἄγγελος for the purposes of preparation in furtherance of God's program. This construct—inclusive of the elements: a) God as a sending agent; b)

---

9. See Tolbert, *Sowing the Gospel*, whose entire study makes mention of Isaiah only eight times, and half of those are in footnotes.

10. The present tense form of the verb here would likely have caught the attention of first-century readers/hearers insofar as it immediately follows the ascription to Isaiah, for whom *sending* as a first-person act is always done by God in future time (Isa 6:8; 10:6; 16:1; 43:14; 66:19; see also 10:16; 19:20; 27:8).

sending as a future act; c) a divine messenger dispatched for purposes of preparing a *way*; and d) preparation specifically in furtherance of God's program[11]—literally dots the landscape of the entire OT corpus (and not just the Exodus narrative), and is constituent of a pattern that finds its culmination in the message and ministry of Jesus. Watts' identification of the Exodus as the formative event in Israel's community identity formation thus fails not because it lies in the wrong direction, but because it does not pursue that direction far enough.

Final Summary

This study has been an endeavor that has roots in a question I initially engaged over fifteen years earlier: where does Mark terminate his opening scene? I have undertaken to propose an answer to that question: namely, that Mark's opening comes to closure at 1:15. I have also attempted to address the issue of the opening unit's function, arguing that it is a prologue crafted by Mark, appended to Peter's memoirs, and serving to highlight the identity of Jesus as the Anointed Son of God. Any study of Mark as a whole will likely attempt to prove a "unified theory" of Mark that addresses each of the major, critical issues commonly associated with the study of this Gospel. Nowhere else are such critical issues concentrated than in Mark's opening unit. As I consider possible next steps for my own engagement of Mark, I once again paraphrase the great Sherlock Holmes, "We have *some* explanations of a *few* of the facts; I am interested in the *only* explanation of *all* the facts." Whether or not such a goal is within reach will remain an ongoing question. In the meantime, I intend to continue my journey with that destination in mind.

---

11. Note especially Gen 24:7, 40; 32:2–4; Exod 23:20; 33:2; Mal 3:1.

Appendix
Translation of Mark 1:1–15

¹ The beginning of the good news of Jesus, the Anointed Son of God.

² Just as it has been written in Isaiah the prophet,

> Behold! I am sending my messenger before your personal presence, who will prepare your way. ³ A voice crying in the wilderness: "Prepare the way of the Lord! Make straight his paths!"

⁴ John appeared baptizing in the wilderness and proclaiming a baptism of repentance for forgiveness of sins. ⁵ And all of the Judean countryside and all of the Jerusalemites were going out to him, and they were being baptized by him in the Jordan River, confessing their sins. ⁶ And John was wearing hairs of a camel and a belt of leather around his waist, and eating insects and wild honey. ⁷ And he was proclaiming, saying,

> The One stronger than me is coming after me, the thong of whose sandals I am not worthy to stoop and untie. ⁸ I baptized you with water; he, however, will baptize you with Holy Spirit.

⁹ And it happened in those days that Jesus came from Galilee and was baptized into the Jordan by John. ¹⁰ And as soon as he came up out of the water, he saw the heavens separated and the Spirit coming down onto him as a dove. ¹¹ And a voice appeared from the heavens:

> You are my Son, my Beloved, in whom I delight.

¹² And then the Spirit compels him into the wilderness. ¹³ And he was in the wilderness forty days, being tempted by the Adversary, and he was with the wild animals, and the messengers were ministering to him.

¹⁴ Now after the arrest of John, Jesus went into Galilee proclaiming the good news of God, ¹⁵ and saying that,

> The time has been fulfilled and the kingdom of God has approached; repent and believe in the good news.

Bibliography

Abbott, William M. "What Happened to Mark's 'Infancy' Story?" *Landas* 14 (2000) 202-16.
Albl, Martin C. *And Scripture Cannot Be Broken: The Form and Function of the Early Christian Testimonia Collections.* Supplements to Novum Testamentum. Leiden: Brill, 1999.
Anderson, Hugh. *The Gospel of Mark.* New Century Bible. London: Oliphants, 1976.
Anderson, Janice Capel, and Stephen D. Moore, eds. *Mark & Method: New Approaches in Biblical Studies.* 2nd ed. Minneapolis: Fortress, 2008.
Arnold, Bill T. "Deuteronomy as the Ipsissima Vox of Moses." *Journal of Theological Interpretation* 4, no. 1 (2010) 53-74.
———. *Encountering the Book of Genesis: A Study of Its Content and Issues.* Encountering Biblical Studies. Grand Rapids: Baker, 1998.
Arnold, Gerhard. "Mk 1:1 und Eröffnungswendungen in griechischen und lateinischen Schriften." *Zeitschrift für die neutestamentliche Wissenschaft und die Kunde der älteren Kirche* 68, no. 1-2 (1977) 123-27.
Auerbach, Erich. *Mimesis: The Representation of Reality in Western Literature.* Princeton Paperbacks 124. Princeton: Princeton University Press, 1968.
Aune, David E. "Inclusio." In *The Westminster Dictionary of New Testament and Early Christian Literature and Rhetoric,* 229. Louisville: Westminster John Knox, 2003.
Barber, Raymond C. "Mark as Narrative: A Case for Chapter One." PhD diss., Graduate Theological Union, 1988.
Barton, John. "What Is a Book? Modern Exegesis and the Literary Conventions of Ancient Israel." In *Intertextuality in Ugarit and Israel,* 1-14. Leiden: Brill, 1998.
Bauckham, Richard. *Jesus and the Eyewitnesses: The Gospels as Eyewitness Testimony.* Grand Rapids: Eerdmans, 2006.
Bauer, David R., and Robert A. Traina. *Inductive Bible Study: A Comprehensive Guide to the Practice of Hermeneutics.* Grand Rapids: Baker Academic, 2011.
Beale, G. K., Daniel Joseph Brendsel, and William A. Ross. *An Interpretive Lexicon of New Testament Greek: Analysis of Prepositions, Adverbs, Particles, Relative Pronouns, and Conjunctions.* Grand Rapids: Zondervan, 2014.
Beavis, Mary Ann. *Mark.* Paideia. Grand Rapids: Baker Academic, 2011.
Best, Ernest. *Mark: The Gospel as Story.* Studies of the New Testament and Its World. Edinburgh: T. & T. Clark, 1983.
Betz, Hans Dieter. *Galatians: A Commentary on Paul's Letter to the Churches in Galatia.* Hermeneia: A Critical and Historical Commentary on the Bible. Philadelphia: Fortress, 1979.

Bilezikian, Gilbert G. *The Liberated Gospel: A Comparison of the Gospel of Mark and Greek Tragedy*. Baker Biblical Monograph. Grand Rapids: Baker, 1977.

Bitzer, Lloyd F. "The Rhetorical Situation." *Philosophy & Rhetoric* 25 (1992) 1–14.

Black, C. Clifton, and Duane Frederick Watson, eds. *Words Well Spoken: George Kennedy's Rhetoric of the New Testament*. Waco, TX: Baylor University Press, 2008.

Black, Donald Stephen. "John, Elijah, or One of the Prophets: How the Markan Reader Understands Jesus through John/Elijah." PhD diss., University of St. Michael's College Faculty of Theology and University of Toronto, 2012.

Bock, Darrell L. "The Words of Jesus in the Gospels: Live, Jive, or Memorex?" In *Jesus Under Fire: Modern Scholarship Reinvents the Historical Jesus*, 73–99. Grand Rapids: Zondervan, 1995.

Boismard, Marie Emile. "Procédé Rédactionnel dans le Quatrième Évangile: La Wiederaufnahme." In *Évangile de Jean*, 235–41. Gembloux, Belgium: Duculot, 1977.

Boring, M. Eugene. "Mark 1:1–15 and the Beginning of the Gospel." *Semeia* 52 (1990) 43–81.

———. *Mark: A Commentary*. New Testament Library. Louisville: Westminster John Knox, 2006.

———. "The Christology of Mark: Hermeneutical Issues for Systematic Theology." *Semeia* 30 (1984) 125–53.

Bruehler, Bart B. "Patterns of Ekphrasis in Luke-Acts." Conference Paper delivered to the Annual Meeting of the Society of Biblical Literature, San Francisco, Nov. 20, 2011.

Bryan, Christopher. *A Preface to Mark: Notes on the Gospel in Its Literary and Cultural Settings*. New York: Oxford University Press, 1993.

Burridge, Richard A. *What Are the Gospels? A Comparison with Graeco-Roman Biography*. Biblical Resource Series. Grand Rapids: Eerdmans, 2004.

Caird, George B. *The Language and Imagery of the Bible*. Grand Rapids: Eerdmans, 1997.

Campbell, Constantine R. *Basics of Verbal Aspect in Biblical Greek*. Grand Rapids: Zondervan, 2008.

Casey, Maurice. *Aramaic Sources of Mark's Gospel*. SNTSMS 102. Cambridge: Cambridge University Press, 1998.

Chajes, Zevi Hirsch. *The Student's Guide through the Talmud*. Translated by Jacob Shachter. London: East and West Library, 1952.

Cole, R. Alan. *Mark: An Introduction and Commentary*. Vol. 2. Tyndale New Testament Commentary. Downers Grove, IL: IVP Academic, 1989.

Conybeare, F. C., trans. *Philostratus: The Life of Apollonius of Tyana*. Vol. 1. Loeb Classical Library 16. Cambridge, MA: Harvard University Press, 1989.

Cook, John Granger. *The Structure and Persuasive Power of Mark: A Linguistic Approach*. Society of Biblical Literature Semeia Studies. Atlanta: Scholars, 1995.

Croy, N. Clayton. *The Mutilation of Mark's Gospel*. Nashville: Abingdon, 2003.

———. "Where the Gospel Text Begins: A Non-Theological Interpretation of Mark 1:1." *Novum Testamentum* 43, no. 2 (2001) 105–27.

Culpepper, R. Alan. *Mark*. Collegeville, MN: Smyth & Helwys, 2007.

Danker, Frederick W., ed. *A Greek-English Lexicon of the New Testament and Other Early Christian Literature*. 3rd ed. Chicago: University of Chicago Press, 2000.

Danove, Paul L. *The Rhetoric of the Characterization of God, Jesus, and Jesus' Disciples in the Gospel of Mark*. JSNT 290. New York: T. & T. Clark, 2005.

Dautzenberg, Gerhard. "Die Zeit des Evangeliums: Mk 1:1–15 und die Konzeption des Markusevangeliums." *Biblische Zeitschrift* 21, no. 2 (1977) 219–34.

Davidsen, Ole. *The Narrative Jesus: A Semiotic Reading of Mark's Gospel.* Aarhus, Denmark: Aarhus University Press, 1993.

Davies, W. D., and Dale C. Allison. *A Critical and Exegetical Commentary on the Gospel According to Saint Matthew.* Vol. 1. ICC. London: T. & T. Clark, 2004.

Dawson, John David. *Christian Figural Reading and the Fashioning of Identity.* Berkeley: University of California Press, 2002.

Dechow, Jens. *Gottessohn und Herrschaft Gottes: Der Theozentrismus des Markusevangeliums.* Vol. 86. Wissenschaftliche Monographien zum Alten und Neuen Testament. Neukirchen-Vluyn: Neukirchener, 2000.

Decker, Rodney J. *Mark 1–8: A Handbook on the Greek Text.* Baylor Handbook on the Greek New Testament. Waco, TX: Baylor University Press, 2014.

DeSilva, David Arthur. *Honor, Patronage, Kinship & Purity: Unlocking New Testament Culture.* Downers Grove, IL: InterVarsity, 2000.

———. "X Marks the Spot? A Critique of the Use of Chiasmus in Macro-Structural Analyses of Revelation." *Journal for the Study of the New Testament* 30, no. 3 (2008) 343–71.

Dewey, Joanna. *Markan Public Debate: Literary Technique, Concentric Structure, and Theology in Mark 2:1–36.* SBLDS 48. Chico, CA: Scholars, 1980.

Dodd, C. H. *According to the Scriptures: The Sub-Structure of New Testament Theology.* London: Nisbet, 1952.

———. "The Framework of the Gospel Narrative." *Expository Times* 43 (1931) 396–400.

Donahue, John R. "Jesus as the Parable of God in the Gospel of Mark." *Interpretation* 32, no. 4 (1978) 369–86.

Donahue, John R., and Daniel J Harrington. *The Gospel of Mark.* Sacra Pagina 2. Collegeville, MN: Liturgical, 2002.

Dormeyer, Detlev. "Mk 1,1–15 als Prolog des ersten Idealbiographischen Evangeliums von Jesus Christus." *Biblical Interpretation* 5, no. 2 (1997) 181–211.

Drury, John. "Mark 1:1–15: An Interpretation." In *Alternative Approaches to New Testament Study,* edited by A. E. Harvey, 25–36. London: SPCK, 1985.

Edwards, James R. *The Gospel according to Mark.* Pillar New Testament Commentary. Grand Rapids: Eerdmans, 2002.

Egger, Wilhelm. *Frohbotschaft und Lehre: Die Sammelberichte des Wirkens Jesu im Markusevangelium.* Vol. 19. Frankfurter theologische Studien. Frankfurt am Main: Knecht, 1976.

Ehrman, Bart D. "The Text of Mark in the Hands of the Orthodox." *Lutheran Quarterly* 5, no. 2 (1991) 143–56.

Elliott, J. K. "Mark 1.1–3: A Later Addition to the Gospel?" *New Testament Studies* 46, no. 4 (2000) 584–88.

———. "Mark and the Teaching of Jesus: An Examination of Logos and Euangelion." In *Sayings of Jesus,* 37–45. Leiden: Brill, 1997.

———. *New Testament Textual Criticism: The Application of Thoroughgoing Principles: Essays on Manuscripts and Textual Variation.* Supplements to Novum Testamentum. Leiden: Brill, 2010.

Ernst, Josef. *Das Evangelium nach Markus.* Regensburg: Pustet, 1981.

Evans, Craig A. "Mark's Incipit and the Priene Calendar Inscription." *Journal of Greco-Roman Christianity and Judaism,* no. 1 (2000) 67–81.

Feneberg, Wolfgang. *Der Markusprolog: Studien zur Formbestimmung des Evangeliums.* Vol. 36. Studien zum Alten und Neuen Testament. Münich: Kösel, 1974.

Ferguson, Everett. *Baptism in the Early Church: History, Theology, and Liturgy in the First Five Centuries*. Grand Rapids: Eerdmans, 2009.

Fishbane, Michael A. *Biblical Interpretation in Ancient Israel*. Oxford: Clarendon, 1985.

———. *The Exegetical Imagination: On Jewish Thought and Theology*. Cambridge, MA: Harvard University Press, 1998.

France, R. T. *The Gospel of Mark: A Commentary on the Greek Text*. NIGTC. Grand Rapids: Eerdmans, 2002.

Frye, Northrop. *The Great Code: The Bible and Literature*. New York: Harcourt Brace Jovanovich, 1982.

Funk, R. W. *The Poetics of Biblical Narrative*. Foundations & Facets: Literary Facets. Sonoma, CA: Polebridge, 1988.

Gabel, J. B., and C. B. Wheeler. *The Bible as Literature: An Introduction*. New York: Oxford University Press, 1986.

Gibbs, J. M. "Mk 1,1–15, Mt 1,1—4,16, Lk 1,1—4,30, Jn 1,1–51: The Gospel Prologues and Their Function." In *Studia Evangelica Vol 6, Papers Presented to the 4th International Congress on New Testament Studies Held at Oxford, 1969*, 154–88. Berlin: Akademie, 1973.

Gillman, John. "De Summaria in Marcus En de Compositie van Mc 1:14-8:26." *Catholic Biblical Quarterly* 51, no. 4 (1989) 760–62.

Gnilka, Joachim. *Das Evangelium nach Markus*. Vol. 1. Evangelisch-katholischer Kommentar zum Neuen Testament 2. Zurich: Neukirchener, 1994.

Grassi, Ernesto. *Rhetoric as Philosophy: The Humanist Tradition*. University Park, PA: Pennsylvania State University Press, 1980.

Green, Donald E. "Evangelicals and Ipsissima Vox." *Master's Seminary Journal* 12, no. 1 (2001) 49–68.

Green, Joel B. *Hearing the New Testament: Strategies for Interpretation*. 2nd ed. Grand Rapids: Eerdmans, 2010.

Guelich, Robert A. *Mark 1—8:26*. WBC 34a. Nashville: Nelson, 1989.

———. "The Beginning of the Gospel: Mark 1:1–15." *Biblical Research* 27 (1982) 5–15.

Guijarro, Santiago. "Why Does the Gospel of Mark Begin as It Does?" *Biblical Theology Bulletin* 33, no. 1 (2003) 28–38.

Gundry, Robert H. *Mark: A Commentary on His Apology for the Cross (1–8)*. Vol. 1. Grand Rapids: Eerdmans, 1993.

———. *Use of the Old Testament in St. Matthew's Gospel*. NovT. Leiden: Brill, 1967.

Haenchen, Ernst. *Der Weg Jesu: Eine Erklärung des Markus-Evangeliums und der kanonischen Parallelen*. Berlin: de Gruyter, 1968.

Harmon, A. M., trans. *Lucian*. Vol. 1. Loeb Classical Library 14. Cambridge, MA: Harvard University Press, 1967.

Harris, J. Rendel, and Vacher Burch. *Testimonies*. Cambridge: Cambridge University Press, 1916.

Havelock, Eric A. "Oral Composition in the Oedipus Tyrannus of Sophocles." *New Literary History* 16, no. 1 (1984) 175–97.

Hays, Richard B. *Reading Backwards: Figural Christology and the Fourfold Gospel Witness*. Waco, TX: Baylor University Press, 2014.

Head, Peter M. "A Text-Critical Study of Mark 1:1, 'The Beginning of the Gospel of Jesus Christ.'" *New Testament Studies* 37, no. 4 (1991) 621–29.

Healy, Mary. *The Gospel of Mark*. Grand Rapids: Baker Academic, 2008.

BIBLIOGRAPHY

Hedrick, C. W. "The Role of 'Summary Statements' in the Composition of the Gospel of Mark: A Dialog with Karl Schmidt and Norman Perrin." *Novum Testamentum* 26, no. 4 (1984) 289–311.

Hengel, Martin. *Studies in the Gospel of Mark*. Philadelphia: Fortress, 1985.

Horsley, Richard A., Jonathan A. Draper, and John Miles Foley, eds. *Performing the Gospel: Orality, Memory, and Mark*. Minneapolis: Fortress, 2006.

Houston, George W. *Inside Roman Libraries: Book Collections and Their Management in Antiquity*. Studies in the History of Greece and Rome. Chapel Hill: University of North Carolina Press, 2014.

Humphrey, Robert L. *Narrative Structure and Message in Mark: A Rhetorical Analysis*. Mellen, 2003.

Hurtado, Larry W. "P45 and the Textual History of the Gospel of Mark." Edited by C. Horton. *Journal for the Study of the New Testament Supplement Series* 258 (2004) 132–48.

Hutton, M., trans. *Tacitus*. Vol. 1. Loeb Classical Library 35. Rev. ed. Cambridge, MA: Harvard University Press, 1970.

Iersel, Bas M. F. van. "Een 'Evangelist' Kijkt Terug: Veertig Jaar Bezig Met Marcus (An 'Evangelist' Looks Back: Forty Years of Reading Mark)." *Tijdschrift Voor Theologie* 39, no. 3 (1999) 228–43.

———. *Reading Mark*. Translated by W. H. Bisscheroux. Edinburgh: T. & T. Clark, 1989.

Incigneri, Brian J. *The Gospel to the Romans: The Setting and Rhetoric of Mark's Gospel*. Biblical Interpretation 65. Leiden: Brill, 2003.

Johnson, Luke Timothy. *The Writings of the New Testament: An Interpretation*. Philadelphia: Fortress, 1986.

Kealy, Sean P. *A History of the Interpretation of the Gospel of Mark*. 2 vols. Lewiston, NY: Mellen, 2008.

Keck, Leander E. "The Introduction to Mark's Gospel." *NTS* 12 (1966) 352–70.

Keener, Craig S. *The Historical Jesus of the Gospels*. Grand Rapids: Eerdmans, 2009.

———. *The Spirit in the Gospels and Acts: Divine Purity and Power*. Peabody, MA: Hendrickson, 1997.

Kelber, Werner H. *The Oral and the Written Gospel: The Hermeneutics of Speaking and Writing in the Synoptic Tradition, Mark, Paul, and Q*. Voices in Performance and Text. Bloomington: Indiana University Press, 1997.

Kennedy, George A. *New Testament Interpretation through Rhetorical Criticism*. Chapel Hill: University of North Carolina Press, 1984.

———. *Progymnasmata: Greek Textbooks of Prose Composition and Rhetoric*. Leiden: Brill, 2003.

Kingsbury, Jack Dean. *The Christology of Mark's Gospel*. Philadelphia: Fortress, 1983.

Klauck, Hans-Josef. *Vorspiel im Himmel? Erzähltechnik und Theologie im Markusprolog*. Biblisch-theologische Studien 32. Neukirchen-Vluyn: Neukirchener, 1997.

Krentz, E. "The Starting Point of the Gospel: The Year of Mark." *Currents in Theology and Mission* 23, no. 6 (1996) 405–15.

Kudasiewicz, J. "'Poczatek Ewangelii Jezusa Chrystusa, Syna Boga' (Mk 1, 1) ('Anfang des Evangeliums von Jesus Christus, dem Sohn Gottes')." *Roczniki Teologiczne* 43, no. 1 (1996) 89–109.

Kuthirakkattel, Scaria. *The Beginning of Jesus' Ministry According to Mark's Gospel (1,14—3,6): A Redaction Critical Study*. Analecta Biblica 123. Roma: Editrice Pontificio Istituto Biblico, 1990.

BIBLIOGRAPHY

Lafleur, Didier. *La Famille 13 dans L'évangile de Marc*. New Testament Tools, Studies and Documents 41. Leiden: Brill, 2013.

Lambrecht, J. "John the Baptist and Jesus in Mark 1.1–15: Markan Redaction of Q?" *New Testament Studies* 38, no. 3 (1992) 357–84.

Lane, William L. *The Gospel of Mark*. NICNT. Grand Rapids: Eerdmans, 1974.

Lang, Friedrich Gustav. "Kompositionsanalyse des Markusevangeliums." *Zeitschrift für Theologie und Kirche* 74, no. 1 (1977) 1–24.

LaVerdiere, Eugene. *The Beginning of the Gospel: Introducing the Gospel according to Mark*. Collegeville, MN: Liturgical, 1999.

Lightfoot, R. H. *The Gospel Message of St. Mark*. Oxford: Clarendon, 1950.

Lohmeyer, Ernst. *Das Evangelium des Markus*. Vol. 1. Kritisch-exegetischer Kommentar über das Neue Testament. Göttingen: Vandenhoeck & Ruprecht, 1959.

Lucas, George. *Star Wars, Episode IV: A New Hope*. 20th Century Fox, 1977.

Mack, Burton L. *A Myth of Innocence: Mark and Christian Origins*. Philadelphia: Fortress, 1988.

Malbon, Elizabeth Struthers. "Echoes and Foreshadowings in Mark 4–8: Reading and Rereading." *Journal of Biblical Literature* 2 (1993) 211.

———. "Ending at the Beginning: A Response." *Semeia* 52 (1990) 175–84.

———. *Hearing Mark: A Listener's Guide*. Harrisburg, PA: Trinity, 2002.

Malina, Bruce J. *The New Testament World: Insights from Cultural Anthropology*. Rev. ed. Louisville: Knox, 1993.

Mansfield, M. Robert. *Spirit and Gospel in Mark*. Peabody, MA: Hendrickson, 1987.

Marcus, Joel. *Mark 1–8: A New Translation with Introduction and Commentary*. AB 27. New York: Doubleday, 2000.

Martin, Ralph P. *Mark, Evangelist and Theologian*. Exeter: Paternoster, 1972.

Marxsen, Willi. *Der Evangelist Markus: Studien zur Redaktionsgeschichte des Evangeliums*. Vandenhoeck & Ruprecht, 1956.

Matera, Frank. J. "The Prologue as the Interpretative Key to Mark's Gospel." *Journal for the Study of the New Testament* 34 (1988) 3–20.

May, Herbert Gordon, and Bruce Manning Metzger, eds. *The New Oxford Annotated Bible with the Apocrypha: Revised Standard Version, Containing the Second Edition of the New Testament and an Expanded Edition of the Apocrypha*. New York: Oxford University Press, 1977.

McCowen, Alec. *Personal Mark*. London: Hamilton, 1984.

Mell, U. "Jesu Taufe durch Johannes (Markus 1,9-15): Zur narrativen Christologie vom neuen Adam." *Biblische Zeitschrift* 40, no. 2 (1996) 161–78.

Miller, Norbert. *Der empfindsame Erzähler: Untersuchungen an Romananfängen des 18. Jahrhunderts*. Literatur als Kunst. Münich: Hanser, 1968.

Mitchell, Margaret M. *Paul and the Rhetoric of Reconciliation: An Exegetical Investigation of the Language and Composition of 1 Corinthians*. Hermeneutische Untersuchungen Zur Theologie 28. Tübingen: Mohr, 1991.

Moloney, Francis J. *Beginning the Good News: A Narrative Approach*. Eugene, OR: Wipf and Stock, 2006.

———. *Mark: Storyteller, Interpreter, Evangelist*. Peabody, MA: Hendrickson, 2004.

Mourlon Beernaert, P. *Saint Marc. Le Temps de Lire 2*. Brussels: Lumen Vitae, 1985.

Muilenburg, James. "Form Criticism and Beyond." *Journal of Biblical Literature* 88, no. 1 (1969) 1–18.

Myers, Ched. *Binding the Strong Man: A Political Reading of Mark's Story of Jesus*. Maryknoll, NY: Orbis, 1988.

BIBLIOGRAPHY

Neirynck, Frans. *Duality in Mark: Contributions to the Study of the Markan Redaction*. Revised. Bibliotheca Ephemeridum Theologicarum Lovaniensium 31. Leuven: Leuven University Press, 1988.

Nestle, Eberhard, and Kurt Aland. *Novum Testamentum Graece*. 27th ed. Stuttgart: Deutsche Bibelstiftung, 1993.

Nightingale, Danelle. "'Don't Be Late!' Assessing the Cost of Missing the Prologue in the Gospel of Mark." *Evangelical Quarterly* 84, no. 2 (2012) 107–18.

Nouis, A. "Proposition de Plan de L'évangile de Marc." *Hokhma* 87 (2005) 32–60.

Oko, Ohajuobodo I. *"Who Then Is This?": A Narrative Study of the Role of the Question of the Identity of Jesus in the Plot of Mark's Gospel*. Bonner Biblische Beiträge 148. Berlin: Philo, 2004.

Ong, Walter J. *Orality and Literacy: Technologizing of the Word*. London: Routledge, 1991.

Osborne, Grant R. "Historical Criticism: A Brief Response to Robert Thomas's 'Other View.'" *JETS* 43 (2000) 113–17.

———. "Historical Criticism and the Evangelical." *JETS* 42, no. 2 (1999) 193–210.

Oswalt, John N. *The Book of Isaiah, Chapters 1–39*. NICOT. Grand Rapids: Eerdmans, 1986.

Oyen, G. van. *De Summaria in Marcus en de Compositie van Mc 1,14—8,26*. Studiorum Novi Testamenti 12. Leuven: Leuven University Press, 1987.

Painter, John. *Mark's Gospel: Worlds in Conflict*. New Testament Readings. New York: Routledge, 1997.

Palmer, David G. "The Markan Matrix: A Literary-Structural Analysis of the Gospel of Mark." PhD thesis, University of Glasgow, 1998.

Perrin, Bernadotte, trans. *Plutarch's Lives*. Vol. 1. Loeb Classical Library 46. London: Heinemann, 1914.

Perrin, Norman, Dennis C. Duling, and Robert L. Ferm. *The New Testament, an Introduction: Proclamation and Parenesis, Myth and History*. New York: Harcourt Brace Jovanovich, 1982.

Pesch, Rudolf. "Anfang des Evangeliums Jesu Christi: Eine Studie zum Prolog des Markusevangeliums (Mk 1,1–15)." In *Die Zeit Jesu: Festschrift fur Heinrich Schlier*, edited by G. Bornkamm and K. Rahner, 108–44. Freiburg: Herder, 1970.

———. *Das Markusevangelium*. Vol. 1. Herders Theologischer Kommentar Zum Neuen Testament. Freiburg: Herder, 1977.

Radaelli, A. "I Racconti dell' Infanzia nel Contesto del Prologo all' Evangelo." *Ricerche Bibliche e Religiose* 14, no. 1 (1980).

Rahlfs, Alfred, ed. *Septuaginta; Id Est, Vetus Testamentum Graece Iuxta LXX Interpretes*. Stuttgart: Privilegierte Wurttembergische Bibelanstalt, 1935.

Renan, Ernest. *The Life of Jesus*. New York: Burt, 1863.

Robbins, Vernon K. *Jesus the Teacher: A Socio-Rhetorical Interpretation of Mark*. Minneapolis: Fortress, 1992.

———. *New Boundaries in Old Territory: Form and Social Rhetoric in Mark*. Edited by David B. Gowler. Emory Studies in Early Christianity 3. New York: Lang, 1994.

———. "Summons and Outline in Mark: The Three-Step Progression." *Novum Testamentum* 23, no. 2 (1981) 97–114.

Rolfe, J. C., trans. *Cornelius Nepos*. Loeb Classical Library 467. Cambridge, MA: Harvard University Press, 1984.

Rolfe, J. C., trans. *Suetonius*. Vol. 1. Loeb Classical Library. Cambridge, MA: Harvard University Press, 1928.

BIBLIOGRAPHY

Samuel, S. "The Beginning of Mark: A Colonial/Postcolonial Conundrum." *Biblical Interpretation* 10, no. 4 (2002) 405–19.

Sankey, P. J. "Promise and Fulfilment: Reader-Response to Mark 1.1–15." *Journal for the Study of the New Testament* 58 (1995) 3–18.

Santis, L. de. "Mc 1,1: Studio di Traduzione." *Angelicum* 69, no. 2 (1992) 175–92.

Sapaugh, Gregory P. "An Appraisal of the Intrinsic Probability of the Longer Endings of the Gospel of Mark." PhD diss., Dallas Theological Seminary, 2013.

Schaff, Philip, ed. *Nicene and Post-Nicene Fathers*. 14 vols. First Series 1. Peabody, MA: Hendrickson, 1994.

Schmidt, Karl Ludwig. *Der Rahmen der Geschichte Jesu: Literarkritische Untersuchungen zur ältesten Jesusüberlieferung*. Berlin: Trowitzsch, 1919.

Schmithals, Walter. *Das Evangelium nach Markus*. Ökumenischer Taschenbuchkommentar zum Neuen Testament 2. Gütersloh: Mohn, 1979.

Schreiber, Johannes. "Die Christologie des Markusevangeliums: Beobachtungen zur Theologie und Komposition des zweiten Evangeliums." *Zeitschrift für Theologie und Kirche* 58, no. 2 (1961) 154–83.

———. *Theologie des Vertrauens: Eine redaktionsgeschichtliche Untersuchung des Markusevangeliums*. Hamburg: Furche, 1967.

Schweizer, Eduard. *Good News according to Mark*. Louisville: Westminster John Knox, 1970.

Scott, M. P. "Chiastic Structure: A Key to the Interpretation of Mark's Gospel." *Biblical Theology Bulletin* 15, no. 1 (1985) 17–26.

Shepherd, Tom. "The Narrative Role of John and Jesus in Mark 1.1–15." In *Biblical Interpretation in Early Christian Gospels: The Gospel of Mark*, edited by Thomas R. Hatina, 1:151–68. Library of New Testament Studies (Formerly JSNTSup) 304. London: T. & T. Clark, 2006.

Shiner, Whitney Taylor. *Follow Me! Disciples in Markan Rhetoric*. SBLDS 145. Atlanta: Scholars, 1995.

———. *Proclaiming the Gospel: First-Century Performance of Mark*. Harrisburg, PA: Trinity, 2003.

Smith, Dennis E. "Narrative Beginnings in Ancient Literature and Theory." *Semeia* 52 (1990) 1–9.

Smith, Stephen H. "A Divine Tragedy: Some Observations on the Dramatic Structure of Mark's Gospel." *Novum Testamentum* 3 (1995) 209.

Standaert, Benoît. *Évangile selon Marc: Commentaire*. Études Bibliques: Nouv. Ser. 61. Pendé, France: Gabalda, 2010.

Stein, Robert H. *Mark*. Grand Rapids: Baker Academic, 2008.

———. "Proper Methodology for Ascertaining a Markan Redaction History." *Novum Testamentum* 13, no. 3 (1971) 181–98.

Stock, Augustine. *The Method and Message of Mark*. Wilmington, DE: Glazier, 1989.

Talbert, Charles H. *What Is a Gospel? The Genre of the Canonical Gospels*. Philadelphia: Fortress, 1977.

Tannehill, Robert C. "The Gospel of Mark as Narrative Christology." *Semeia*, no. 16 (1979) 57–95.

Taylor, R. O. P. *The Groundwork of the Gospels*. Oxford: Blackwell, 1946.

Taylor, Vincent. *The Gospel according to St. Mark: The Greek Text with Introduction, Notes, and Indexes*. 2nd ed. London: Macmillan, 1966.

BIBLIOGRAPHY

Telford, William. *Writing on the Gospel of Mark*. Guides to Advanced Biblical Research 1. Dorset, UK: Deo, 2009.

Thomas, Robert L. "Historical Criticism and the Evangelical: Another View." *JETS* 43, no. 1 (2000) 97–111.

Thomson, Ian H. *Chiasmus in the Pauline Letters*. JSNTSup 111. Sheffield: Sheffield Academic, 1995.

Tolbert, Mary Ann. *Sowing the Gospel: Mark's World in Literary-Historical Perspective*. Minneapolis: Fortress, 1989.

Trevijano Etcheverría, Ramon M. *Comienzo del Evangelo: Estudio sobre el Prólogo de San Marcos*. Burgos, Spain: Aldecoa, 1971.

Votaw, Clyde Weber. *The Gospels and Contemporary Biographies in the Graeco-Roman World*. Philadelphia: Fortress, 1970.

Wallace, Daniel B. "An Apologia for a Broad View of Ipsissima Vox." Danvers, MA, 1999.

———. *Greek Grammar beyond the Basics: An Exegetical Syntax of the New Testament*. Grand Rapids: Zondervan, 1996.

Wallis, Ethel E. "Mark's Goal-Oriented Plot Structure." *Journal of Translation and Textlinguistics* 10 (1998) 30–46.

Wasserman, Tommy. "The 'Son of God' Was in the Beginning (Mark 1:1)." *Journal of Theological Studies* 62 (2011) 20–50.

Weeden, Theodore J. *Mark: Traditions in Conflict*. Philadelphia: Fortress, 1971.

Whiston, William, trans. *The Works of Josephus: Complete and Unabridged*. New updated ed. Peabody, MA: Hendrickson, 1987.

Wilkin, Robert N. "Toward a Narrow View of Ipsissima Vox." *Journal of the Grace Evangelical Society*, N.p. Accessed October 1, 2013. http://www.faithalone.org/journal/2001i/wilkin.html.

Winn, Adam. *Mark and the Elijah-Elisha Narrative: Considering the Practice of Greco-Roman Imitation in the Search for Markan Source Material*. Eugene, OR: Pickwick, 2010.

Witherington III, Ben. *New Testament Rhetoric: An Introductory Guide to the Art of Persuasion in and of the New Testament*. Eugene, OR: Cascade, 2008.

———. "Paul Thru Mediterranean Eyes: A Review (Part One)." *The Bible and Culture*, August 18, 2012. http://www.patheos.com/blogs/bibleandculture/2012/08/18/paul-thru-mediterranean-eyes-a-review-part-one/.

———. *The Gospel of Mark: A Socio-Rhetorical Commentary*. Grand Rapids: Eerdmans, 2001.

Yarbro Collins, Adela. "Establishing the Text: Mark 1:1." In *Texts and Contexts: Biblical Texts in Their Textual and Situational Contexts: Essays in Honor of Lars Hartman*, edited by Tord Fornberg and David Hellholm, 111–27. Oslo: Scandinavian University Press, 1995.

———. *Mark: A Commentary*. Hermeneia. Minneapolis: Fortress, 2007.

York, John O. *The Last Shall Be First: The Rhetoric of Reversal in Luke*. Sheffield: JSOT, 1991.

Young, David Michael. "Whoever Has Ears to Hear: The Discourses of Jesus in Mark as Primary Rhetoric of the Greco-Roman Period." PhD, Vanderbilt University, 1994.

Zimmermann, Heinrich. *Jesus Christus: Geschichte und Verkündigung*. Stuttgart: Katholisches Bibelwerk, 1973.

Zmijewski, Josef. "Markinischer 'Prolog' und Täufertradition: Eine Untersuchung zu Mk 1,1–8." *Studien zum Neuen Testament und seiner Umwelt* 18 (1993) 41–62.

www.ingramcontent.com/pod-product-compliance
Lightning Source LLC
Chambersburg PA
CBHW051745230426
43670CB00012B/2164